THE NETHER SIDE

OF

NEW YORK;

OR, THE

VICE, CRIME AND POVERTY

OF THE

GREAT METROPOLIS.

By EDWARD CRAPSEY.

NEW YORK:
Sheldon & Company, 677 Broadway.

1872.

PREFACE.

SOME of the articles which make up this volume originally appeared in "The Galaxy," and were so favorably received by the press and public as to seem to excuse their reproduction, with additions, in this more enduring form. In submitting them to the public thus amplified, I claim for them no other merit than that they tell the truth of matters which have rarely had that fate. The accidents of my profession of journalist having brought me in personal contact with the Nether Side of New York, I determined to give the public the results of my observations, but I did not attempt the task until four years had been expended in acquiring the information necessary to its proper fulfilment. With such an advantage I ought to have approached the facts as nearly as is possible, and I think I have; I know that I have presented those I have gathered without extenuation or exaggeration.

It will be noticed that the statistics quoted in this volume are for the several years from 1868 to 1871. When the articles were originally prepared for the magazine the latest attainable facts were used, and the condition of the city remaining substantially the same during these several years, I have concluded that a more general and satisfactory view of the burdens of the metropolis could be obtained from these statistics of separate years, and I have, therefore, left them unchanged; if all the figures used had been those of any one of these years the exhibit would not have been more favorable, and no injustice is done by the method adopted.

The happy appropriateness of the title under which these articles first appeared, and which is preserved in that of the book, having been often complimented, I desire to say that I am not entitled to any credit therefor. It was the suggestion of Messrs. William C. and Frank P. Church, the editors of "The Galaxy," to whom I am under many obligations, beside this of finding me a name which had the great merit of freshness. Thanking them for the invaluable assistance I have received from them, I also desire to acknowledge my indebtedness to the newspaper press in all parts of the country, as the notices which my efforts have received have encouraged me to persevere in dealing with these repulsive subjects, in the hope that I might furnish a basis of fact for the operations of the social reformers of the future. To this end only have my labors been directed, and I hope that my work shows that I have at least honestly endeavored to attain it.

E. C.

CONTENTS.

THE NETHER SIDE OF NEW YORK.

GENERAL FACTS.

VERY many and diverse causes have contributed to make possible the alarming facts which will be found in this volume. New York being an anomaly among cities, owing to certain physical conditions and to some social and political peculiarities, it is only just that these should be briefly stated.

Covering an island about nine miles in length with an average breadth of two and one-half miles, in which are contained twenty-two square miles, and having twenty-one miles of available water front, the city has unequalled accommodations for commerce, but only limited facilities for the healthful housing of a huge population. As yet not more than half this area is built upon, and at least a fifth of this half is wholly devoted to trade, so that the nine hundred and forty-two thousand two hundred and ninety-two persons found by the last Federal census to be living on this island, are crowded into an area of about nine square miles, or at the rate of nearly 162 to the acre as an average for the entire city, although in some portions 732 are compressed within that limited space. To accommodate this population the city has 291 miles of paved street surface, 275 miles of sewers, 340 miles of Croton water pipes under this surface, and 10,000 street gas-lamps lighted at the public cost. The streets are constantly traversed by 12,000 licensed vehicles, 1,000 horse-cars, 267 omnibuses, and many thousands of private vehicles of every kind. These are general facts hardly pertinent to my purpose, but of sufficient interest to pardon this mere mention.

Of the population shown by the last census to be upon the island, 510,553 were native born, and in the remainder were found representatives of nearly every country upon the earth. From Ireland had come 201,999; from Germany, 80,494; from England, 24,398; Prussia, 31,464; France, 8,240; Bavaria, 12,571; Baden, 6,724; and taking other nationalities in alphabetical order shows the following: Africa 36, Arabia 3, Asia 10, Australia 64, Austria 2,743, Belgium 328, Bohemia 1,487, Canada 3,450, Central America 16, Canary Islands 1, China 103, Cuba 1,207, Denmark 680, Hamburg 611, Hanover 3,698, Hesse 7,739, Italy 2,789, India 19, Japan 1, Mexico 56, Malta 4, Madeira Islands 10, New Zealand 2, Norway 373, Poland 2,392, Portugal 90, Russia 1,139, Scotland 7,551, South

America 202, Spain 453, Sweden 1,569, Switzerland 2,169, Turkey 38, Wales 587, and West Indies 388. Many of the smaller nationalities have been omitted, but the figures given show a mixture of people unparalleled anywhere else on earth, and to them must be added 13,093 negroes, of which number 448 were not natives of the United States, but represented as to their places of nativity 29 different countries and all the continents.

After a perusal of these figures, it is scarcely necessary to state that every creed and clime, every race and condition has its representatives in New York, but to show how constant and vast has been the alien element poured into this community, I append a table showing the arrivals of emigrants at the port of New York during the twenty-two years ending in 1868:

Year	Arrivals	Year	Arrivals
1847	129,062	1858	78,589
1848	186,176	1859	79,322
1849	220,603	1860	105,162
1850	212,756	1861	65,539
1851	289,601	1862	76,302
1852	300,992	1863	156,884
1853	284,945	1864	182,296
1854	319,223	1865	196,352
1855	136,233	1866	233,488
1856	142,342	1867	242,731
1857	183,773	1868	213,686

Here is a total of 4,038,991 aliens landed at this port in these twenty-two years, of whom, it is true, 1,597,805 came from Ireland, 1,536,649 from Germany, 498,978 from England, 100,595 from Scotland, 74,405 from France, and 62,608 from Switzerland, leaving only 168,351 from all the other nations of the earth. Of these millions nothing, with few exceptions, but the dregs settled in the metropolis where they landed. All the rest, representing nearly all that was valuable in this avalanche of humanity, was poured upon the untilled lands of the West, where a mighty empire sprang from their loins with the amazing swiftness of necromancy. The thrifty emigrants who came to us forehanded and determined to wring competence from the new republic, merely made New York their stepping stone to fortune; the emigrants who exhausted their stores in securing their passage, and landed penniless perforce, staid with us to add to the dissonance of this mixture of peoples. In time many of these became self-sustaining, and they or their children pushed forward into the ranks of our most substantial citizens, but a large proportion, as was inevitable, became public burdens, and permanent additions to the vice, crime, or pauperism of the metropolis.

In the facts thus far narrated, we have the first of the causes which have made New York a reproach to all the nations. Upon the foundation of ignorance and helplessness found in this diversity of population, constantly fed by arriving emigrants, all that we have of turbulence, poverty, vice, and crime has been reared. I do not mean to say that without this foundation, we would have only peace, plenty, and virtue, for such a statement would be a most unwise economy of truth; but I do mean to assert, and hope to show, that without it our evils would have been less virulent. While these social evils have been with other communities, as it were, of the varioloid type, with us they have been variola of the most pronounced character; and we have this diversity of races, this constant influx of poverty and ignorance to thank for it. True, our civilization culminated in commercial and political rascals who were "native here and to the manner born," but they achieved their bad pre-eminence by the fact that more than half the population of the city which they mastered were the easy prey of unscrupulous demagogues because they were not rooted in the soil by birth or by competency acquired on it. In other words, I trace back the social evils of New York to that political profligacy which was made possible only by the circumstance that New York was a camping ground rather than a city.

The fact that the city became in time merely a collection of Bedouins, was inevitable from the topography of its site, and the peculiarities of its people. Having length without breadth, it was certain that when the compact village below Wall street should become a vast metropolis, stretching miles away to the northward, the inhabitants would be confronted with the problem of city transit. It came in due time, and when the city had its straggling suburbs at Fourteenth street, omnibusses supplied all the needs of the easy-going people of that decade. But when the town, putting on seven-league boots, strode northward at a rate which has had no parallel in the growth of cities, except in the marvellous instance of Chicago, the problem became again a vexation. Then came the introduction of street-railroads on the surface of the streets on which the cars are drawn by horses, and the people, by this innovation, seem to have exhausted their capacity for improvement in this direction. After a few years, the street railroads became wholly inadequate to the swift and comfortable carriage of the population from their homes to their business, and publicists clearly saw that the lack of such means of transportation was telling terribly against the moral and commercial prosperity of the city; yet nothing was done. At the present time nearly a generation of human life has elapsed since the introduction of those street railroads which so fully supplied the needs of a primitive epoch, but which were soon found to be only a temporary expedient for the relief a comparatively small population, yet they still remain the sole resource of the people. The results of this neglect to meet a most vital want were as natural and speedy as they were hurtful to the best interests of the city.

It was worse than a two-edged sword which the metropolis had turned against itself. When it was no longer possible for the people to make the journey between their homes up-town and their business down-town in a reasonable time, they sought to evade the journey altogether. It happened, unfortunately for the city, that just as this problem of transportation became most pressing, the derangement of values consequent upon the protracted war of the great Rebellion, became most flagrant, and affected rents so disproportionately, that it soon became a question whether anything less than the revenues of a principality would suffice to keep a roof over a man's head in the city of New York. It was certain that whoever retained a predilection for civilized home-life, and was able to get away, would fly from this wrath which had already come, and they did fly so quickly, and in such numbers, that the city was soon denuded to a great extent of that invaluable balance-wheel to political action, the middle classes, and New Jersey, Long Island, and contiguous counties of the State of New York, became prosperous and virtuous at the expense of the metropolis of the western world. This is a practical, and in the sense of sacrificing public good to private benefit, a selfish people. Every man of moderate income saw that while he could house his family more decently and at less cost in any one of the suburban towns of New Jersey, he could reach them sooner and with less hardship, even if twenty miles away, than he could if they were only a tenth of that distance up-town. Therefore an exodus began to these towns, which has continued for several years, to the detriment of the city to a degree that is hardly yet realized. Thousands of men who during business hours were engaged in our marts, became rooted in a foreign soil, had all their home-associations elsewhere, were utterly indifferent as to the conduct of municipal affairs, and spent or invested without the city the money they acquired within it.

Evil, and evil only, could result to the municipality from such facts as these. The same causes which had operated to drive out the middle classes had huddled the poorer artisans and laboring population in unhealthful homes, and given to New York its crowning shame as well as gravest danger, in the tenement system. In the body of this work I have endeavored to present this system as it deserves, and do not intend at this point to speak of it in detail. Dealing now rather with causes than their effects, I can only point, out briefly as I have, how these tenements were produced. Their blighting effect upon civic virtue was made more destructive by reason of the fact that while they breeded vice and squalor in their inmates, the system of which they were the growth produced an increasing indifference to all social and political problems upon the part of the wealth and intelligence of the city. So entirely had this become the case, and so threatening had become the condition of the city in consequence, that so long ago as 1857, the prevailing alarm allowed the dominant political party to venture on the hazardous experiment of ruling the city, in part from without itself, and matters of police and excise were vested in Commissioners appointed by State authority. This measure, for the moment, seemed to give the desired relief, but it in the end increased rather than diminished the evil it was intended to eradicate. Citizens who had most interest in the good government of the city, more than ever neglected their civic duties, and became accustomed to look to the State to assume their functions, and this feeling was greatly increased when, a few years later, the State assumed control of matters of public health, through Commissioners, whose efficiency soon became noted the world over. The very excellences of these Commissions made them inimical to the public good, as it was evident that such anomalous expedients could not be permanent under a republican government, and by assuming duties which the citizens themselves should have discharged, they increased the indifference to public affairs among the great body of respectable people. There was little occasion, it was thought, to look after civic matters so long as the city had a most excellent police, a stringent excise law rigidly enforced, and an admirable sanitary code wisely administered. This much the State had done, and there was an increasing belief that it would continue to do as much if not more.

With its middle classes in large part self-exiled, its laboring population being brutalized in tenements, and its citizens of the highest class indifferent to the common weal, New York drifted from bad to worse, and became the prey of professional thieves, ruffians, and political jugglers. The municipal government shared in the vices of the people, and New York became a city paralyzed in the hands of its rulers. Nothing was done to improve, adorn, or strengthen it. The commerce of the world, floating through its grand water-gate, and up its beautiful bay, continued to be landed on wharves that would disgrace a coastwise village. Its pavements, never good, became unworthy of an impoverished community. An island, it remained without bridges, and having length without breadth, it could not, or would not, devise adequate means of city transit. With princely municipal revenues, the public buildings became dilapidated and the public places were badly adorned, or not adorned at all. Favored with an equable climate and a healthful site, the death-rate remained abnormal, because of defective sewage, unventilated tenements, and unclean streets. Maintaining a costly police force, thieving increased, because the administration of correctional law had fallen into itching palms. Numbering among the people thousands of citizens whose record for integrity and culture would stand against the world, many of the high places in the municipal government were filled with marvels of venality, uncouthness, and ignorance of everything but political chicanery. In short, the city which had been most gifted by nature, had been most abused by man, and what greatness it possessed had been achieved in despite of untoward circumstances.

There can be no wonder that a city thus afflicted became the prey of thievery and debauchery; but worse remained behind. The history of New York during the years 1867, 1868, 1869, 1870, and down to the middle of 1871, ought to suffuse the cheek of every American citizen with the blush of shame. The State still adhering to the pernicious system of caring for the city, led to a union of the corruption in both political parties, and gradually one of these two fell under the domination of an infamous cabal, which soon became known and dreaded as the Ring. Learning from a past depravity the cohesive power of public plunder, this Ring was established and unblushingly maintained by the conversion of public revenues to private or partisan uses. Scarcely deigning to conceal its rascality from the general view, the Ring prospered, and soon became absolute master of the city. It named the incumbents of municipal offices from the highest to the lowest, and relegated to the popular voice only the empty form of ratifying its nominations. Through its machinations a government professedly republican became more autocratic and more corrupt than any rule ever before inflicted upon any people. It was omnipotent, and used its omnipotence to extend and perpetuate its power by debauching the public conscience. It was the source of power and plunder. Its appointees knew its arts, and so successfully practised them, that the whole municipality became a close corporation of venal rascality. While the general condition of the city was so bad that even skilled labor could with difficulty keep a roof over its head, the Ring and its favorites were rioting in suddenly acquired wealth, and constantly exhibited themselves to the public gaze loaded with diamonds and guzzling costly wines, like the vulgar knaves they were. Salaries were increased to an extent so great as to be infamous, yet officials not only lived at a rate far beyond them, but made large investments. Only by the foulest tools could these infamies be wrought. Men who were fit only to be ushers at minstrel shows were made State Senators, and the keepers of gin-shops were manufactured into legislators for the great State of New York. Among the police magistrates were the meanest of political tricksters, and a man who had been brought back from a distant State to answer for a felony, was made Auditor of the public accounts.

And there was scarcely a protest against all this iniquity. Not only did the dominant party permit its honored name to be loaded with an undeserved odium, but there was a universal conviction that the government was based upon thievery, and a universal indifference to the fact. Prominent citizens, of all shades of political opinion, took office under the Ring, and it seemed there were many of good repute whom $10,000 per annum would induce to become the apologists or defenders of apparent venality. There was never a time in the history of any people when public morality had sunk so low as during these disgraceful years in the imperial city. There was not only general acquiescence in this government, but general desire to share in its booty. It was rare to hear it denounced, and if any one did denounce it he was declared to be angry because he was not in the Ring! It was everywhere announced that all governments were corrupt, and that of New York was no worse than others. It came to be accepted as a matter of course that municipal office should be a short-cut to fortune, and it occasioned no surprise that a year or two should change bankrupts into millionaires. Yet the members of the Ring did not put their safety altogether in the indifference of the public. There was always danger that the public conscience might be awakened (as it was at last), and to guard against the mishaps which might follow, the most cunning and shameless frauds were perpetrated at the annual elections to make them result in conformity with the wishes of the Ring. Such farces as the elections of 1868 and 1869 were never before acted in the faces of a free people. The press, as a rule, denounced these frauds, as it had in a general way all the doings of the Ring, but without much effect. The people seemed contented with being swindled, and at any rate they could not be roused to defend themselves until, in 1871, they were confronted with evidence that could not be doubted. Then they arose in their might and crushed the Ring as a giant would break a straw.

During these distressful years when, in addition to this deep sleep of the public conscience, drinking-dens had multiplied to an alarming extent, and poverty had increased in the same ratio, it must be admitted that crimes of violence did not increase. The explanation is not to be found in the stern administration of primitive law, but in the fact that the thugs of the city found employment in politics equally congenial and more remunerative. In some respects the judiciary of the higher grades escaped the prevailing epidemic. I have facts to narrate in this volume which seem to require explanation, but I am too thankful for the fact that it was still possible to get justice in the higher courts, in some cases at least, to neglect to mention it. During this time the city was startled with some atrocious homicides, and there would have been many more undoubtedly if these murderers had not found the courts insensible to their influence. In the worst of these cases the assassin, who was a powerful tool of the dominant party, was hanged, and he has never had an imitator of the peculiar atrocity of his crime. There were several highway robberies of startling boldness, but some of the footpads being caught, were punished with such extreme rigor that the crime was afterwards of rare occurrence. There was an uneasy feeling in the public mind that the general peace and individual safety were held by the frailest of tenures, and every crime of violence which was unusually virulent or daring, provoked a storm of popular wrath, that may have had much to do with the speedy and severe punishment of the offenders. I prefer to believe, as I have good reason, that the judges holding the General Sessions and Oyer and Terminer themselves partook of the general disquietude, and acted in all these cases from a genuine desire to repress crime rather than in obedience to popular clamor. But whatever may have been the motives, their action was eminently timely, as without it the city would have fallen utterly under the sway of thieves and thugs. Matters had already become so threatening that an aged citizen had been robbed and murdered in broad daylight at his own door; two policemen had turned footpads on patrol and stolen the money of a stranger they pretended to be guarding; and lesser crimes, but of equal significance, were constantly occurring. But, upon the whole, owing partly to the fact that many of the thugs were devoting themselves to reaping the spoils of office, and partly in consequence of the severity with which they were punished when they followed their natural bent, crimes of violence were surprisingly few during this terrible epoch.

But covert crime largely increased. The operations of pickpockets, burglars, sneak thieves, and "confidence" rogues became daily more extensive and more enterprising. Street cars and all public places were so infested with the light-fingered that watches and wallets parted from their owners with alarming frequency, and the public were startled with such stupendous triumphs of thievery as the Lord-Bond robbery and the Ocean Bank burglary. Petty crimes became almost countless, and the warfare of the outlaws upon property became more enterprising and successful than had ever been waged before in any civilized community. It was inevitable that this result should follow from the almost universal method adopted in dealing with these foes of society. I will present facts concerning the detective manner of handling the great rogues, which will entirely explain why they escaped unscathed, and it is only necessary in this place to state certain defects in the police and judicial systems, which gave such length of tether to crime. These defects were partly inherent in the systems, but were chiefly chargeable to imbecile or corrupt administration. As to the police, there were many and grave faults. The city being divided into thirty-two precincts, of which twenty-nine embraced territory, there was a force of only 2,325 rank and file, to cover this vast area. As a consequence the "beats" of patrolmen were, as an average, so extensive, that no possible amount of vigilance could have enabled these officers to give proper guardianship to the property placed in their charge. But it is scarcely probable that even a sufficient number of men of the kind of which the force was largely composed, and governed as they were, would have produced results any more satisfactory. There were few incentives to the faithful performance of duty. There was, indeed, a medal for meritorious conduct, but although often deserved it was never awarded but once. Promotion was declared to be for merit, but the men soon found that it could be obtained only by partisan favor. In dealing with breaches of discipline the Commissioners were so arbitrary and inconsistent that no well-defined precedents could be establlshed, and an idea went abroad among the men that pique, or supposed political necessities had controlling weight in determining their fate when brought up on charges. These corroding influences from headquarters were strengthened from the precinct station-house. There the captain was an autocrat, who could, and many of whom did, destroy whatever of efficiency headquarters had left. The pernicious detective system permeated all the precincts, as in each was found a man called the "ward officer," who was the favorite of the captain, and whose exclusive right it was to "work up" all reported robberies, but if it was one so trivial or desperate that nothing could be made out of it, it was loftily refused and turned over to a patrolman. This ingenious contrivance cut in two directions with deadly effect. The patrolman, who, getting the first clue to a robbery, found the case taken from him and given to the favorite, had his interest in the performance of his duty destroyed, and afterward avoided rather than sought such clues. The captain, with his "ward officer," taking exclusive control of all these cases, made the pursuit of criminals a corporation so close as to fully explain how so many of these officials could expend annually more than their salaries, and yet have balances at the end of the year. It was inevitable that such a process should result in few captures of criminals and in fewer convictions. I may here state a general fact, which of itself will go far to account for everything to be found in this volume concerning criminals:

unless the thief was taken in the act he was rarely taken afterward, and the percentage of cases where he was apprehended in the actual commission of his offence, was naturally very small.

But there never was any certainty that even the malefactor taken *in flagrante delictu* would get his deserts. Police courts, the world over, are marvels of stupidity or corruption,and those of New York are not exceptions to the rule. There are nine magistrates, holding five separate travesties on law and justice. Each one of these magistrates is the creature of profligacy to the extent that he was elected to his office by popular vote, at a time when political corruption was most flagrant. A majority of them are the natural offspring of such official parentage. With one exception they are not lawyers, and a majority are as ignorant of matters generally as they are of law. It would be amazing if such tribunals did anything to repress crime except occasionally and by accident. That thieves with political influence should find favor in these parodies on court, is as natural as it is notorious, and that mistakes having the same effect are often honestly made, is equally notorious. I will have occasion to show the working of these courts more in detail and it will be seen that they are often as unduly severe as they are sometimes inexcusably lenient, and that upon the whole the condition of society would be measurably improved by their destruction.

Very much has been alleged of the encouragement to crime by the administration of the District Attorney's office, but I take occasion hereafter to state what little is known, or I might perhaps more justly say, suspected in this matter. I have gone briefly over some general facts which are more than sufficient to explain the prevalence of crime and turbulence among us. The conformation of the city, the lack of city transit, the exodus of the middle classes, the constant influx of emigrants, the abasement of the lower classes by the tenements, the corruption of politics made possible by all these facts, and the paralyzation of the police with the inefficiency of the minor tribunals, are reasons in abundance in mitigation of our social condition, and go far to exculpate the great body of our people from the reproach that would otherwise belong to them. The primary causes have been beyond their control, and this fact gives them the right to combine an axiom of scandal with one of medical practice, and plead that if they are no better than they should be, they are doing as well as call be expected under the circumstances.

PROFESSIONAL CRIMINALS.

HAVING resolved to give the public some trustworthy information concerning our New York criminal classes, the difficulties of my task presented themselves at its very beginning. I wished, for instance, to know the total of the criminal population, and the numbers of each class, but there were no published statistics upon the subject, and no one person who would admit that he was possessed of the information. I sought, next, to learn the value of the property yearly stolen, and the amount recovered; but there were no police reports to tell me, and no police captain who would even hazard an estimate. Thus far I was not very much surprised; but I must confess my astonishment when every official consulted pretended to a total ignorance of the number of receivers of stolen goods and haunts of thieves in the Metropolis. I therefore felt that there was serious need for *somebody* to know something of matters so important.

I availed myself, first, of the meagre facts officially published, and on consulting the report of the Police Commissioners, found the rather startling statement that 78,451 arrests had been made during the year 1868. But an analysis of the table showed that 66,880 had been taken in custody for such comparatively trivial matters as intoxication, disorderly conduct, and various misdemeanors, leaving only 11,571 as the total arrests for every degree of crime, from homicide to malicious mischief. A still further examination of the table showed that there had been 4,927 arrests for petit larceny, 2,413 for grand larceny, 303 for picking pockets, 255 for receiving stolen goods, 630 for burglary, 132 for robbery, and 78 for murder. But when these figures had been collated no progress had been made in determining the number of criminals in New York, or the number of crimes committed. As an example, take the 303 arrests for picking pockets. Any one familiar with the city knows perfectly well that the figures indicate nearly the total number of professional pickpockets regularly plying their vocation in our crowded places, but that they do not approximate by many hundreds to the number of watches and wallets stolen during the year by these industrious gentlemen. Nor was I impressed with a high sense of the value of this official table when I found it reporting 78 murders in 1868, for I knew from an examination of the Coroners' records that no more than 48 murders had been committed, and that 61 was the highest number of homicides in any one year since 1856. The discrepancy is very great, and cannot be explained by the fact that murderers flying from other places have been arrested in the city and returned for trial to the places where the crimes were committed.

Not finding even fundamental data in the official publication, I made inquiries from all those police officials whom I knew to be most conversant with the subject. It is a very poor police captain who does not know his own precinct sufficiently well to give an almost absolutely correct estimate of the number of professional thieves living within its boundaries; and from the figures thus gathered I am certain I have arrived at very nearly the exact truth. The result will surprise many people, and seem incredible to the uninformed generalizers who always exaggerate when they know absolutely nothing; but it is nevertheless a fact that in all New York there are in round numbers not more than 2,500 professional criminals of every kind and grade. I do not include the hundreds driven by want or sudden temptation to the commission of offences, and who cannot justly be considered as members of the criminal class; but I do embrace every person, male and female, who depends exclusively upon the fruits of theft for a livelihood. The number seems small in comparison with the depredations upon property; but such is the industry and daring of New York "cross-men," and they have enjoyed such immunity from punishment, that if they were as numerous as has been generally supposed no man's goods would be safe for a day.

The great body of the outlawed come under the general name of "sneak." The accomplished bank-robber, and the skilful burglar, may object to the name as a badge of ignominy; but that is because they have never thoughtfully considered the nomenclature of their calling. The term "sneak" includes all that is determined, patient, plausible, scheming, thoroughly educated and able in roguery, no less than it does all that is small, mean and grovelling. Sneaks differ in degree; but they have one common characteristic which gives them their distinctive name. That outlaw is a sneak who does not, at the outset of his crime, proclaim his nefarious purpose by some word or act. The bank-robber and the hall-thief are alike in this respect, and hence are equally sneaks. With this explanation, due to offended pride, I can marshal the sneaks in due order of precedence.

Bank-sneaks of the first class do not number over fifty persons, and their ranks are rarely recruited, as the qualities necessary for successfully "working the racket" are not often found combined in one person. Few as they are in numbers, they are not exclusively the property of New York, but infest in turn every large city, or, in the words of a policeman who knows every one of them, "they jump into a town, work the street for a couple of days, and then hop away." The bank-sneak is the highest possible criminal development, and brings to his use so much of patient research, so profound a knowledge of character, such readiness of resource, such perfect mental equipoise, that he seems worthy of being that favorite of fortune which his high qualities have made him. The bank-sneak is popularly called the bond-robber, and the mention of such achievements as the Lord bond robbery, and the Royal insurance robbery, shows that he is in a line of business entirely safe and hugely profitable. He is a shrewd operator who manages to realize fifty per cent. on other men's capital, and this is a common event with the bank-sneak. He is never caught in the act of committing his crime, but invariably escapes, with or without the valuables he seeks to steal, but usually with them. Having obtained the property, if the detectives should get on his trail, his future proceedings are limited to negotiations with the despoiled owners, which are certain to result in an amicable arrangement whereby he secures immunity for his offence, and gets fifty per cent. on the transaction. Even if he is arrested, and the stolen property found in his possession, the negotiation nevertheless proceeds and is completed, notwithstanding the police may have sufficient evidence to secure his conviction. Bankers and detectives seem to love not justice less but money more, and they cheat the law to satisfy their greed. If the bankers can get all their property back without making any promises, they are as eager as Shylock to give the rascal only the letter of the law; but if the rascal can manage to retain even a tithe of their valuables, he has a certain hostage for their good behavior. Hence results the fact, so damaging to the community, that of late years not one of the prominent and adroit bank-sneaks has been sent to State Prison in New York, whatever may have been their fate in other States.

Damper-sneaks are a little company not more than one hundred in number. By "damper," a thief means a safe, for the reason that it is supposed to put a damper upon his hopes. Hundreds of business men in New York can tell from costly experience how damper-sneaks operate. A man of intense respectability of dress and demeanor, enters a broker's office, and asks to look at the directory, or sometimes to write a note. Permission being given him, he takes care to put himself inside the railing, and as near the safe as possible. If its door is ajar, he stands examining the directory, or writing for a moment or two, when two of his confederates enter, and the broker is immediately engrossed by the pressing needs of his new customers. While he is thus engaged, the first sneak, seizing his opportunity and whatever valuables he can lay hands upon, passes out of the office, always pausing as he goes to thank the broker for his courtesy. Presently the confederates leave, to make further inquiries before concluding a bargain, and it is always some moments, and often hours, before the broker discovers his loss. Robberies of this kind are constantly occurring, and the damper-sneaks probably have a more certain and a larger income than any other class of thieves. Bank-sneaks steal far greater amounts at a time; but their thefts are less frequent because their opportunities are more rare. Tin boxes, containing large amounts in bonds, are not habitually left exposed to the grasp of the bank sneaks, who have been following them for hours, perhaps, and from place to place, but the damper-sneaks can safely count upon a carelessness of the business community which it seems impossible to cure. Safe-doors are left open during business hours, and while bankers persist in leaving their valuables thus exposed to the enterprise of a most adroit and active class of rogues, they yet join in the hue and cry against the police when a robbery is committed which their imprudence alone has rendered possible.

Safe-blowers do not have more than seventy-five names upon their muster-rolls, but the little army is far more dangerous to the hoarded wealth than its numbers indicate. Commonly known as burglars, their skill is first called on to gain entrance to a building, which is generally accomplished by means of false keys made from impressions in wax, previously taken from the genuine keys. The "blowers," being in the building, proceed with a rapidity and an attention to detail made possible by long experience. First, they lower the windows of the room about an inch to prevent the breakage of glass, and next they wrap the safe in wet blankets to deaden the noise of the expected concussion. The preliminaries thus arranged, they drill holes in the door of the safe near the lock, and these having been filled with powder, a fuse is attached; the explosion takes place, the safe is torn open, and three minutes suffice for the operators to seize its contents and escape from the building. This is the most hazardous of all robberies, and is never resorted to unless the outlaws are sure that the contents of the safe are sufficiently valuable to compensate for the risks incurred. Hence, it is always prefaced by a careful, and often protracted, scenting of the selected premises, with the design of obtaining exact information of the profits to be expected of the contemplated adventure.

Safe-bursters, do not out-number the blowers, and gain access to the building by the same means; but henceforward are more artistic and less daring. In common with all other classes, they work in "mobs" of three or four persons; but they go prepared to accomplish their designs, rather by dint of science than by brute force. First, the safe is clamped securely to the floor, so as to be made perfectly immovable against any pressure; next, holes are drilled in the door, and in these jack-screws are fitted, to be worked by levers. The operation is entirely noiseless and thoroughly effective. No safe was ever made strong enough to withstand the tremendous power thus applied, and it is generally the work of a few minutes only to make the shapely strong-box a mass of iron shreds. So complete is the wreck that non-professionals, looking upon it, insist that gunpowder was used, and wonder why the police did not hear the noise of the terrific explosion. In point of fact, there had been no explosion and no noise of any kind. The bursters, like the blowers, never take unremunerative risks, and never attack a safe until sure of what it contains. The attack having been made is almost certain to be completely successful, and the operators are as sure to escape undetected, with all of the valuables.

Safe-breakers are the lowest grade of operators upon the vaunted burglar-proof receptacles, and are also the most numerous, as they number about two hundred. They rely solely upon main force both in entering a building and in working upon the safe, as they pry open the first with a "jimmey," or small hand-bar, and belabor the latter with a hammer until it falls to pieces. Although thieves in the crude state, they are not altogether idiots, and so wrap the hammers with old cloths as to materially deaden the noise. They are less successful than the other classes, and are more frequently "coppered"—that is, arrested. They are, too, a hap-hazard set of knaves, and even when they have opened a safe, and evaded arrest, are often not recompensed for their trouble, for it has frequently happened that they have over-tasked their muscles in breaking down iron walls that enveloped nothing whatever of value.

Bed-chamber sneaks, are the silent, invisible partners of blowers, bursters, and other first-class burglars, as well as of forgers, and are only about fifty in number. Their particular "racket" is to obtain the means of entering dwellings and stores without noise or violence, and they are the most insidious of all outlaws. They require for success in their line, more of nerve, endurance, and plausibility than the great mass of rogues can claim, and hence the large demand for their services, and the many robberies in which they have been found to be partners. Their energies are devoted to obtaining impressions in wax of the true keys, from which false keys can be made. The sneak watches a store for days, until he learns who has the custody of the keys, and, whether it be proprietor, clerk, or porter, he follows that person to his home until he finds a chance of entering the house unobserved and secreting himself in the bed-chamber of the proposed victim. On these occasions the sneak never steals or displaces anything, and being so adroit that he never awakens the inmate of the room, the fact that an impression of the keys has been taken is not known until after the robbery. When the keys of a dwelling, instead of those of a store, are wanted, the sneak ingratiates himself with the house-servants, and while deluding those susceptible minds with the soft words of scheming love, deftly takes a fac-simile in wax of the desired key. He never purloins the key itself, for he is entirely successful in his purpose only when it is accomplished without creating any suspicion that a dishonest enterprise is afoot. These sneaks do not wait for orders for particular keys, but keep constantly on hand a large and well-assorted stock of the most desirable wares in their line. They are the prime movers in nearly all the burglaries, and procure the information as to the valuables upon which the crimes are based, and give this, with the false keys, to their "pals," the burglars.

Second-story sneaks are not more than one hundred in number, and owe their name to a recently-devised expedient for reaching the coveted valuables of honesty. Formerly they worked what was called the "eatable lay," and for a time quite a profitable "lay" it was. Generally working in couples, they chose for their operations the hour when the dinner-table was spread, and sauntering through some quiet, respectable street, selected a house where the basement door was ajar. One posting himself there, the other ascended the stoop and rang the front-door bell. Up went the servant, and while the ringer detained her with persistent inquiries for some mythical Jones or Smith, asserted to reside in the neighborhood, his confederate below walked into the deserted dining-room, and walked out again with the spoons and silver-ware concealed under his coat. But the Metropolis has so advanced, and the basement floors of houses having silver are now so infested with servants, that the "eatable lay" has fallen into desuetude, and second-story sneaks have arisen. They can only work in secluded streets, and during the season when the dinner-hour of six o'clock is after dark. While the inmates of the house are all down-stairs at dinner, the sneak boldly scales one of the pillars of the stoop, and thus reaches a second-floor window, which he opens with an admirable little apparatus specially prepared for the purpose. Once within the house, he has usually an easy task before him, for he finds all the doors unlocked, and roams unimpeded through all the upper rooms, rummaging all the closets and bureaus, and seizing whatever he can find. Having gathered all that is portable and valuable, he goes down the pillar again, or sneaks down the stairs, and makes his exit by the front door, to rejoin his "pal," who has meantime been engaged in an operation which he styles "piping off the cop," by which he means that he has been watching the movements of the policeman, in order to intercept him with some plausible device if he should give signs of approaching the house while the sneak is working it. This sort of robbery has lately become quite common, and the diamond thefts in dwellings, which seemed so inexplicable, were all done by these sneaks.

Chance-sneaks are an army about eight hundred strong, and stand at the very bottom of the scale of villainy, the scorn of all speculative thieves, the butt of all rascally ridicule, and the aim of all police endeavor. They differ in degree among themselves, but are all equally without adroitness and originative capacity. They are poor, thriftless, aimless creatures, drifting helplessly about the streets by day and by night, watching for a chance to dart into a hallway and snatch a coat, to sneak behind some counter and rifle a till, or to purloin a hat, or pair of boots, or some trifling article from the street display of a store. These chance-sneaks, as a rule, have evinced an amazing lack of sense in the perpetration of their crimes, and in their proceedings afterward. They have way-laid men who have not had a dollar to be stolen, and they have committed burglary upon retail shops which were almost certain to contain nothing worth carrying away. They have kept a key which was the sole result of a highway robbery, and they have neglected to throw away a marked penny which was the only result of a laborious burglary, and the trifle, which any intelligent thief would have cast from him on the instant, served, in both cases, to detect the criminal. In common with all chance-sneaks, these blunderers are continually tumbling, from sheer mal-adroitness, into the clutches of the law, and their ranks are thus constantly depleted by arrests, but are as rapidly filled up with fresh recruits. Chance-sneaks are the most easily manufactured of all villains, the only necessary ingredient being a willingness to steal.

I have now disposed of the classes known as sneaks, but many other sorts of criminals are waiting for presentation. To me there is a fascination in this orderly review of the great host living beyond the pale of the law, and at war with all honesty, and hence I am emboldened to believe that what is not tiresome to write will not be wearisome to read.

Pickpockets in New York are almost without equal as cunning, daring criminals. They have, too, the great virtue of industry, and ply their trade with such unintermitting zeal that each one of them seems multiplied by a score. There are not more than three hundred of these light-fingered operators, notwithstanding a prominent detective lately announced his belief in the existence of a thousand. Nor would his statement seem incredible to the casual observer who should spend a day at the Central Detective Office and listen to the many "squeals for stuff," as the singular language of the place styles complaints that pockets have been picked. But when this casual observer learns that the New York pickpockets are the most industrious thieves upon earth; that a pair of them will "work" half a dozen different lines of stages and street cars in the course of the same day, and then be on hand in the evening in places of public resort, he will, perhaps, begin to wonder why the three hundred do not every day steal every watch and wallet in the city. The adroitness and impudence of our pickpockets are matchless; and although they are so often arrested that many of them are probably in custody several times in every year, it is so difficult to fix their crimes upon them that it is a rare event for any expert professional to be convicted. In "mobs" of two or three, they infest the street cars, when they are overcrowded. Standing upon the rear platform where every one passing in or out must push past them, when a good watch-chain is discovered upon a vest they hustle the passenger violently about under pretence of making room for him, and, in the ensuing confusion, the watch and chain abruptly change owners. Sometimes they repeat this operation several times upon the same car, within as many minutes, and when they leave a car it is only to get upon another, and continue to ply their trade. They are so rarely taken in the act of crime that during the year 1868 only twenty-five persons were brought to trial for assaults with intent to steal as pickpockets, and of this small number two escaped conviction by reason of the insufficiency of the proof. About one-fourth of the pickpockets are females, who frequent dry-goods shops, churches, funerals, fairs, and other places crowded with ladies. These females are equally gifted with the males in the stealthy, light-fingered art.

The dexterity of these rascals is astonishing. As a case in point I must cite the old gentleman who had involuntarily contributed several watches to the fraternity, and becoming tired of their constant demands upon him, finally had his watch so strongly welded to the chain that even pickpockets could not separate the two, and to this precaution added that of fastening the chain securely to his vest. One day he entered a Broadway stage, and presently feeling a tug at his watch, turned around so as to give the thief every chance to prosecute his task. The tug was twice repeated, and a moment afterward the seat next to him was vacated, the clerical-appearing man who had occupied it having left the stage. The old gentleman laughed immoderately over his triumph, and explained to his astonished fellow-passengers: "That fellow who just got out is a pickpocket. He took three pulls at my watch, but you see he didn't get it!" Again the old gentleman's face was full of merriment; but happening to thrust his hand into his trowsers pocket, a sudden change came over his features, and he cried out: "But the rascal's got my pocket-book, with $500 in it!"

This experience is that of many, and there are thousands of persons, scattered all over the globe, who know from personal episodes how adroit, bold and industrious are the New York pickpockets. There are others at home who can tell that these chevaliers, more than all other thieves, are possessed of political power and, in some localities, are a controlling element in ward caucusses and nominations. The multitude of ward roughs, who do the voting, and the fighting necessary to effective voting, look up to the well-dressed, suave pickpockets as superior beings, and the latter accept the reverence as so much grist to their mills. They use the roughs to force their favorites to power, and fill high places with creatures dependent on their bounty and ready to do their bidding. Much has been asserted, and more imagined of the political power of thieves in New York, all of which may not be true; but it is certainly a fact that whatever of such power belongs to professional criminals is almost exclusively the property of the pickpockets, who are no less dangerous at the ballot-box than in street cars.

Shoplifters constitute another grand division of the army of rogues, and number not more than two hundred persons, fully one-half of whom are females, who are by far the most successful in this line of business, as, from their costume, they have better opportunities for carrying away the stolen goods from under the very eye of the owner. These female shoplifters always operate in pairs, and one of the two invariably has under her dress an immense pocket, sustained by a girdle around her waist, which will easily swallow two or more pieces of muslin, or packages of similar bulk. Entering a shop together, one of them engages the attention of the shopkeeper, the other slips a package of goods from the counter into her capacious pocket.

Forgers, speaking of them as professionals, are hardly a class, so few are they in number. They do not exceed twenty-five, but it must be remembered that the figures include only the professionals, and that the amateur forgers are four or five times as numerous. The forger's first step is to inform himself of the average of the victim's bank account; his next to take a bed-chamber sneak into the speculation. His partner contributes to the stock of the concern one of the cancelled checks of the victim, some of his ink, and a b ank check, all of which he steals from the victim's office. Provided with these art cles, the forger works patiently, until he produces a perfect fac-simile of the victim's signature. Then the check is made out, generally for a sum less than $500, and the forger summons his second partner in some bank-sneak who has had a run of bad luck, and being temporarily in difficulties, is ready to turn his hand to any promising job. As the bank-sneak can assume any shape at will, and preserve his nonchalance under the most adverse circumstances, it is his business to present the check at the bank and receive the money for it. The forger himself never enters the bank, but is invariably lurking in the vicinity; so if the fraud is successful, the sneak is certain that the eye of his principal is upon him from the moment he leaves the bank, and that he has no chance to secure more than his legitimate share of the proceeds of the operation. By such means as these the forgers operate, and although few in number, they are so industrious and so skilful that the banks of the city are yearly victimized to the extent of thousands of dollars. Very recently the city was congratulated upon the decline of the crime of forgery, and the report of the Police Commissioners was cited as showing only 113 arrests for the offence during the past year. But these figures included hardly one of the professional and dangerous forgers, and did not even approximate the number of times the crime had been committed. Banks very rarely prefer justice to their own interest, and if a forger is content to cheat them out of small amounts they pocket the loss in silence, and never report the matter to the police at all. But the fact that such and such banks have been defrauded by forged checks leaks out through various channels, and the police have not therefore fallen into the error of believing that the forgers have retired from business. Sometimes the forgers strike so heavily that the bank forgets its caution and "squeals" with exceeding liveliness. This was the case about two years ago, when the City Bank paid a check for $75,000 purporting to be signed by Cornelius Vanderbilt, and endorsed by Henry Keep. So excellently well were these signatures made, that the check was unhesitatingly paid, notwithstanding its large amount, nor was it discovered that both names were forgeries until after some time had elapsed. The cashier of the bank remembered distinctly the features and person of the man who presented the check, and made a pen-and-ink sketch of both that enabled Detective George Elder to follow the forger through several States, and finally to arrest him in an interior town of Illinois. Elder also recovered nearly all the money of the bank, and hence the forger is now doing the State some service in the Sing Sing Prison to which place he was committed under the name of Henry Livingston. But while this case is one of the most remarkable forgeries upon record, and brought Livingston temporary, but widespread notoriety, his partial success has not induced any of his *confrères* to imitate his example. They have chosen rather to follow the safe and beaten path.

Confidence-operators exist only because fools and their money can be easily parted. Strictly speaking, they are not thieves, but belong rather to the category of swindlers; nor can the majority of those detected in the offence be justly called professionals. Any impecunious person, whose moral perceptions are slightly blunted, may be driven by temporary distress to some indirection in raising means for a pressing emergency without intending to commit a crime. But there are about one hundred men and women in New York who depend for subsistence solely upon the credulity of their fellow creatures. By means of some plausible tale they manage to filch a very comfortable living out of other people's pockets, and some of them elude the vengeance of their victims for months or years. A recent case is the most striking illustration of the manner in which these cheats achieve greatness that the police annals can give. A woman, past middle life, of unprepossessing appearance, and by no means of winning address, was lately taken before a police magistrate, on a charge of false pretences, made by a man whom she had induced to lend her a small sum of money, by the statement that her uncle had recently died in Germany, leaving her a large fortune which she desired to settle upon the children of her first husband. To accomplish this purpose she wished the complainant to act as guardian of the children and trustee of the estate, and the money advanced was to pay a lawyer for drafting the papers necessary to the transfer. After her arrest, several other victims appeared against her, and it was developed that the gross amount of her frauds by this shallow device was upwards of $3,000. In every case the persons she applied to had snapped eagerly at being invested with the control of the apocryphal fortune, and had readily dropped the substance they had to snap greedily at its shadow.

Receivers of stolen goods, or "fences," as the thieves more tersely name them, not only make thievery possible, but are the only persons who ever become rich from its proceeds. The thief might steal cart-loads of costly silks and not be a dollar the richer, were there no fences to take the "lush" off his hands, and work it again, by degrees, and unsuspected, into the regular channels of trade. The thief chaffers with the "fence," threatens him, sometimes with physical hurt, and sometimes with the loss of his custom, but all the time knows that he is utterly in the power of the fence, who is the inevitable evil of his calling. Thieves are always without money, and cannot afford to quarrel with men who stand to them somewhat in the relation of bankers, and hence fences and thieves maintain amicable relations despite the fact that the thieves know that the fences cheat them every day worse than they did the day before. If the thief ever gets from the fence one-fifth of the value of the stolen goods he considers himself the luckiest of villains, and if he ever gets more the fence looks upon himself as the weakest of fools. The fences manage to keep up a semblance of pursuing a legitimate calling. They stand as a cordon of pickets between roguery and honesty, and, while distrusted by both, neither can absolutely dispense with them. Very rarely indeed is a first-class fence fairly caught, and more rarely still convicted. In New York the doctrine that "the receiver is as bad as the thief," has been practically discarded. Thieves use fences to "work off" stolen goods, and detectives use them to trace and recover stolen property. Between the two, fences find not only safety, but great profits. It is a fortunate thing for the city that there are no more than one hundred of these professional receivers; as they multiply, so do robberies increase. Any pawn-broker or junk-dealer is liable to, and very often does, become innocently a receiver of stolen goods; but the amount of property that can be worked off through them is inconsiderable; for in going to them the thief incurs a risk he will not take until all other expedients fail. It may be surmised, therefore, that the extirpation of professional receivers would very materially lessen the number of sneak robberies and burglaries. There is sufficient probability of this result to make the experiment worth trying; but there is no hope that it will be tried until detectives shall abandon the practice of using one criminal to entrap another.

There are other classes of criminals who must be briefly reviewed and dismissed. "Buckhoos"—the word was never before written, and I am not sure as to the orthography—is the name given to a small band of prowlers in the Fourth Ward, who have qualified themselves for their "lay" by one short voyage, whereby they pick up a stock of sea phrases sufficient to enable them to become boon companions of sailors ashore, and thus lure them to the dance-houses, where they are mercilessly robbed. As different as can be from the "buckhoos" are the butcher-cart robbers, once known as hog-thieves, who gain their title by the fact that they have a butcher cart with a fast horse attached, standing near the scene of an intended robbery, and jumping into the cart the moment their crime is accomplished, rarely fail to outstrip pursuit. Formerly these fellows devoted themselves exclusively to hog stealing, and a very profitable and pleasant occupation they made of it. Driving through the upper parts of the city, when a hog was seen in the street the cart was stopped, out jumped the thieves—usually two—and seizing the hog, threw it into the cart and drove off at a spanking gait, before the astonished animal had time to even begin to squeal. Very industriously, indeed, did the thieves work this "racket," and they only abandoned it when the raw material was exhausted, and not a hog was to be seen in the streets. As the hog-thieves went down, the "smashers" came up, and the peculiar plan of operations that gave these last their name, is of comparatively recent origin. Their first point is to provide a plate of iron about nine inches square, with a handle upon one side, and armed with this to smash in the show-windows of jewellers, or the protecting glass of banking-houses, and steal the valuables behind the glass. Akin to the "smashers" are those desperate thieves the police style "hangers-up," who steal upon a man in some private place, bind him hand and foot, and after robbing him leisurely and effectually, go away, leaving him to loosen himself as best he may. The most notable case of this kind is the Bowdenheim Bank robbery, when the thieves entered the house of the cashier, bound and gagged the whole family, and having secured the keys of the bank, robbed it without molestation. But I cannot possibly name within reasonable limits all the little coteries of the lawless, who have gained distinctive names by remarkable deeds, but who in the walks of their everyday crime belong to some one of the grand divisions enumerated.

It is singular that while the police authorities of London can report that there are in that city 4,336 habitual criminals, and 1,740 houses of bad character, including 1,064 brothels, the same authorities in New York profess that it is utterly impossible to obtain similar facts, in the much more easily policed city under their charge. Under the old Municipal Police system, the captains of wards were required to make reports of all known and suspected disreputable characters within the limits of their commands; but under the Metropolitan *régime*, this excellent practice was soon discontinued, and the precise executive head of the Police was not ashamed, on a late occasion, to declare that he had no idea as to the number of the criminal population of New York, and that it was impossible to obtain the information. The task thus decreed to be impossible, has been accomplished in these pages, and solely by the agency of police captains and detectives, who would have been compelled to report the same facts to the Central Police Office, had they been ordered to do so. The central authorities have indeed had a vague idea that it was incumbent upon them to know something of the criminals they are popularly supposed to have under surveillance, and hence there is a regulation requiring officers arresting persons known to be professional criminals, to have their photographs taken for the "Rogue's Gallery." How rigidly this regulation has been enforced, and how valuable are its results, can be imagined when it is known that only 498 persons have thus far been photographed, and that the number is made up almost exclusively of common-place chance-sneaks, shop-lifters, and confidence-operators, and includes very few of the adroit and daring outlaws known to be at large in the streets. No bond-robber, or safe-burster, or thief of high degree, whose name is known in police circles the nation over, has ever been seized by the camera for the official collection. The bald fact is sufficiently suggestive, and I have never heard any explanation attempted. The "Rogues' Gallery" is of some little value as it is; but it could so easily be made a potent and complete agency in detective work that its paucity of faces is one of the many official mysteries crowding the marble pile in Mulberry street, known as "Police Headquarters."

CASUAL CRIMINALS.

AT a public meeting in 1871, the Rev. Henry W. Bellows declared that there are in the city of New York 30,000 professional thieves, 20,000 lewd women and harlots, 3,000 grog shops, and 2,000 gambling establishments. Such statements as these, by a gentleman so distinguished as Dr. Bellows for strict adherence to attainable facts, prove the urgent necessity there is for this series of articles. In the present chapter I am to deal with that large casual class which gives rise to these gross exaggerations, and I cannot do a better public service than to say, by way of preface, that the professional criminals are less than 3,000, the public prostitutes living in 601 houses of ill-fame and using houses of assignation, not more than 5,000, the licensed grog-shops over 7,000 in number, and the gambling establishments, including 92 faro banks and all the places where lottery tickets are sold, less than 600. We are bad enough as it is, but if we were in anything like the condition as to our criminal, disorderly, and pauper classes asserted by common rumor, New York, rich and powerful as she is, could not sustain the burden.

No class is more costly or in a certain way more offensive to the metropolis than that which drops into crime, as Mr. Wegg did into poetry, as an occasional interlude to more reputable employment. In consequence of the intense energy of its journals in collecting and commenting upon news, New York has acquired a reputation for lawlessness which, upon a candid consideration of all the facts, is found to be in a measure undeserved; and it is further to the credit of the city that nearly all the bad repute which rightfully belongs to it is due to its amateur instead of its professional criminals.

In every great community made up of heterogeneous materials, there are always a large number constantly hovering on the outermost edge of the law, where only the slightest influence is required to push them beyond it; and this is especially true of New York. No modern city has a population so mixed and in some portions more dense, or is so liable, from certain peculiarities in its system of government, to foster the disorderly classes which produce all of the casual crimes and much of the squalor of the great city. A population in which all nationalities are not only represented but intermingled, which is struggling with bitter intensity for bare subsistence, and which imbibes from a vicious political system a dangerous disregard for the rights both of person and property, is not one which can be expected to rigidly observe all the obligations of the law. The wonder is not that the prisons of the city are constantly crowded, and that its police force is overtaxed by the disorderly classes, but that these lawless elements do not entirely defy restraint. A stranger wandering at random about the city, if competent to correctly judge palpable facts, will be amazed to encounter so little violence when he sees everywhere the most abundant provocation to outrages.

The city has 7,500 licensed places where intoxicating liquors are sold, and the majority are dens where only the vilest stuff can be found. The best of fermented beverages has been contemned as maddening draughts of Hippocrene, and it is not strange that the use of such as those retailed in New York should result in a single year in 32,721 arrests for intoxication, and in 14,935 for disorderly conduct; in arrests for assault and battery to the number of 6,799, and for the more serious crime of assault where a deadly weapon was used 875 during the same period. This vast army of casual criminals has been steadily increasing from year to year, and by keeping pace with the increase in the number of liquor dens has shown the source of its recruitment. It is this army of casuals, rather than the comparatively small squads of professional thieves, which keeps the vast machinery for the administration of correctional law in constant operation, at an annual expense to the tax-payers of the city of nearly $4,000,000.

The maintenance of police force alone cost $2,837,836 in 1869, exclusive of building. And owing to the lavishness of New York in paying the highest possible rates for the least possible service, the five police courts cost nearly $200,000, the Court of Special Sessions only about $20,000, and the Court of General Sessions an enormous total which has never been distinctly divulged to the general public, but must approximate $150,000. This police force and these tribunals would rot in idleness had they only the professional outlaws to restrain or punish, and would scarcely be endured by the public which supports them. The fact is therefore evident, that a view of the nether side of New York would be incomplete without this presentation of the casual criminals.

There is the high authority of a proverb for the declaration that "when wine is in, wit is out," and it is not strange that the stuff sold in the bar-rooms of New York impels men to play such fantastic tricks with the established usages of society as occasionally get them inside a prison. These constitute the most numerous, as they are the least reprehensible and most unfortunate, of our casual criminals. It is a terrible thing to get so drunk in New York as to fall into the hands of the police, for the debauch is followed by something much more serious than the splitting headache which is said to be its usual result. Men of property and general respectability can speak with the wisdom of sad experience of the depletion that awaits the unfortunate taken in the act of committing the misdemeanor, known as "being in the public street in a state of intoxication." So long as he is in the hands of the police, the culprit guilty of heinous offence is entirely safe. If he is arrested during hours when the magistrate is sitting, he is rushed at once upon his fate by being taken immediately before that official, provided he is not too drunk; but at other hours he is locked up to await the next session of the court. When taken away his valuables, which had all passed into official keeping when he was incarcerated, are returned to him, and he is led away as a lamb to the slaughter.

As producers of travesties upon law and justice, the police courts of New York are unequalled. Some of them occasionally regard the statutes provided for the cases presented before them, but it is always safe to suppose that the most of them will be a law unto themselves in any event, but especially so when dealing with intoxication. There are five police courts in the city, four of which are provided with two magistrates who sit alternate weeks, thus making in reality nine separate tribunals, and with two or three exceptions it makes little difference to the inebriate which one he is taken before. If he is a poor miserable wretch, he is summarily dismissed with a commitment for ten days; but if he exhibits signs of being worth the plucking, he soon realizes how dreadful a thing it is to get drunk. The forms of law are of course rigidly observed, but the law has no stronger conviction than that it is proper to "fight the devil with fire," and is provided with a vast armory of weapons by which evil may be wrought with the possibility of some ultimate good being achieved. In criminal practice none of these weapons is so potent or so often used as the "commitment for examination," which means anything or nothing as the exigencies of each case may demand. When dealing with intoxication, it means that the culprit stays in the prison below during the pleasure of the magistrate, who meantime informs the inquiring friends of the prisoner that he is fined $10. The law awards that sum, and the judge so relentlessly exacts it when there is the faintest chance of getting it, that it always comes before the prisoner goes. There are many cases where the unfortunate has the money on his person, when of course this device of temporary commitment is not used, as he hands over at once the amount demanded, and is at liberty to go and sin as often on the same terms as he may please. When he has not the money at hand, he finds to his great sorrow that the penalty of the law is only a small part of the tolls he must pay on the road to liberty. He must communicate with his friends, and the court messenger never stirs without a fee. He is so unmanned by his new and dreadful position as a prisoner, that he is an easy prey to the harpies in the shape of shyster lawyers who infest these courts, and who persuade him that their influence or advocacy is a pearl of great price, and he pays for it accordingly. If in the end, when all expenses are counted up, he gets out for less than $50, he is fortunate, and the money is the least of the losses entailed by his debauch. He has ever afterward the consciousness that he has been a criminal, however casually, and he has seen how great a mockery is the administration of justice which he enjoys, and he is never thereafter worth as much to himself or the community. There is nothing so likely to make a man forget his obligations both private and public as an experience, no matter how slight, in the police courts of the great city.

But the hapless man who only gets drunk sees only the surface of a depravity that is wholly visible to but one class of criminals who habitually violate the law, but only casually encounter punishment. There are over six hundred houses of public prostitution in the city, and the inmates of at least half of them are made by the officials to understand in some way that they are criminals. In this case the police force is not free from reproach, for it is asserted as a general fact that blackmail is levied upon many of these houses as the price of toleration, but in some cases tribute is exacted by the process familiarly known as "pulling." Armed with a warrant which authorizes him to arrest the proprietress for keeping a disorderly house, a police captain or sergeant makes a sudden raid upon the selected den at an hour when it is certain to have the most inmates, and carries off captive everybody he finds in it. The prisoners being arraigned before the magistrate issuing the warrant, the penniless are discharged, those promising something better committed for examination, the proprietress held in nominal bail to keep the peace or for appearance at a trial which is never to occur, and that is all the public ever knows of the affair. It is to the credit of some of the magistrates that they will not issue these warrants, and to the police captains or sergeants that few of them will have anything to do with the process if they can avoid it. There are a few, however, who seek it with an avidity that shows their purpose, and the frequency with which they use it is sufficient explanation of the anomaly presented in a small salary covering large expenditures. The same means have been employed to bleed the gamblers, and one police sergeant, who won the plaudits of the newspapers for his incessant efforts to put an end to the sinful game of faro, suddenly concluded his labors to that end by absconding with another man's wife and some thousands of dollars which he had never earned. This was an extreme case, but in a modified form it is one that almost any luckless gambler, or any one of those sorrowful wrecks of womankind that float into the streets at nightfall, can tell you is constantly occurring. Baited but hardly hampered by authority, known to be constantly beyond the pale of the law, but only molested at the dictates of capricious greed, there is but one class of casual criminals more to be pitied than these poor Mag dalens.

The second division of the army of casuals, comprising 14,935 persons arrested in a single year for disorderly conduct, is something of an annoyance, but scarcely a discredit to the metropolis. The misdemeanor is a vague if not glittering generality, and depends exclusively upon the fancy of the policeman making the arrest. There is no citizen whom it is safe to insure against being seized to answer the charge at the station house. The man of the most sterling worth and soundest discretion is liable to become involuntarily involved in some street dispute, or to be one of many others happening to be spectators of something occurring in a thoroughfare, which an arriving policeman, who knows nothing of the facts, may consider provocative of a breach of the peace ; and in that case it usually happens that if there is any one in the crowd having less to do than any one else with the disturbance, that one is taken to answer for it. All of these casuals are not of this character, but where they are worse it is rarely that they are guilty of anything more serious than a disposition to wrangle without sufficient provocation. The crowding of men together generally leads to disputes that provoke or threaten breaches of the peace, and it is therefore natural that the tenement houses, where dozens of families are crowded into a limited space, should produce by far the larger portion of the annual crop of arrests for disorderly conduct. The offence never having malice as an ingredient, and being of a character so undefined that the most cautious citizen can never be certain of not committing it, there is every reason to believe that the substantial ends of justice would be served by omitting it from the statutory list of acts liable to penalties. Its presence in the law gives the police patrolmen a discretionary power that few use discreetly, and its absence would inflict no greater evil upon the community than to stay the uplifted hand of the law until some actual crime had been committed. Generally prevention is better than cure, but in this case it is so impossible to say what is to be prevented, that the proverb does not apply.

The next division of the casual host numbers only 6,799, and its turpitude is greater only in the degree that blows are more criminal than hot words. "Assault and battery," as the law terms it, although there is rarely any battering and usually but little assault about it, is the simplest, most natural, and least reproachful of the actual crimes of which the law takes cognizance. To strike another a blow with the "closed fist," as the complaints allege, is certainly an overt breach of the peace, "against the peace and dignity of the State, and contrary to the statute in such case made and provided," but it does not brand the perpetrator as the most heinous of malefactors, nor even stamp him as a dangerous character. When a man gets into an affray and uses no other than natural weapons, there may be much good left in him, and he is deserving of much greater consideration than is generally shown these violators of the law. Any of us are liable to let passion get the better of discretion, and so give the blow which the law declares a punishable misdemeanor; but it should not follow, as it often does, that if the casual criminal happens to be one able to satisfy the offended statute with exemplary damages, he should be mulcted accordingly. And he is further to be commiserated from the fact that whatever penalty is taken is exacted by the forms of law perhaps, but contrary to its letter, for the statistics show that final disposition is made of more than half these cases in the police courts. In the year only 2,242 of these cases were examined in the Special Sessions, and it is fair to presume, from the general knowledge to be obtained of those institutions, that a large proportion of the remaining 4,557 had a most sorrowful experience. Yet in many of the cases the offence in itself was trivial, and would have been fully punished by the brief imprisonment which must always be endured before a magistrate is reached.

But these remarks apply to only a portion of those arrested for assault and battery, as there are many who get less of punishment than they deserve. Nothing breeds so fast in a great city liberally supplied with drinking saloons, as a reckless turbulence which is so akin to that malicious disregard of human life which is the essential ingredient of murder, that the difference is scarcely perceptible. A large proportion of the assaults being bar-room fights, an offence that is venial in itself becomes alarming in its suggestion of the enormous number of apprentices in the art of homicide which the city harbors. There are thousands of youths between fifteen and twenty-one years of age constantly roaming the streets, who give the city nearly all of its disrepute, and furnish nine-tenths of its murderers. Their first lawlessness is committed by the blow with the "closed fist," but after a short season of this weak warfare on mankind they are apt to be armed with deadly weapons, and from being annoying pests become grave perils. They are casual criminals only during the brief years of boyhood, and soon ripen into habitual vagrants, thieves, or ruffians, and in each case become public burdens. Sodden with vile liquor, ready to give insult without provocation, indescribably filthy in language, person, and habits, they are entitled to a great deal less of grace at the hands of the authorities than they get. For they who deserve the most receive the least of the penalties meted out to the crime of assault and battery, and so generally escape all punishment that they comprise nearly the whole of the great number of cases where the offender is paternally told to go and sin no more, which injunction is so little regarded that the admonition must be and is often repeated.

The next division of the casuals, represented by 875 arrests during the last year of which police statistics have been published, is composed almost exclusively of those ruffians who have naturally advanced from the fist to the bludgeon, knife, or pistol. There is nothing unnatural in the fact that there have been this number of deadly affrays in New York in a single year, nor is there in it full justification of all the reproach which has been heaped upon the city, but there is certainly in it a warning that must be heeded. The fact that murder is attempted 875 times in a single year, and avoided in all but about sixty cases by the accident that the inflicted wounds do not happen to prove fatal, is one of grave import, which is in no wise lessened by the other fact that almost without exception these felonious assaults are committed by casual and not by professional criminals. In the long list of metropolitan murders during the past dozen years, the celebrated Rogers and Nathan crimes are almost the only ones done by professionals. Ninety times in a hundred homicide, attempted or completed, has liquor as the first cause, and is the work of those youthful ruffians who, being reputably employed during the greater part of their time, are the most dangerous of all lawless characters during their periodical debauches.

The latest murder reported at the time this article is written, is a most startling illustration of this general truth. Several young men, all under twenty-one years, all having trades at which they worked in the intervals between their drinking-bouts, and none of whom were known to be thieves, on a late Sunday entered a lager-bier saloon in First avenue. They demanded liquor, which being furnished they answered a request for payment by a combined attack upon the barkeeper, who having been knocked down, kicked, and beaten until he was disabled, one of the party, holding a pistol close to his head, fired a shot which produced death, and thus ended a wanton outrage with deliberate murder. These youths had barely escaped this horror scores of times before on the same day, during the whole of which they had been roaming, frenzied with drink, from saloon to saloon, everywhere demanding liquor and invariably refusing to pay for it. The terrible significance of this tragedy is not abated by the knowledge that while the Metropolitan Excise law was in force it could not have occurred when it did; for it makes little difference to a city where rum-crazed ruffians reel through the streets heavily armed, whether they use their deadly weapons on Sunday or some other day.

If this were an exceptional case, it might be dismissed as a frightful anomaly; but it is unfortunately an occurrence which happens every day, in a form modified certainly by the chances of each affray, but with the ingredient of murder present in every instance. Almost every hour of every night some of these reckless ruffians are roaming about the city, loaded with revolvers or knives, ready to use their weapons on all occasions; and if they get through the night without an affray, it is due to accident rather than purpose. Out of the ranks of these lawless youths have come all those noted desperadoes of whom the late Dave O'Day was a leading example, and who have made New York a reproach the world over. Yet these men are not criminals in the professional sense, as they do not gain their livelihood by their lawlessness, but by some legitimate employment, and their crimes are committed during their respites from labor. They are simply the natural products of a civilization that fires its recklessness with rum, then arms it with a pistol, and, turning it into the street to see what will come of it, pretends to be horrified when blood comes of it. There was a ghastly scene one morning in a basement eating house at the corner of Canal and Hudson streets, where a party of infuriated beasts had endeavored to bring a spree to a satisfactory end by the murder of their host, but had one of themselves killed in his stead, and the city duly shuddered when presented with the horrible details. There was a companion picture to this warning scene presented a few months later, when Dave O'Day, who was a chief actor in the first, died as he had lived, by the hand of violence. Again the city was appalled, and her rivals pharisaically rejoiced that they were not as she; but in neither case did the city strike, or her contemners advise her to strike, at the system which made possible these horrors, which were only exaggerations of incidents occurring every day.

It is true that there must be some turbulence in a great city of mixed population, but it is also true that there are more displays of violence in New York than should be permitted. The experiment of restraining the liquor traffic was only a partial success, and that experiment having shown that in spite of all restriction a certain number of people will get drunk, and, being drunk, will disregard all law, divine or human, it should also have suggested the propriety of devising some more effectual safeguard for human life. If the ruffians only killed each other, there might be enough in this result to recompense the community for the trampling on the law involved in reaching it; but it unfortunately happens that the wrong man is generally killed, and it is therefore absolutely essential that something effective should be done to prevent them. It may be interfering with personal liberty to a dangerous extent, to make the mere carrying of any deadly weapon a felony; but all police experience goes to show that this device will decrease the number of felonious assaults more than two-thirds; and that anything short of it will have no effect whatever in checking them. The law prohibits the carrying of what it terms "concealed weapons," but only such things as slung-shots are included in the designation, and it is a remarkable proof of the efficacy of the provision that the use of a slung-shot is a very rare occurrence in New York. The ruffian avoids the weapon with scrupulous care, because he knows that he is always liable to be arrested for intoxication or disorderly conduct, and if it is found upon him when searched at the station-house, the more frivolous charge is abandoned and he is sure of severe punishment for this violation of the statute. There can be no doubt that if the law included firearms and dangerous knives the effect would be the same; and with their teeth thus drawn, our drunken brutes would be comparatively harmless. As the experiment is manifestly worth trying, and would entail *no* hardship upon the reputable citizens who never carry arms of any kind, it is singular that it has never been ventured upon.

There is another class of casual criminals, and it is the one, with perhaps a single exception, which is "more sinned against than sinning." In a single year 7,031 persons have been arrested in the city for the crime of theft, of which number 2,122 were accused of grand larceny, and 4,909 of petty pilfering. In the former case, sympathy would in nearly every instance be wasted if bestowed upon any of these prisoners, as they are offenders who have subsisted by crime for years and are beyond the chance of reformation. To one of any experience in the methods and appearance of criminals, there is generally little difficulty in recogizing these veterans in warfare on mankind; but when a number of alleged petty thieves are arraigned at the bar of a minor tribunal, the casual is liable from mere carelessness to be considered as a professional and thus suffer gross injustice. The hardened thief is always so ready with a harrowing tale of pinching want and sudden temptation, that when it is the saddest truth that ever fell from human lips it comes to incredulous and unsympathetic ears. Yet in a city so over-crowded with struggling poor as this, a large proportion of the petty thefts are committed by persons more deserving of charity than censure. The professional outlaw who is worthy of being ranked as a public danger strikes at higher game than the unfortunate who, urged to crime by starvation, purloins some trifling article; and although it would not be safe to say that the pettiness of the theft removes it in a moral sense from the list of crimes, these cases are always sufficiently questionable to claim more careful investigation than they often receive. I have seen more of such cases than I desire to ever see again; for whether the plea be true, or, being false, is so told as to appear true, there is more pleasant entertainment than to hear it unavailingly uttered at the bar of justice, and I have heard it so uttered scores and scores of times.

Once it was a woman whose rags and gaunt face, made terrible by the wolfish eyes, ought to have been full confirmation of her story, who told of a husband dying more from want than sickness, and of three children crying for bread. She had begged for it without avail, and at last had stolen it. The crime was a venial one at best, but the outraged law that could be so merciful at times to the brawler or murderer could not forgive this trivial transgression, and the suffering woman was sent to jail. Again it was a boy, not more than ten years old, who, dwarfed by penury, was small and puny. He, too, had the ravenous eyes and hollow cheeks which the full-fed professional thief cannot counterfeit, and he, too, told a story that, corroborated as it was by his appearance, ought to have gained him forgiveness rather than punishment. In this case it was a shop boy who toiled sixteen hours in each twenty-four for a pittance barely sufficient to keep life in his little body, and who had struggled hopefully until his widowed mother, stricken down by sickness, was starving at home. Then he stole a dollar from the till of the shop, and being detected by his master was handed over to the police and sent to the House of Refuge as an incorrigible young rascal. What became of the mother I never knew, but most probably she starved to death, which is by no means an uncommon occurrence. Only yesterday, when looking over the mortuary tables for the week, I found marasmus credited with the taking of three lives, two of them being adults; want of proper food was most likely the origin.

There was another case more sorrowful than either of these, for it handed a rarely beautiful young girl, in whom honest and virtuous instincts were yet strong enough to rebel against her fate, over to a life of shame and crime. Probably, it must be admitted, it was a diseased heart that had led her astray; for being poor and vain, she had stolen a trifling ribbon from the shop where she was employed. She had not the excuse of actual want nor of a desolated home; but she was for all that only a casual in crime, and the law might, wisely tempering justice with mercy, have bid her go and sin no more. But the law on such occasions always seems to act as if it were very much afraid that criminals are about to disappear from the earth, and therefore does its best to secure a future supply by so dealing with novices in wrong as to make sure that they shall become more experienced. So in this case the unfortunate girl was sent to prison, where her beauty made her fatal friends. She came out with that convict stain which the uncharitableness of the world makes indelible, and she was naturally forced to take refuge with her prison associates. The last I heard of her she was a professional shop-lifter, and the companion of a noted sneak thief. Such as she is the law made her, and as she is certain to afford it a reasonable amount of occupation, it ought to be satisfied with its work.

These may be called extreme cases, but they are such as are liable to occur, and, for all any one knows to the contrary, do occur every day. Nor is it unusual for apparently able-bodied men to plead pinching want as an excuse for larceny, and although it is not to be expected that they should receive the same sympathy as women and children, their tales are often literally true. Thousands of men annually drift into the great city, victims of the delusion that it is an open mine to every comer, and it would be strange if many of these were not forced to beggary and some to crime. Generally they are men who are untrained in any skilled industry, and totally unfitted for those higher spheres of human labor in which there is plenty of room in town and country alike. Therefore these men become casual thieves for the means of subsistence, chiefly because they have not the means to get away from the city where they have first discovered their helplessness. Such men might be nothing but public burdens anywhere, and certainly are nothing else in the city; yet it is impossible to be entirely unmoved when they tell how they have sought for work without finding it, and were finally driven to theft. Be the measure of their sin what it may, they are entitled to mention as forming a large company in the host of casual criminals.

There is yet one other class of these incidental doers of evil that is apt to make a man of common humanity snap his fingers in the face of the law that is responsible for its existence. Poverty is closely akin to crime the world over, but an ordinance of the city of New York makes it an offence punishable with arrest and imprisonment to beg in the public streets. It is pleaded in extenuation of this device for the propagation of crime, that the city bountifully provides for its really poor, and the law is intended to suppress only the charlatans who have made beggary a profession. Whatever its purpose, it has worked evil and evil only. It is more often enforced against children, who have been sent into the streets by their parents to beg than against any one else. It is freely granted that these children are a great annoyance in public places, and that the parents spend the money thus obtained in rum, and yet the wisdom of the ordinance is denied. For it happens when the law is put into practice that it is chiefly used to rid the fashionable theatres of these children, who gather at the entrances to solicit alms of the arriving patrons. This is, of course, at an early hour of the evening, when the courts are closed for the day, and the child then arrested is necessarily taken to a station house. If held, as many of them are, they are locked up for the night in cells, where they are surrounded with thieves, prostitutes, and drunkards, and where they are exposed in a single night to more corrupting influences than any child ought ever to encounter. It is impossible that they should be unharmed by this experience, and the fact is that they are often made by that one night thieves or vagabonds for life. They might be such without it, but the ordinance is entitled to the credit of changing a doubt into a certainty, and might itself be suppressed because of that merit with profit to the public. The time may come when law-makers will realize what a very serious thing it is to lay hands upon children and thrust them into prisons, and when they do the land will be burdened with fewer of both casual and professional criminals.

The principal divisions of the casual army have now been reviewed, but there are several small bands of skirmishers, one of which must be briefly mentioned. Meanest of all the casuals are the blackmailers, whose achievements are a libel upon crime. Any respectable burglar would scorn to watch his neighbor or friend for the purpose of taking him in the act of a peccadillo, which being known would destroy his family peace or standing in society, and then charging the highest attainable price for his silence. Yet this is what the blackmailers do whenever the opportunity is presented, and it is only because of the infrequency of this that they are not always professional instead of being generally casuals, who spy out the infirmities of friends as a means of profitably employing the odd hours of their worthless lives. Seldom punished, as those entrapped in their meshes dread the publicity that punishment involves, and will not prosecute them, the blackmailers, who are sometimes men, but oftener women, ply a trade that is as safe as it is infamous; and cases have been known where it was so remunerative as well, that a single victim has been plucked of thousands of dollars. More heartless and depraved than any professional thief, these human vampires are a pest of civilization, which would not be endured were their deeds less infamous or their numbers greater. Fortunately for themselves and to the credit of humanity, no class of criminals is so small or has so few recruits.

As a proof of the existence of these amateurs in villainy, I can mention one case which I obtained from an authentic source. A young butcher who was doing a prosperous business, happened to notice an elderly gentleman standing on a corner in a somewhat unsavory quarter of the city looking furtively about him. On this occasion the matter did not receive especial attention, but happening to see the same gentleman at the same place acting in the same way on several subsequent days, the butcher turned the matter over in his mind until he came to the conclusion that there was money in it. Leaving his legitimate business to his subordinates, he devoted himself to watching the elderly gentleman whose appearance to a close observer like the blackmailer, showed that he was worth plucking. For several days the self-imposed dirty task of the butcher was barren of the desired result, but he was finally rewarded by seeing the gentleman meet a lady, and in tracing them to a house of assignation which he saw them enter together. This was satisfactory as a step forward, but he was yet ignorant of the identity of either party, and had yet much work before him. He waited until the pair came out, and after they separated, as they did soon after leaving the house, he followed the man to his home which he found to his great relief to be the abode of wealth. Not yet possessed of all the facts required for his operations, he watched again, until he traced the pair once more to the house of assignation. Again he waited until they reappeared, and this time followed the woman to her home, which was a difficult task, as she took a very tortuous route, but he kept close upon her through all her turnings, and finally traced her to a highly respectable house in Brooklyn. He had now laid the foundation for his operations, which were simple in the extreme but as effective as they were simple. His first step was to write a letter to the man telling him that he knew of his liaison and demanding an interview. That was of course immediately granted, and when they met the blackmailer demanded $1,000 as the price of his silence, and the money was given him. The woman was then approached, and she too finding herself in the nets of the toiler, paid him $500. She was not again molested, but the man was fleeced again and again until he had been robbed of nearly $10,000, and he was finally compelled to fly from the city in order that he might save any of his property. The butcher meantime prospered on his spoils, and was so utterly without conscience that he boasted of his exploit, and announced his purpose to repeat at the expense of new victims whenever the opportunity should be presented.

This may have been an extreme case, and I hope for the credit of humanity that it was; but I have the names and dates of others of the same general character which are scarcely less flagrant in their incidents. It seems incredible that men will pay such large sums as hush money when they are detected in crimes or peccadilloes, but the fact is indisputable. There are many cases on the police records to show that where only breaches of financial trusts have been involved, the fears of the culprits have been so worked upon that they have surrendered far more than the product of their transgressions to the blackmailer. Cases of this kind have led to many suicides and to numerous "mysterious disappearances," where the victims finding their condition at last to be intolerable seek refuge in death or in sudden flight to unknown parts, and are never seen again in their old haunts. I can most forcibly illustrate how general and abject is the fear of these vampires by narrating a case which was told me by one of the two persons immediately concerned. A merchant of mature years and most reputable standing, who was married and had a large family, formed an illicit connection and established his paramour in a house in a retired street. This house soon excited curiosity as to its inmates, which was, however, very difficult to gratify. One stormy winter night a gentleman happened to pass the house at the instant the door was opened and the merchant was about to step out. The latter seeing some one in the street stepped hastily back and closed the door. This roused the curiosity of the gentleman, who posted himself in the shadow of a tree and waited for the other to come out. When he did so the gentleman stepped briskly out so that the two met and stared at each other in the light of the street lamp. The gentleman seeing an entire stranger laughed inwardly at his foolishness, and dismissing the incident from his mind, went his way. It so happened that the next day the gentleman, who was an insurance surveyor, had business with the firm of B. & Co. The moment he entered the counting room and said to Mr. B., "Well, I've come to see about that matter," that gentleman turned color and stammered out that it was all right. The surveyor, who had not recognized the merchant as the person he had seen the previous night, said he supposed that it was all right, but he wished to see that it was. Mr. B., with great trembling, took him into a private room and eagerly asked how much he wanted. The astonished surveyor, looking more carefully at his questioner, recognized him and hastened to inform him that he was not a blackmailer, but was an insurance surveyor who had called to see about some new heating arrangements in the store, which bore upon the insurance. A sigh of relief escaped the merchant, and becoming satisfied that his secret was safe with its new possessor he regained his composure.

There is little need to multiply these illustrations of the extreme meanness of which human nature is sometimes capable, but as blackmailers are more often women than men, I must fortify myself with at least one citation. A young man of general good character and excellent position and prospects, who was the paying teller of a bank, was so unfortunate as to become entangled in the meshes of a woman who had not even beauty to offer as an excuse for her frailty. She soon began to extort money from him by threatening to expose him, and at last became so importunate that she appeared regularly every week in the street before the banking-house to receive her hush-money, which every week she increased in amount. The savings of her victim had been exhausted, and he had made one abstraction from the funds of the bank, when fortunately for him a police captain who knew the woman happened to notice her before the bank, and by waiting and watching possessed himself of her purpose. He then took her in custody, and by dint of threats which he knew he could never fulfil, he managed to frighten her from her prey, and the young man was saved.

These cases might be multiplied endlessly, but I have said enough to justify my general denunciation of these harpies. With the exception of these few monsters, the casual criminals are entitled more to pity than censure. They are the victims of circumstances, or of a recklessness born of a legal blunder, and their crimes, even when so serious as the shedding of blood, never have their origin in total depravity.

HARBOR THIEVES.

SAUL and Howlett are among the most noted names in the criminal annals of New York. Members, and in some sense leaders of a gang of daring pirates infesting the harbor of the metropolis, they crowded years of infamy into the short span of boyhood, and achieved the bad eminence of the gallows on the 28th of January, 1853. Saul was then only twenty years of age, and Howlett was even a year his junior.

Young as they were, they were early patriarchs in crime. And yet, while hundreds of outrages upon persons and property were reasonably attributed to them, only one was at last and with great difficulty legally brought home to their doors. That one was a brutal, wanton murder, committed on the night of the 25th of August, 1852, on board the ship Thomas Watson, then anchored in the East river, when they killed Charles Baxter, the watchman of the vessel, who had detected them in the act of robbing it. The crime had no human witness, and the two boy desperadoes, with a drunken associate sprawled helplessly in the bottom of their boat, rowed leisurely ashore, carelessly counting up the gains of the night, and without a thought that they had done their last murder.

General suspicion and bad repute rather than direct evidence led to the dragging of that sad tragedy on the lonely ship into the light of law and retribution. Prior to that night Saul and Howlett had been well known to the police as harbor thieves, and were suspected of several mysterious homicides which had occurred within a few months on the water fronts ; but no positive proof of their complicity in any of these outrages, with the then imperfect appliances of the detective police, could be obtained against them. Still they were so much suspected that keen policemen of all ranks kept as close watch of them as was possible.

Early in the evening of the 25th of August the two were seen by a patrolman in a bucket-shop of the Fourth Ward. The officer's attention was particularly directed to them by the fact that William Johnson, one of their associates, was beastly drunk, and he stood for some moments before the door debating with himself the propriety and necessity of taking that wrecked robber to the station-house. Finally, concluding that the trouble would be greater than the possible reward, he passed on and left the party.

From that carouse, protracted to a late hour, the two pirates passed to the robbery of the Watson, leaving Johnson, who was drunk to uselessness, stretched in the bottom of their small boat alongside. While rifling the vessel the faithful watchman was encountered, and murder followed as a natural incident of the robbery. They left the ship unseen, but also left a hat behind them ; and that fact, reinforced by independent witnesses to many of their movements on shore immediately preceding and succeeding the murder, finally entangled them in the meshes of the law, the crime was traced to them, and they at last with something of bravado confessed the truth.

Baxter's murder being something more than an ordinary crime, and the feeling it excited being intensified because it was the last of several similar crimes which had crowded upon each other's heels, called forth extraordinary exertions upon the part of the police. The best men of the force were put upon the case, with George W. Walling, now an inspector and valued veteran of the police service, at their head. Their investigations at last led them into a maze of crime then unequalled and since unparalleled in the history of the city. It was found that Saul, Howlett, and Johnson were only three of a regularly organized band of a dozen harbor pirates, most of whom were boys under eighteen years of age, but all of whom were experienced criminals who had incurred almost every penalty of the most comprehensive crimes act. Young as they were, they had formed *liaisons* with abandoned women, and made them their partners in outrages no less than in love. They infested the rum-shops near the piers, lying in wait for prey, and no sum of money, large or small, ever met their eye but they dogged the possessor from the den to waylay and rob him at the first suitable spot. They sent their women at night into the fashionable and brilliantly lighted promenades, to lure to their hands higher game than came naturally to their haunts. They lurked on the deserted piers or in the adjacent streets to intercept and fleece boozy sailors or belated landsmen. At the dead of night they stole off in small boats by twos and threes, and, boarding the vessels lying at anchor, rifled them with impunity. To the ships moored to the piers they were a constant menace and continual loss, as they went on and off them at pleasure, carrying away everything movable.

Every night for many months was occupied in these spoliations, and there is now little doubt that every night had its murder. The people about the piers and water fronts of a commercial city at night are generally rovers, whose disappearance causes no remark. The river is at hand to receive the body, and gives it back to the eyes of men only when all traces of violence done in life are effaced. The work of murder was thus made one of comparative safety. With the ordinary footpad or the burglar homicide is a last resort, as he must always alarm the law by leaving the body of his crime to tell of his deed; but the harbor pirates secured safety rather than hazard by acts of violence; and sufficient evidence of their habits was procured to make it certain that murder was a means commonly used to destroy the proofs of lesser crimes. A man robbed and left to go his way might prattle to a policeman on the next block; but a man robbed, murdered, and thrown over a pier, was certain not to tell of the lesser grievance and very rarely to make known the greater. The logic was conclusive to the piratical mind and practically acted upon.

No one will ever know what human lives these ruthless outlaws destroyed; but from confessions made by different members of the band, meagre details of some of their deeds were obtained. One of these cases was a most atrocious crime, where a stranger was lured into an alleyway by one of the women and struck on the head with a slung-shot by her male confederate as he stood talking to her. His pockets were rifled, and the two wretches, without taking the trouble to see if he was dead or merely stunned, dragged him to the river a few rods away and threw him in. Another case was where two of them met a German at midnight on the deserted Battery, and although any thief of mettle would have disdained to meddle with so pitiful an object, they attacked him, one of them dealing the poor, homeless wanderer, as he in fact was, a blow with a slung-shot which instantly killed him. Having obtained twelve cents as the entire reward of their crime, they threw the body over the Battery wall; but it lodged upon the ice, where it was found next morning, to furnish a horror to the city and an insoluble mystery to the detectives. Another case brought home, but, like all the others, without legal evidence, to the miscreants, was a wholesale and equally unprofitable and needless homicide. Four of the pirates in a small boat encountered three sailors rowing to their ship anchored in the North river, stopped them, robbed them of the few pennies they had, and then, without other cause or excuse than to get their boat also, threw the poor wretches overboard, and they were drowned. These five murders were certainly chargeable to the gang, as was shown by the police reports written out at the time and filed in the District Attorney's office. These have since disappeared, however, and nothing can be now obtained but the outlines of that terrible era in the history of New York as it survives in the memory of the officers who made the investigations. This narrative, being obtained from that source, necessarily lacks the details of horrors which have never been fully divulged, and which, being only partially suspected, sent a shudder through the metropolis.

If hanging ever did any good, it was in the case of Saul and Howlett. That crisp January morning when they were strangled by due process of law in the yard of the Tombs prison, where so many since that time have suffered, was the last of their band and its methods. Since that time murder as a cover of robbery has been utterly unknown in the harbor or about the piers, and for a long time even property was comparatively safe. Piracy at the door of a great city was ended by a judicial homicide, and the apologists of a barbarism had an argument that comes in their way only once or twice in a lifetime. But they made more use of it than the facts warranted; for although the execution certainly put an end to habitual harbor homicides, it by no means extinguished river robberies. For a time, it must be admitted, there were few of these depredations; but the thieves soon became normally active, and the average of losses at their hands soon rose to what it had been, and continued to increase until the establishment of the harbor police, under the metropolitan system, made their calling more hazardous and their gains less certain. But the improved surveillance—or rather the fact of police protection to vessels in the harbor, as prior to that time there had been none at all—has made no other change. The harbor thief of to-day differs from his predecessor of the Saul and Howlett epoch in the fact that he habitually threatens murder and never does it, while the prototype habitually did murder and never threatened it; in every other way the ruffian of Slaughter-house Point or Hook Dock is as vicious, dangerous, and as much an annoyance and expense to the community as the worst rascal on record.

No criminal class is so troublesome and costly in proportion to its numbers as the harbor pirates. There are not more than fifty of the professional water thieves; but they so multiply themselves by industrious plying of their vocation that each of them answers for ten. All of these are so well known to the police that the gang and haunts of each are stored away in the memory of experienced officers, which, by the way, is the only record of criminal matters in New York I have been able to find. One only of these gangs, and that but few in numbers, infests the North river, having a rendezvous at the foot of Charlton street. There is sufficient reason for this paucity of marauders, as the west water front of the city is provided with covered, well-lighted piers, and, being occupied almost exclusively by ocean steamers, which are well guarded, offers little opportunty for depredation. The Charlton street thieves have therefore been driven into regular piracy, and, provided with a small sloop of excellent sailing qualities, ravages the shores of the North river almost to Albany. Good sailors and thorough thieves as they are, "Flabby" Brown, "Big Mike," Patsey Higgins, Mickey Shannon, "Big Brew," and "Slip" Locksley, who are all the members of the North river gang, have for several years levied wholesale contributions upon the farms and hamlets on the banks of the lordly river, and especially during the past summer became a romantic terror in the boldness and rapacity of their operations, and the rumor born of a fervid imagination that they were led by a female buccaneer of marvellous beauty and great adroitness. Having this extraordinary aid, their forays were unusually successful, and the gang can probably get through the winter when up-river raids are impossible without discomfort.

The harbor thieves proper are all found on the East river side of the city, congregating, when not at work, principally at "Slaughter-house Point," as the intersection of James and Water streets is named in police parlance, Hook Dock, at the foot of Cherry street, and at the foot of Roosevelt and of Rivington streets, the desperadoes of the river being found at the first two localities.

Thieves are gregarious to an unusual extent, and water thieves have the quality developed to an extent extraordinary even in their class. Each of these gangs is so entirely distinct in every respect, that a member of one will rarely be found with one of either of the others. Yet their depredations are entirely similar and committed in precisely the same way, and their habits in their leisure hours are in no way dissimilar. Their days are spent in sleeping, cheap drinking, petty gambling, or dickering with junkmen for the disposition of plunder on hand or to be acquired; and their evening recreations are confined to the Bowery drama or coarser pleasures. Social outcasts in every sense, they have no domestic ties they feel bound to respect, and like the mass of thieves in general, they are improvident to the recklessness of none of them being forehanded with the world, although some of them have been successful depredators for years and are known to have committed robberies which should have made them rich long ago. Their crimes, as a rule, are safer and more remunerative than those of any other class of criminals. The burglar oftener makes large hauls, but he runs more risk of capture; while the pickpocket less often has his booty captured by the police, but the average product of each of his operations is much smaller. The water thief of the first class steals only staple commodities, and, taking them in such shape that they cannot be identified by the owner, incurs very little risk of punishment or loss, even should he be captured, as he often is, with the stolen property in his possession. But while this peculiarity of their calling adds largely to the vexation and losses of importers, it does not increase the gains of the thief, who, in his eagerness to clutch a little money almost throws his booty away to the junkman, and wastes in exceedingly squalid pleasures the small reward of cunning persistence and daring which would make him of large account in the world's economy if legitimately employed.

No man works harder or under more disadvantages than the river thief; and none suffers more from exposure to the weather, unless it be the police who are constantly on the alert to circumvent him. Six to eight years will wear out all but the most hardy and drive them into the congenial haven of a junk-shop, from whence they make occasional forays upon shipping in the old way; and it is amazing that the river thief lasts as long as he does. Light is as fatal to his acts as darkness to that of the photographer; and so thoroughly is gloom an essential of his calling, that he can endure nothing stronger than the glimmer of stars. Even this he abhors, and he will frequently postpone a promising enterprise from time to time, waiting for a night when the darkness shall be so impenetrable that the great ships throbbing on the pulsing river are utterly isolated in the black chaos. If in addition to the darkness he can have elemental turmoil to drown the sound of his oars or of his stealthy movements aboard ship, he has a season especially suited to his needs. Therefore, meteorological conditions that enforce other men to quiet drive him into abnormal activity. When the very blackest shadows of night have settled on the harbor, and a great wind is whistling through the forest of masts and driving the sobbing tide before it, he is abroad. If a beating rain be added to the darkness and wind, he is still better pleased; or if a heavy mist usurps the place of all three, he is equally contented, for it hides his movements from prying eyes, and his sense of hearing is so wonderfully acute that, drifting with the tide in the dense fog, he thinks he can distinguish the thud of police oars from all others, and thus forewarned is able to avoid the dreaded Nemesis that relentlessly pursues him through the damp folds of fog as well as through rain and tempest. Whether the result be due to accident or the finesse of the thief, it is certain that misty nights, of which we fortunately have very few, are peculiarly fatal to property in the harbor, and equally propitious to the thieves, who are rarely detected when favored by this atmospheric condition.

Weather favoring, the river thieves, in triplets or quartets, glide out in small boats from under some pier near their haunts, and by rapid pulling shoot out into the middle of the stream. Whether bound to the Brooklyn wharves for choice sugar or Java coffee, or to the lower New York piers for fine rice, they invariably first seek mid-stream, and dally there long enough to baffle conjecture as to their intentions, in case their suspicious departure from the pier had been noticed. That object accomplished, they pull slowly and watchfully to their destination, and always pounce upon their prey from the water side by gliding alongside the ship to be rifled, and clambering up by a rope which carelessness has left hanging over the side; or, if this be wanting, they sneak around to the pier side and reach the deck by the lines. The hands of a vessel discharging cargo, being overworked during the day, are the soundest of sleepers; and when the thieves get on board, finding probably the entire crew, including perhaps the watchman—who has at least been driven to cover by the inclement night—in profound slumber, they incur little risk of interruption during their subsequent proceedings. They do not disdain to purloin any staple article; but especially delighting in coffee, sugar, and rice, it is to vessels discharging these cargoes that they are most partial. They never carry off a pound of either in the original package, but, always going with bags of their own which are devoid of trade-marks, fill them by abstracting from the importing cases or bags to the utmost capacity of their boat, and then pull away to a point convenient to the shop of a junkman selected beforehand as the purchaser of the plunder. It is when thus returning laden with spoils that they pass the critical period in their operations, as, being deep in the water, they make slow progress and are liable to be overhauled and captured by the police. This seeming catastrophe occurs to some of them, on an average, about four times per week; but it rarely results in anything more serious than temporary inconvenience. The thieves are lodged in the nearest station-house, and the plunder is sent to the Property Clerk at police headquarters; but when the plunderers are arraigned next day before a magistrate, they have the easy task of answering an intangible suspicion.

They were found in possession of goods supposed to have been, and which had in point of fact been stolen; and the police rarely fail to discover to a moral certainty the precise cargo from which they had been purloined. But the legal proof of theft is as rarely obtained, for the magistrates stick to the precise technicality of the law, which is perhaps right enough, and demand that the property shall be positively identified. It is not enough that the importer shall testify that on the night the thieves were taken he lost property precisely similar in quality and quantity to that found in their possession, but he must swear absolutely to his ownership of the property thus found. One grain of coffee, sugar, or rice, or one bale of cotton with the wrapper stripped off, is too much like every other grain or bale to permit a conscientious person to take such an oath. So the case falls, the prisoners are discharged, and, being prompt to demand the return of their property, as they call it, the courts are compelled to follow the technicality to its logical conclusion and comply with the demand.

Sergeant Edwin O'Brien, who is the most experienced and valuable of the harbor police, during last year made fifty-seven arrests upon the river, in every one of which cases he captured noted thieves having in their possession at the time property which had undoubtedly just been stolen; and yet he secured but three convictions out of the whole number. In all these cases the prisoners had stolen, as usual, in bulk, transferring to bags of their own—a process technically called "skinning"; and as they thus left behind trade-marks which could be sworn to, the owners were unable to identify except in the three cases where consciences were stretched to the point of making oath to the property itself.

Some years ago, however, the thieves were caught in an unexpected trap, and numbers of them compelled to do the State considerable service. They were just then particularly attentive to ships anchored at Quarantine, and, having a long pull before they could reach a covert, were very often captured with their plunder. But in every case the question of identity baffled the law, and the sole result of police interference was the relief of the thieves from the severe manual labor of getting their spoils to a market, as the police took possession of goods as well as thieves, and brought both to the city, where they were speedily compelled to surrender both. But at last O'Brien hit upon the happy thought of ignoring the larceny and prosecuting the outlaws for violating the Quarantine laws in boarding vessels under surveillance; and, being fortunate enough to obtain the proof in several instances, got his prisoners convicted, and thus frightened their fellows off the Quarantine grounds. In some other cases the thieves have been circumvented, when found in possession of stolen goods, by abandoning the charge of larceny and pressing that of smuggling; and in all such cases the thieves were unable to say when or where they paid duties, and so lost their plunder, the goods being forfeited to the United States. The mention of these facts has been made solely with the purpose of showing how difficult it is to bring these marauders to any kind of punishment.

Among the first-class river thieves whose methods and dangers have been told, there are some who stand out in bold relief from their fellows as desperate and successful outlaws. James Lowry and Tom Geigan, two of this class, are relics of the Saul and Howlett gang, to which they belonged as "kids," being then mere boys not more than ten years of age, but already noted for aptitude in crime. During the seventeen years which have elapsed since that terrible epoch they have been constantly engaged in harbor depredations whenever at liberty. Both have often been arrested; both have been subjected to several brief terms of imprisonment and have returned, to be again, as they have been all these years, the terrors of the East river. During their long careers they have stolen property to the value of hundreds of thousands of dollars; yet they have always lived on scanty allowance, and, it is said, are as poor now as when they served Saul and Howlett by crawling into cabin windows. Both are men of extraordinary physical powers, which are yet unimpaired, notwithstanding their years of exposure, during which they have scarcely been visited by the rheumatism, which is the common and most terrible foe of all their tribe, as it cripples and drives out of the vocation more river thieves by seventy times seven than the law ever did or ever can. Both are men who have made thievery an art, and have practised it with supreme indifference to everything but their own safety and profit.

Some years ago a cruel act of piracy was committed on a vessel off Riker's Island. The ship was boarded by thieves, who, finding themselves discovered and resisted, killed the mate and shot the captain as he was coming up the companion-way, inflicting a serious wound. Lowry was arrested for complicity in this crime, but the proof was defective and he was finally discharged; but whether guilty or not, he has never evinced much reluctance to resort to violence to secure his safety. Like all his fellows, he has had frequent rencontres with the police, where shots have been exchanged between the parties; but as this interchange of bullets has always been at long range and in the darkness of a wild night, wounds have rarely been inflicted by them on either side. In these affairs Lowry and Geigan have been no better or worse than their comrades, and their preëminence is due rather to their long service and uniform success as thieves than to any specially noteworthy deeds. Lowry, however, seems to be bent just now on distinctive renown, as he has become so embittered by police interference that he has sent word to O'Brien that he will kill him when he next attempts to arrest him.

In addition to these staple thieves—to invent a name for them—there are other classes equally annoying to general shipping; and chief among them are the tackle thieves. These are among the most forlorn of pilferers, whose ambition never soars above the purloining of rope ends, blocks, and other small articles which can be picked up on the decks of ships, which are of little value in themselves, and must be disposed of by the thieves for the merest pittance. These thieves generally select vessels anchored in the stream for their operations, clamber up the sides with the agility of practised athletes, noiselessly gather whatever booty is at hand, and, slinking away as stealthily as they came, are rarely detected on board.

Another gang is called the "Daybreak Boys," from the fact that none of them are a dozen years of age, and that they always select the hour of dawn for their depredations, which are exclusively confined to the small craft moored in the East river just below Hell Gate. They find the men on these vessels locked in the deep sleep of exhaustion, the result of their severe labors of the day; and as there are no watchmen, they meet little difficulty in rifling not only the vessels but the persons of those on board. If there is any such thing as a watch or money, it is sure to disappear; and it has often happened that one of these vessels has been robbed of every portable article on board, including every article of clothing, and the crew have awakened in the morning to find themselves in the distressing dilemma, as to clothing, of Falstaff's company. While this species of robbery is extremely provoking and a great hardship to the poor men who are its victims, it brings little profit to the precocious thieves, who will frequently obtain only coarse sustenance for a day in exchange for a boat-load of plunder, which costs them several hours of hard labor to steal and get to the junkman who buys it.

Very different from these abject "Daybreak Boys," both in the method and results of the thefts, is another class, which is perhaps the meanest of all, as it takes its booty by indirections which defy the law. "There are no thieves on these waters," say the police, "so bad as the lightermen;" and they will cite stubborn facts to show how these trusted servitors of commerce habitually and flagrantly betray their trusts. It must be admitted that they are sorely tempted, and it would be strange if they came off altogether with clean hands. Taking on cargoes at Harbeck's stores, Brooklyn, to be transported to the foot of Thirty-fourth street, North river, for shipment by rail, they have exclusive charge of thousands of tons of merchandise for a time long enough to deplete every package of a quantity so small that the abstraction is not noticed; but in the aggregate the thefts are enormous, and give rise to acrid disputes and often to litigation between sellers and buyers, on account of discrepancies in weight. The loss in every bag of coffee of a pound in weight between the importers' wharf and the railroad pier is a marvel impossible to explain if the lightermen honestly perform their functions; but this obvious explanation of a constantly-recurring fact is one which all parties unite in ignoring.

Such in brief and general terms are the several classes of harbor thieves as they exist to-day; and each class is to be credited with some specially notable crimes.

The most remarkable of all these cases is also one of the most recent. The mate of a schooner trading to Brazil, when last at Para, having his eye open to a speculation on private account, purchased four splendid anacondas, one being twenty-one feet in length, one fifteen feet, and the other two fourteen feet each. He escaped all the perils of the sea and arrived in the harbor of New York with his snakes all in fine condition. The news of the extraordinary arrival spread with great rapidity among the dealers in such articles, and during his first day in port the mate had numerous advantageous offers for his reptiles. He toyed with all, however, hoping for something better; but among the bidders were two men who were especially pertinacious, and at last forced from him a refusal of the snakes until next morning, and got him to accept five dollars to bind the bargain. That night six men in two small boats went alongside the schooner, and, getting on board, administered chloroform to the captain, whom they found asleep in the cabin, and then removing the hatches got out the box containing the snakes and carried it ashore. The police, of course, having little difficulty in working up such a case as this, speedily had snakes and thieves in custody. But the pirates, even under such untoward circumstances, proved themselves shrewder than the law; for it then appeared that the men who had paid five dollars to bind the bargain for the purchase were noted river thieves, who led the raid on the schooner and in whose possession the serpents were found. Under these circumstances they claimed to be *bona fide* holders, and the affair was held to be a civil one; the mate, being denied the redress of criminal process, was worsted in the subsequent proceedings and lost his snakes.

Another notable case was an unusual achievement of the Daybreak Boys, four of whom, prowling on the North river in the middle of the day, happened to come upon a small boat containing three small boys out for a pleasure sail. The young thieves, in the true spirit of piracy, pulled alongside, and, by the utterance of many oaths and the brandishing of several knives, cowed the boys into submissiveness while they robbed them of their pocket money and the silver watch one of them had. Two of the thieves then took possession of the boat, and, taking two of the boys with them, while the other was put ashore on the piratical craft, made them row to the foot of Thirty-fourth street. It happened, however, on their arrival, that a detective officer whom one of the boy-prisoners knew was on the pier, and his aid being invoked the infant thieves were taken in charge; and their two companions being subsequently arrested, the piracy ended in a term of imprisonment for all concerned in it.

It is important to commerce and interesting to the general reader to know what means have been adopted to limit the depredations of marauders who have been shown to be active, audacious, and successful to a degree that makes them a public danger, although so few in number. Prior to 1857, when the metropolitan *régime* was established, there was no police protection whatever to the shipping in the harbor. Shortly after that event the harbor police was instituted upon a plan that gave the largest possible amount of protection with the force and appliances at hand. There was a station-house on shore, and the force was subjected in all respects to the rules governing the land police, the only difference between the two being that the harbor men patrolled the rivers and bay in small boats instead of walking the streets. There were fifty-seven men in the command, which enabled the captain to have at least six boats constantly on patrol. These were of course inadequate to give absolute protection to the extended water front of the city, but were so great an improvement on no protection at all that there was immediately a very decided diminution in the number of robberies. This system of water police had thoroughly proved its efficiency and was being rapidly improved, when the Commissioners gave aid and comfort to the thieves by its abrogation and the adoption of a new system. The shore house was abandoned, the force reduced, and a steamer provided which was to make twenty miles an hour, run down or pick up all the thieves as fast as they came out of their holes, and generally make river robbery an impossibility. But the boat, when brought into use, had great difficulty in making headway against a strong tide, was never fast except when tied to the pier, showed Falstaff's "alacrity in sinking," and speedily became, as she remained to the end, the laughing-stock of thieves and honest men alike. During the ten years she was in service she was instrumental in making but one arrest, and that was due rather to the stupidity of the thieves than the prowess of the steamer.

But so far as interfering with piratical operations is concerned, the result would necessarily have been the same with any large vessel. Captain James Todd, who was in command of the harbor police for more than ten years, although doing his best to utilize his large steamer, was forced to do all his effective work by small row-boats. No thief is so clumsy that he cannot keep clear of large steamers under all circumstances, and none so adroit that he can ever be sure of escaping the row-boats which follow him into slips, under piers, behind ships, and into all his coverts. The steamer has therefore been exclusively employed in spending the public money, in which she has been remarkably successful, in displaying the city flag in the harbor, and in making a great "sound and fury signifying nothing;" and all the real work has been done, as it always must be done, by small boats. This service, with the small force allowed since the introduction of the steamer, which is supposed to work miracles, is one of extreme hardship and very inadequately performed. In consequence of the peculiarities of the currents around New York, the tide being flood only four hours, while it is ebb eight hours in the North river, makes the patrolling of that river, which includes miles of piers, one of extreme difficulty; while the greater facilities for thieving on the East river, where tidal hardships are not encountered, renders the surveillance of that side no less onerous than the other. Only one boat can be sent out on each river at a time, and as it must enter all the slips at night, the tour of duty of six hours is frequently exhausted before the boat has traversed more than half the space allotted it.

Harbor thievery can never be wholly extinguished, but it can be most hampered by a return, with one important modification, to the organization of the harbor police originally adopted. The numerical force should be at least fifty, including officers; there should be the station-house ashore, as before; the steamboat should be entirely dispensed with, and steam launches should be substituted for row-boats for patrolling purposes. With these changes, the advantages of which are too obvious to require enumeration, the harbor thieves would find their occupation almost entirely gone.

WHY THIEVES PROSPER.

THE thieves of New York cost the honest people of the city nearly seven millions of dollars a year. They always have money, and are always spending it with reckless improvidence. Yet we are told, in the report of the Police Commissioners, that the value of the property lost in 1868 was only $4,755,077 83, and that of this sum $4,383,567 13 was recovered, leaving only the trifling balance of $371,510 70 as the total loss for the year. Accepted without question, these figures are creditable to the police. But, as matter of fact, this reported total loss is apparent only; the thieves are to be charged with much more than the $150 each given officially as their annual income.

The figures of the Commissioners are obtained by computing in one account property reported as stolen and that reported as lost under the one head of "property lost." Now as the lost is nearly always found, and thus appears on both sides of the account, while the stolen very rarely requires a second entry, it is apparent that the official figures are altogether deceptive. Even if the Commissioners kept a separate account of the property stolen, the result attained would not be exact, since they can only carry upon their books the robberies reported to them, and every one knows that not a day passes when scores of pockets are not picked, and not a night when buildings are not entered and rifled, and the police left uninformed of the facts. The crimes reported either to the police or in the newspapers being only a part of those committed, we must go outside of reported figures, and, by a close observation of the outlaw classes, make our own estimate.

As a rule, the New York thief is well dressed and well housed: it is a singular fact, by the way, that when the thief comes in the shape of an actual purchaser he seldom attempts to ply his vocation, but pays full price for what he buys. It is plain, therefore, that he must have money, and nothing is more certain than that he does have it. Some of our thieves squander princely incomes every year, while others starve and pinch on a bare sufficiency, but their average expenditure is certainly $4 a day each; and, as every dollar thus spent is the product of thievery, it is plain, allowing them to realize the par value of their thefts, that being about 2,500 in number, their first cost to the city is about $10,000 per day, or $3,650,000 per annum. But it is well known that this par value is something the thief never gets, and that these figures, therefore, are not true representatives of the property stolen. This vast sum is, too, merely the first cost of the criminals, who make necessary besides all the enormous outlay for the police and criminal judicial establishments to preserve the public peace and protect the citizen in his property. The amount annually extracted from the tax-payers for the support of these establishments is about $3,212,000, which, added to the former amount, makes the total cost of the criminal and disorderly classes to the city $6,862,000 annually. The crumb of comfort to be found in the fact that the cost of the police and judiciary should be equally divided between the criminal and disorderly classes, is eaten up by the other fact that the amount received by the thieves for stolen property is far less than the value of their thefts.

Although the thieves are not credited with their full dues on the books of the Police Commissioners, they gain nothing by these large additions to their incomes, which the authorities are afraid to acknowledge, even to themselves.

Whether the receipts of a thief be four dollars or four thousand in the course of a year, he is generally penniless. A more improvident, reckless spendthrift than the professional criminal does not live. To take no heed of the morrow is the only scriptural injunction he can be relied upon to observe. His money comes easy, but it goes with such marvellous ease and rapidity that he can hardly remember that he has had it. In his way he is just and generous, and when his pockets have been filled by some lucky venture he first pays his own pressing debts, and next helps some less fortunate comrade out of the sloughs of pecuniary despond. If he has anything left after these demands of honor are satisfied, he plunges into the excitement of gaming, and almost invariably leaves his surplus with some faro-dealer. He is undoubtedly a devotee to some extent of wine and women, but is economical in both of these indulgences. Rarely a drunkard, he is still less often a licentious debauchee, and the presumed co-partnership between harlotry and thievery is a delusion. Sometimes, indeed, a thief is found living illicitly with a woman, but she is almost certain to be an adept in some purloining art, and to contribute her full quota to the joint income.

But even if the thieves never approached the gaming-table, and never expended a dollar for the gratification of sensual appetites, they would still be an impecunious race, for no class is so ruthlessly stripped. They are common game for detectives and lawyers, and when once entangled in the meshes of either, expect to be robbed of their last penny—and are rarely disappointed in their expectation. If they are thieves of the lesser order they are sure to be plucked and go to prison afterward; if they belong to the ranks of the educated and adroit operators, and happen to have a large amount of money on hand when caught, by due discretion in its use they can compound the most flagrant crimes. For the present administration of correctional law in New York may be thus epitomized: *Obtaining conclusive evidence of guilt against a thief; arresting him; wresting from him the last possible dollar, and then turning him loose to repeat his crime and again experience its condonement.* There are exceptions, of course, but this is the usual end and aim of detective endeavor. Such being the perils that surround the stealthily-won products of thieves, we cannot wonder that they are, as a class, usually impecunious, or refrain from joining in the general amazement recently occasioned by the announcement that a noted depredator had just died worth $60,000. It is doubtful, however, whether the general public will share in the poignant regret aroused in the detective breast by this piece of news—at least, not for the same reason.

There are statistics to show that our thieves wage their crusade against society without much cause to fear the terrors of the law. Somebody once made a curious calculation of how many thousands of bullets must be fired before one man is hit in battle. Let us consider how vast an amount of property must be stolen before one thief is locked up in State Prison. It being a well-established fact that the adroit, practised, and therefore dangerous thieves, very rarely come under the jurisdiction of the courts, it is plain that the subjoined figures apply almost exclusively to mere tyros, who, not having learned how to "square it" with the officials, or else not doing business on a scale sufficiently large to justify the latter in allowing them to do so, are promptly tripped up by the vigilant police, to emblazon the terrible severity of an unyielding justiciary in vindicating the laws. This is a grave charge, but it cannot be refuted by the mention of any considerable number of noted burglars, or bond-robbers, or pickpockets, who have experienced deprivation of personal liberty during the past few years.

This fact being kept in constant remembrance, the following tabular statement is submitted to show the number of cases disposed of in the courts of criminal jurisdiction in the City of New York during the year 1868, and also the totals of arrests for the same offences, for the same period, as they appear in the annual report of the Police Commissioners. In order that the subject may not be encumbered by extraneous matter, the figures are presented only in the cases of certain felonies, although the same proportion is apparent up and down the whole gamut of crime:

OFFENCE.	ARRESTS.	DISPOSED OF.	MISSING.
Arson	65	3	62
Bigamy	13	1	12
Burglary	630	154	476
Forgery	113	24	89
Larceny, grand	2,413	347	2,066
Larceny, petit	4,927	2,834	2,093
Picking pockets	303	49	254
Receiving stolen goods	255	3	252
Robbery	130	11	119

These figures afford cumulative evidence that comparisons are odious; but they are also suggestive, and when closely examined show, either that the police annually make hundreds of arrests without the slightest cause, or that the judges are continually unloosing the bonds of criminals. It is an unpleasant dilemma for either side, but it may be further said that two of the four police courts—the only ones where such data were obtainable—sent to the District Attorney during the year, 473 cases of grand larceny, 163 of burglary, and 46 of highway robbery. By reference to the table it will be seen that these two committing tribunals supplied that official with more of these felonies than he can account for altogether. It is true that the police justice must hold for trial when a *prima facie* case is presented, and that the grand jury may fail to indict, or having found bills, that the District Attorney may deem the proof insufficient, and dismiss the charge. But when all these allowances are made they fail to account for the grand total of 5,423 cases of crime, which, during a single year, evaporated into utter nothingness between the police station-houses and the bars of the courts. The Police Commissioners report that they have had them, but the magistrates and the District Attorney do not appear to have ever been informed of, much less to have encountered this avalanche of crime.

A portion of the vast discrepancy between the arrests and the cases brought to a conclusion in the courts may be explained by the fact that the table of the Commissioners is not so compiled as to be accurate authority. Year after year the Commissioners have published their table of the number of persons arrested as "offences during the year," and have thus sought to ignore the very palpable difference between the number of crimes and the number of persons arrested for crime. They report a grand total of 78,451 offences during the past year, when a little scrutiny makes it apparent that they mean only that so many persons have been dragged to the station-houses on various charges, frivolous or serious, as the case may be. The mode by which the totality of wickedness is reached is a very simple but effective method of evading the truth; for if a dozen footpads waylay a citizen in the street, and the dozen are arrested, the one highway robbery is increased a dozen times when it gets into the report. Nor is this singular method of gathering statistics the only wrong the Commissioners inflict upon the city. Not a day passes that patrolmen do not take prisoners into nearly every one of the thirty station-houses of the city, the charges against whom dissolve under the first examination, and the accused are discharged by the officer in charge. But all these cases go upon the record, and do duty in the annual report as so many offences, when in fact they may be nothing more than proofs of the malice of accusers or the stupidity of patrolmen. There are, indeed, many more such felonies as burglary and larceny committed annually than appear in the reports; but the Commissioners are not thereby justified in reporting false charges as true, and, by counting both false and true over and over again, making a table of haphazard guesses when they should submit a record of undeniable facts.

But while this official method of dealing with figures is accountable for a part of the discrepancies between arrests and dispositions, it is not justly chargeable with the whole sin. The police do undoubtedly arrest many criminals who are committed by the magistrates for trial, but who are never heard of again anywhere in the labyrinthic realms of justice. There are many cases where thieves have been arrested with the most convincing proofs of their crime at hand, and yet have never been tried. On many occasions, the police magistrates, in the bright heyday of suddenly-developed virtue, have committed notorious thieves without bail, and the same thieves have been upon the streets next day and every day since, so far as that particular charge is concerned. It is well known that the four police courts commit for trial a number of persons sufficient to keep the courts of last resort constantly busy; and yet, although those mills of justice grind exceeding slow, their hoppers, in the shape of prisons, rarely overflow. It is known that there are a score or more of first-class rascals in the city, who frequently fall into the hands of the law they daily outrage, and yet have never been confronted with a jury to pass upon their crimes. It is known that while the shadowed army of roguery is *en route* from the committing magistrate to the worshipful judge, nearly a fifth are lost; but the general public have not been able, even with the help of some research, to learn what becomes of them. They may find a safe refuge in the office of the District Attorney; they may succeed in compromising with the complainant, or they may even throttle justice in the short journey from the grand-jury room to the box of the petit jury. The District Attorney, however, can probably explain how it is that so many complaints for felonies, that are seemingly defended by impregnable proofs, are abandoned without even a pretence being made to sustain them. He, in conjunction with the Police Commissioners, the Recorder, and the City Judge, can resolve the enigma presented in 8,849 arrests for crime in a year and only 3,426 cases of the same crimes disposed of in all the courts during the same time. There seems enough here to make credible the assertion of the Superintendent of Police, made during the heat of a late election canvass, that there are 10,000 indictments quietly laid away in the office of the District Attorney; but whether that be true or not, there is certainly sufficient in these unrelenting figures to warrant every official in New York, having to do in any way with criminals, in rising to a personal explanation.

These charges are of such serious character that, notwithstanding they are based upon official reports, they seem to demand some specific cases as illustrations. All that I use are of recent date, and are culled from a long list of similar cases, with a view of showing not only the relations existing between criminals and the authorities, but also of showing the audacity and adroitness of thieves as well as the general lack of conscience in dealing with one of the gravest matters of public concern.

One of the latest cases on the books shows very clearly the enterprise of burglars and the methods of detectives. A bank in Maryland was entered by burglars, and robbed of securities of the value of $120,000. In due course of time, and by means which, of course, have never been divulged, these securities were traced to New York, and to the possession of two notorious burglars. In its preliminary stages, the case promised to be a praiseworthy exception to the rule in modern detective work, for the New York officers schemed in an entirely legitimate way for the recovery of the bonds and the capture of the thieves. No criminal was used as a decoy, and no promise of immunity was made to any one. The burglars were patiently "shadowed," and by the employment of a regular broker their desire to sell the stolen securities was ascertained. A suitable office was prepared, and the burglars finally invited to a last meeting with the broker, for the purpose of closing the transaction. They came according to appointment, and the officers, who were secreted in an adjoining room, sprang in upon them at the moment they were about to pass over the property. Thus far, the case was as the first dawn of coming purity, and there was especial cause for congratulation, in the fact that honesty had proved the best policy. The capture of the burglars with $99,500 of the stolen bonds in their possession at the moment of arrest, afforded a reasonable presumption that at least two of the great bond-robbers would now find their way to a prison. But it was only a presumption, and by no means a realized fact. As a first step, the identity of the burglars was rigorously concealed by the officers under false names, and matters were then speedily arranged to the satisfaction of all immediately concerned. The success of the New York officers had diverted from the Baltimore detective firm, first employed in the case, the large reward offered for the recovery of the bonds; but there were still $20,000 out-standing, and the Baltimore firm clutched at this remnant with a sharpened, because disappointed appetite. A farce was then played by the adroit detectives, whereby it was made to appear that the burglars had waived their legal rights, and consented to return to Maryland for trial, without the intervention of a requisition from the Governor of that State; and the New York officials having taken a receipt for their bodies, a Baltimore officer started with the captives for that city. The journey must have been expeditiously performed, and a trial of marvellous dispatch been followed by a speedy acquittal; for the ink was scarcely dry upon the New York receipt before both men had snapped the leashes of the law, and were promenading Broadway, unfettered and unwatched. The apparent mystery is easily solved by the knowledge that the $20,000 had been recovered, and the affair concluded to the satisfaction of everybody, except, perhaps, the public, whose laws had been outrageously cheated. The robbers were content, for they had escaped the penalty of their crime; the detectives were hilarious, for they had pocketed over $16,000 in rewards, and the bank was assuredly satisfied, as it had regained nearly all of its property at a reasonable price.

As another instance of detective work may be cited a case where no question of money was involved, but the officer entered into a covenant with a thief merely to oblige a friend. A gentleman having lost his watch, reported the fact at the Central Police Office, and expressed great anxiety to regain it, as it was an old family possession. Thereupon the official in charge sent for a noted thief, stated the case in detail, and asked him if he "could get to it." Thief did not know, but would try, and started out upon the special detective duty to which he had been assigned. But presently he was brought before the official who had sent him forth. He was now in custody of a verdant patrolman, who had found him prowling about the streets in a suspicious way, and, knowing him to be a thief, had taken him in charge. Matters were explained, and the thief again went out upon his mission; but, having occasion to visit a different part of the city, was again captured and taken in by an officious patrolman. This time the thief desired written authority for his movements; but while this was prudently declined, he was told that if again molested he might use the official's name. Finally, the watch was recovered, but the man who stole it was never molested. "Set a thief to catch a thief," is a precept the New York police cannot obey, even if so inclined; for, although the thieves are always ready, as a matter of business, to assist in the recovery of stolen property, they will never aid in effecting the arrest of a "pal."

Sometimes the authorities prove relentless when they have a malefactor "dead to rights"—as, with a keen sense of satire, they style having conclusive evidence against him—and are pressed by public clamor for a rigorous enforcement of the penalties of the law. But even when the malefactor encounters this extremity, he is by no means in immediate peril. He may delay the crisis indefinitely, and hope for eventual succor from the law's delays. Some months since, one of the most noted and adroit of the New York pickpockets was thus got "dead to rights," and, unfortunately for himself, fell into the clutches of a patrolman instead of a detective. As the public mind was, just then, greatly excited against criminals of all grades, it was confidently predicted that the unlucky pickpocket would be convicted, and sent to Sing Sing within a week. But the prophets did not take the resources of the thief into consideration. Within the time specified, some of his confederates had spirited away the chief witness against him. The culprit gained time by this expedient, and the *quidnuncs*, guided by long experience, were as ready to prophecy that he would escape altogether; but the case was destined to prove anomalous in all respects, and after many weeks' delay the malefactor was finally tried, convicted, and actually sent to Sing Sing.

Another case, illustrating the same point, but showing a different termination, was that of the youth who lately gained cheap notoriety as a bond-robber, was tried and convicted. He was only an amateur thief. He was a clerk in the house which was robbed, and having been used by the professionals to assist in effecting the robbery, was afterward shrewd enough to cheat them out of a large portion of the proceeds. He fled with his spoils, and after a long pursuit was captured, tried, and convicted, chiefly because he refused to enter into negotiations for the return of $30,000 of the stolen property, which the detectives could not find. He declared this sum to be worth five years in Sing Sing, and seemed to accept his sentence as a purely business transaction. But he was shrewder than he was thought, and after gaining great renown as a bond-robber, tried, convicted, and sentenced, declined, after all, to go to prison and herd with common criminals, in recompense for his reputation and profits. He was removed from the City Prison by a deputy sheriff, to be taken to Sing Sing, and after two days' absence that deputy coolly returned and reported that his prisoner had escaped. The case was too flagrant to be overlooked, even in New York, and the investigation which followed showed that the deputy must have connived at the escape, although it was never ascertained what price the prisoner had paid for his liberty. The deputy, being put upon trial, pleaded guilty, and was awarded a term of four years in State Prison. That was the last ever heard of the case; and the outraged law, which had expected a great bond-robber, was forced to be content with a mere deputy sheriff.

There is another case, where no sheriff or judge was ever called to account for defrauding the law of its dues. One evening, two bold pickpockets assaulted a Brooklyn gentleman in a Broadway stage and tore a diamond pin from his shirt front, but were arrested the next moment as they were running from the stage. The gentleman appeared at the station-house to make his complaint against his despoilers, and was probably aware of the devious ways of justice in New York, as he resolutely announced that he would make every effort to send them to State Prison, as he considered that it was full time for an example to be made of some of the daring freebooters of the city. As he was a man of considerable political prominence, it was thought that something would come of this resolution. The next morning the two pickpockets were duly committed by the police magistrate for trial at the General Session ; but that was the last of the case. It is not known how the matter was arranged, but it is certain the culprits were never tried, and did speedily regain their liberty. Happily, however, one of them soon afterward visited Philadelphia, and, being well known as a thief, was seized by virtue of a wholesome law of Pennsylvania, and sent to jail for ninety days on general account.

A somewhat similar case was that of two bold rogues who entered a disreputable house, and having lured two of the women into the hall, and in close proximity to the door, snatched their jewels from their persons, and rushed into the street ; but when the hue and cry was raised, a policeman happened luckily to be at hand, and both were arrested in full flight, and at only a short distance from the house. All these facts were duly set forth in the complaint before the magistrate and the two men were committed for examination. A raid was instantly made on the complainants by the friends of the prisoners, to induce a withdrawal of the charges, and so incessant were the importunities and so liberal the offers, that they were at last induced to consent, and repairing at an unusual hour to the police court, when there was sure to be no impertinent observer, executed the necessary papers, and the two felons were promptly discharged. It may be that in this case no official was guilty of anything worse than allowing the thieves to compound a felony with the complainants, which is, however, so constantly and unblushingly allowed that the authorities will probably be astonished and indignant to find it rated as a fault.

The next case illustrates an almost every day occurrence in police circles, and shows how the machinery of the criminal law is used to enforce the payment of civil debts. The accounts of a young man occupying an important position in an insurance company became so entangled that a charge of embezzlement was easily founded upon their intricacies, and late on a Saturday afternoon he was arrested and locked up in a police cell. The next day was Sunday and he was not taken to court. His father, who was permitted to see him, became empowered as an ambassador, and negotiations were opened with the insurance company, and were carried on with such vigor and success that early on Monday morning the prisoner was discharged, as the matter was declared to have been settled. The details of the settlement, of course, were not allowed to be known ; but it did transpire that the company had been paid the full amount it claimed, and the young man saved from public reproach, since he was never tried for his alleged crime, and very few ever knew of his arrest.

We come now to the last of these curious cases, which is also the most flagrant. A man having a nursery a short distance from the city established a stand in one of our markets, for the sale of shrubs and plants, and engaged a young man as salesman, but first required him to deposit $500 as security for his honesty. After a time the returns of sales were not satisfactory to the nurseryman, and he spoke of the matter to a friend, who happened to be a prominent detective. The friend surmised at once that the salesman was embezzling the receipts. The detective said he could fix him, and was as good as his word. Going to the stand in the character of a purchaser, he paid over a marked five dollar bill, and without giving the salesman time to make return of the transaction, appeared in his detective character, and upon arresting him of course found the marked money upon him. The clerk was carried off to a cell, and kept there, in bold violation of the law, forty-eight hours before he was taken before a magistrate. But the time was needed, and it was busily employed. First, an attorney was allowed access to the cell of the prisoner, to assure him that he was certain to go to prison for five years, unless he settled with the complainant by assigning to him the $500; and the prisoner consenting to this, was taken before a police magistrate, who was asked to discharge him on the ground that no proof could be obtained against him. But the magistrate happened to be in an inquiring mood, and finally arriving at something near the truth of the affair, ordered the $500 to be paid into court. What eventually became of that money is a mystery; it is only certain that the unfortunate salesman never was burdened with a dollar of it again.

Space will not allow the further multiplication of these citations. Even thus hastily dealt with, the inherent corruption of the correctional administration of law in New York has become apparent; but how thoroughly rotten or imbecile are the whole police and judicial systems has been but faintly shadowed. Reformation must come, and speedily, or honesty, instead of being the best, will be the very worst possible policy in a city handed over utterly into the hands of thieves. The law, as it is, if vigorously, intelligently, and honestly administered, might suffice to repress crime and corruption to a certain extent, but some special amendments are needed before any material reformation can be expected.

The first necessity is to utterly eradicate the present detective system. Corruption has become so universal that it can only be stayed by the law's making it a felony for a police officer to receive any reward whatever beyond the salary attached to his position. In some way the attention of the police officer must be diverted from the property stolen to the person stealing it. Somehow the brokerage in crime upon the part of officials, which is constantly increasing, must be stopped, and there is no way of effecting the reform of which there is such terrible need, except by the law putting the detectives and magistrates, who pander to crime or share in any way in its gains, upon the same footing with the original thief.

In these remarks I do not intend to malign individuals, but rather to attack a system of doing public business which has become so universal that it has compelled many good men to look upon themselves as something worse than the criminals they are supposed to pursue. To cut off the detective from all hope of receiving any reward for recovering stolen property, may appear a harsh measure, and would probably prove so in many cases, but there is no other way of exterminating the evil. But it is absurd to expect that men fitted by experience, knowledge of criminals, and the rare and peculiar acumen required for detective work, can be had for the mere pittance now paid them. The law virtually declares the Central Detective Squad a fraud and a sham, by allowing its members only the same pay given the inexperienced patrolman from the day he begins police duty. It is presumed these detectives are called to higher duties than are required of the patrolmen, and there is no good reason why the pay of police officers should not be graded according to the experience and capacity demanded by the position. Cut off the outside rewards, give honest wages, and it may be possible to obtain honest detective work.

When the law has weeded out corruption, it should clothe its officers with additional power to secure the outlaws. Lately a police captain sought to rid his precinct of the professional thieves who infested it, by arresting a number of them as vagrants, but the move was a complete failure. When taken before the magistrate every thief could show money and goodly raiment, and no policeman could make oath that he might not have worked on some day named by the shrewd counsel he had funds enough to employ. What is needed, therefore, is a law, provided with proper safeguards against its abuse, establishing the same summary proceedings against thieves, as are now in force with reference to vagrants. If upon proper proof that a man is a professional thief, the magistrates were compelled to send him to the penitentiary for a short term, the outlaws who now crowd the thoroughfares of New York would very soon be driven into honesty, or other cities. As it is to-day, general repute counts nothing against the criminal until he is charged with some specific offence; as it would be then, there would not be an hour of his life when he would not be transgressing the law, and could not be awarded its penalty. Such a law would be abused to some extent, perhaps, but it could be made to drive out the hordes of professional outlaws. But certainly the city can well afford to take the risk of the abuses of such a law in order to gain its benefits. Society has the right of self-protection; and something must be done if thievery is not very soon to become the most profitable and best-protected of industrial pursuits.

But in apportioning the profligacy of which I speak, the people, and more especially men engaged in extensive mercantile and financial affairs, must be held in no small degree responsible for its existence. Very often when police and magistrates would be content with recovering only a portion of the stolen property, provided the thieves were punished, the despoiled parties insist upon an entire reversal of proceedings. They strive, and scheme, and dicker with outlaws to regain the last possible penny, and sell their own honor and the safety of the community by shamelessly promising immunity for crime in exchange for all but a small per cent. of their stolen treasures. Very often the detectives find the losers insuperable obstacles in the way of justice. There is much pertinence in the shrewd saying of a late officer, that the detectives can, indeed, run a thief to earth, but only the person robbed can pen him there; and that it is chiefly the fault of the robbed that thieves go free that men calling themselves honest may get their due. No statutory provision can be made to reach the men whose greed is so perilous to public safety; but it can be hoped that when the law has put the seal of infamy upon its officials engaging in such work, the citizen will be shamed into honesty, and cease to rush into personal negotiations with thieves when a detective with a remnant of conscience left in him has refused to act as his go-between. But the official circle must at any rate be purified; and that done, some improvement in public morals is certain to result. The evil will not be extinguished, but it will be so far abated that the experienced, educated, adroit thief will be less an object of envy than now.

What I have said may perhaps explain why such affairs as the Lord bond robbery and the Ocean Bank burglary can constantly occur and yet no thief capable of such work ever be made to know by his personal experience that in the eye of the law his deeds are crimes. When I have added what is known of private detectives, they cannot possibly continue mysteries.

PRIVATE DETECTIVES.

BROADWAY is a street of marvels and mysteries, where all tricks of trade have place and the last resorts of scheming knavery are found. These are of many kinds, of which some have mounted to the decrepitude of lofts, while others are lodged in the dignity and prosperity of second floors. One of these latter is situated in the commercial heart of the city. It is a Private Detective office.

The visitor going up the broad stairs finds himself in a large room, which is plainly the main office of the concern. There is a desk with the authoritative hedge of an iron railing, behind which sits a furrowed man who looks an animated cork-screw, and who, the inquiring visitor soon discovers, can't speak above a whisper, or at least don't. This mysterious person is always mistaken for the chief of the establishment; but, in fact, he is nothing but the "Secretary," and holds his place by reason of a marvellous capacity for drawing people out of themselves. A mystery, he is surrounded with mysteries. The doors upon his right and left—one of which is occasionally opened just far enough to permit a very diminutive call-boy to be squeezed through—seem to lead to unexplored regions. But stranger than even the clerk or the undefined but yet perfectly tangible weirdness of the doors is the tinkling of a sepulchral bell and the responsive tramp of a heavy-heeled boot. And strangest of all is a huge blackboard whereon are marked the figures from 1 to 20, over some of which the word "Out" is written; and the visitor notices with ever-increasing wonder that the tinkling of the bell and the heavy-heeled tramp are usually followed by the mysterious secretary's scrawling "Out" over another number, being apparently incited thereto by a whisper of the ghostly call-boy who is squeezed through a crack in the door for that purpose. The door which the call-boy abjures is always slightly ajar, and at the aperture there is generally a wolfish eye glaring so steadily and rapaciously into the office as to raise a suspicion that beasts of prey are crouching behind that forbidding door.

Nor is the resulting alarm entirely groundless, for that is the room where the ferrets of the house who assume the name of detectives, but are more significantly called "shadows," are hidden from the prying eyes of the world. A "shadow" here is merely a numeral—No. 1 or something higher—and obeys cabalistic calls conveyed by bells or speaking-tubes, by which devices the stranger patron is convinced of the potency of the Detective Agency which moves in such mysterious ways to perform its wonders. If any doubt were left by all this paraphernalia of marvel, it would be dispelled from the average mind when it came in contact with the chief conjurer, who is seated in the dim seclusion of a retired room, fortified by bell-pulls, speaking-tubes, and an owlish expression intended to be considered as the mirror of taciturn wisdom. From his retreat he moves the outside puppets of secretary, shadows, and call-boys, as the requirements of his patrons, who are admitted singly to his presence, may demand. It is he whose hoarse whispers sound sepulchrally through the tubes, who rings the mysterious bell, and by such complex means despatches his "shadows" upon their errands. It is he who permits the mildewed men in the other ante-room to be known only by numbers, and who guards them so carefully from the general view.

By these assumptions of mystery the chief awes the patrons of his peculiar calling, of whom there are pretty sure to be several in waiting during the morning hours. These applicants for detective assistance always sit stolidly silent until their separate summons comes to join the chief, eyeing each other suspiciously and surveying their surroundings with unconcealed and fitting awe. One is of bluff and hearty appearance, but his full face is overcast for the moment with an expression half sad, half whimsical; it is plain that a conjunction of untoward circumstances has raised doubts in his mind of the integrity of a business associate, and he has reluctantly determined to clear or confirm them by means of a "shadow." Next to him is a fidgety furrowed man, bristling with suspicion in every line of his face, and showing by his air of indifference to his surroundings that he is a frequenter of the place. He is in fact one of the best customers of the establishment, as he is constantly invoking its aid in the petty concerns of his corroded life. Sometimes it is a wife, daughter, sister, niece, or a mere female acquaintance he wishes watched; sometimes it is a business partner or a rival in trade he desires dogged; and he is never so miserable as when the reports of the agency show his suspicions, whatever they may have been, to be groundless. It is but just, however, to the sagacity of the detectives to remark that he is seldom subjected to such disappointment. Whatever other foolishness they may commit, these adroit operators never kill the goose that lays their golden eggs. Beside this animated monument of distrust is a portly gentleman, his bearing in every way suggestive of plethoric pockets. Paper and pencil in hand, he is nervously figuring. He makes no secret of his figures because of his absorption, and a glance shows that he is correcting the numbers of bonds and making sure of the amounts they represent.

It is plain that this last is a victim of a sneak robbery, and, the unerring scent of the chief selecting him as the most profitable customer of the morning, he is the first visitor called to an audience. Large affairs are quickly despatched, and it is soon arranged how a part of the property can be recovered and justice cheated of its due. Very soon a handbill will be publicly distributed, offering a reward for the return of the bonds, and it will be signed by the Agency. The thief will know exactly what that means, and the affair being closed to mutual satisfaction, the thief will be at liberty to repeat the operation, which resulted in reasonable profit and was attended with no risk.

There is also in the room a sallow, vinegary woman of uncertain years, and it seems so natural that a man should run away from her, we are not surprised that, being voluble in her grief, she declares her business to be the discovery of an absconding husband. But near her is another and truer type of outraged womanhood, a wasted young wife, beautiful as ruins are beautiful, whom a rascal spendthrift has made a martyr to his selfishness until, patience and hope being exhausted, she is driven to the last extremity, and seeks by a means at which her nature revolts for a proof of but one of those numerous violations of the marriage vow which she feels certain he has committed. It is a cruel resort; but the law which permits a man to outrage a woman in almost every other way frowns upon that one, and she is driven to it as the sole method of release from an intolerable and degrading bondage. In such cases as this might perhaps be found some justification for the existence of private detectives; but they themselves lo not appear to know that they stand in need of extenuation, and so neglect the opportunity thus presented to vindicate their necessity by conducting this class of their business with, even for them, remarkable lack of conscience. Anxious always to furnish exactly what is desired, their reports are often lies, manufactured to suit the occasion, and once furnished they are stoutly adhered to, even to the last extremity. Frequently the same Agency is ready to and does serve both parties to a case with impartial wickedness, and earns its wages by giving to both precisely the sort of evidence each requires. Sometimes it is made to order, with no other foundation than previous experience in like affairs; but sometimes it has a more solid basis in fact. Two men from the same office are often detailed to "shadow," one the husband and the other the wife, and it occasionally happens that they have mastered the spirit of their calling so thoroughly that they do a little business on private account by "giving away" each other. That is to say, the husband's man informs the wife she is watched, and gives her a minute description of her "shadow," for which information he of course gets an adequate reward, which the wife's man likewise earns and receives by doing the same kindly office for the husband. In such cases there are generally mutual recriminations between the watched, which end in a discovery of the double dealing of the Agency, and not infrequently in a reconciliation of the estranged couple. But this rare result, which is not intended by the directing power, is the sole good purpose these agencies were ever known to serve. Lord Mansfield, it must be admitted, once seemed to justify the use of private detectives in divorce suits, but he was careful to cumber the faint praise with which he damned them by making honesty in the discharge of these delicate duties a first essential. Had he lived to see the iniquitous perfection the business has now attained, he would undoubtedly have withheld even that quasi-endorsement of a system naturally at war with the fundamental principles of justice.

The waiters in the reception-room are never allowed to state their wants, or certainly not to leave the place, without being astonished by the charges made by the detective for attention to their business. Whatever differences there may be in minor matters, all these establishments are invariably true to the great purpose of their existence, and prepare the way for an exorbitant bill by a doleful explanation of the expenses and risks to be incurred in the special affair presented, dilating especially upon the rarity and cost of competent "shadows." Now the principal agencies estimate for them at $10 a day, whereas these disreputable fellows are found in multitudes, and are rarely paid more than $3 a day as wages; their expenses, paid in advance by the patron, are allowed them when assigned to duties, as they frequently are, involving outlay. The general truth is that these agencies, being conducted for the avowed purpose of making money, get as much as possible for doing work, and pay as little as possible for having it done. In their general business of espionage they may make perhaps only a moderate profit on each affair they take in hand; but in the more delicate branches of compounding felonies and manufacturing witnesses fancy prices obtain, and the profits are not computable. It is plain, knowing of these patrons and prices, that reasonable profit attends upon the practice of the convenient science of getting without giving, which, notwithstanding its prosperity and antiquity, is yet an infant in the perfection it has attained. Awkward, flimsy, transparent as they ever were, are yet the tricks and devices of the knaves who never want for a dollar, never earn an honest one, but never render themselves amenable to any statute "in such case made and provided." To say that the master-workmen in roguery who do this sort of thing are awkward and transparent seems to involve a paradox; but whoever so believes has not been fully informed as to the amazing gullibility of mankind. The average man of business now, as always before, seems to live only to be swindled by the same specious artifices that gulled his ancestors, and which will answer to pluck him again almost before the smart of his first depletion has ceased. Only by a thorough knowledge of this singular adaptation of the masses to the purposes of the birds of prey, can we intelligently account for the vast bevies of the latter which exist, and are outwardly so sleek as to give evidence of a prosperous condition. When we know that the "pocket-book dropper" yet decoys the money even of the city-bred by his stale device; that the "gift enterprises," "envelope game," and similar threadbare tricks yet serve to attain the ends of the sharpers, although the public has been warned scores and scores of times through the public press, and the swindlers thoroughly exposed, so that the veriest fool can understand the deception, we need not be amazed at the success which attends the practice of these arts. The truth is, that a large proportion of the victims are perfectly aware that fleecing is intended when they flutter round the bait of the rogues; but they are allured by the glitter of sudden fortune which it offers, and bite eagerly with the hope that may be supposed to sustain any gudgeon of moderate experience of snapping the bait and escaping the barbed hook. Human greed is the reliance of the general sharper, and it has served him to excellent purpose for many years. But some of these operators must depend on actuating motives far different from the desire of gain in money; and chief among them are these private detectives, who draw their sustenance from meaner and equally unfailing fountains.

It is not upon record who bestowed a name which is more apt than designations usually are. The word detective, taken by itself, implies one who must descend to questionable shifts to attain justifiable ends; but with the prefix of private, it means one using a machine permitted to the exigencies of justice for the purpose of surreptitious personal gain. Thus used, this agency, which even in honest hands and for lawful ends is one of doubtful propriety, becomes essentially dangerous and demoralizing. Originally an individual enterprise, the last resort of plausible rascals driven to desperation to evade honest labor, it has come to be one of associated effort, employing much capital in its establishment and some capacity in its direction. All the large commercial cities are now liberally provided with "Detective Agencies," as they are called, each thoroughly organized, and some of them employing a large number of "shadows" to do the business, which in large part they must first create before it can be done. The system being perfected and worked to its utmost capacity, the details of the tasks assumed and the method of accomplishment are astonishing and alarming to the reflecting citizen, who has the good name and well-being of the community at heart. Employed in the mercantile world as supposed guards against loss by unfaithful associates or employees, and in social life as searchers for domestic laxness, these two items make up the bulk of the business which the private detectives profess to do, and through these their pernicious influence is felt in all the relations of life. Were they however only the instruments of rapacious and unreasoning distrust, they might be suffered to pass without rebuke as evils affecting only those who choose to meddle with them; but as they go further and the community fares worse because they are ever ready to turn a dishonest penny by recovering stolen property, which they can only do by compounding the crime by which it had been acquired, it is evident that they are a peril to society in general no less than a pest to particular classes.

It is a shame and danger of our country that love of property is permitted to so overbalance all other considerations, that it is the almost universal police experience when a robbery is reported that the loser makes the recovery of his property the first and nearly always the only object of his solicitude. He is ready to do anything short of sending good money after bad, to recover what he has lost, and will invariably sacrifice the right of society to punish the thief, to regain even a portion of his treasures. He hampers the officer of the law at every step if that official endeavors to secure the criminal rather than his plunder. Indeed, there is no obstacle to the proper administration of justice so insuperable as these greedy victims of thievery. A case which has just occurred so plainly illustrates this grave public danger, that its statement will not be unprofitable. A gentleman on his way home about two o'clock one morning was knocked down in Bleecker street with such violence as to inflict a permanent injury to his jaw, and then robbed of his watch and money. He was of course indignant at the police inefficiency which had permitted such a crime, and loudly demanded the recovery of his property and the punishment of his assailant, just as all such victims do at first. After much labor the police finally established the identity of the highwayman, but found also that he had left the city. He was, however, one of the best known of a gang of ruffians who have made the once aristocratic Bleecker street one of the most infamous and dangerous localities of New York; and a watch being kept for his reappearance, he was arrested within an hour after his return to his old haunt. But almost within the same hour one of the fellow's comrades visited the victim, returned him his watch, and made prodigal promises of further recompense if the prosecution was not pressed. As a consequence, the victim, who had before averred that he could swear to the identity of his assailant beyond mistake, now became doubtful, and when forced to admit that the prisoner was the man, flatly refused to prosecute. The whole power of the law had to be used to make him appear, and when finally the highwayman pleaded guilty in the Court of Oyer and Terminer, and was sentenced to a term of ten years in State's Prison, the victim had the effrontery to stand up before the judges of the land and plead, as well as his broken jaw would permit, for the pardon of the outlaw. While this case is in some respects an extreme one, it is by no means uncommon, and the District Attorney of New York can certify that thieves find their surest refuge in the cupidity or maudlin sympathy of their victims.

The private detectives are ever ready to aid and abet this willingness to compromise with robbery and to assist in the work of making thievery safe and profitable. The Police Commissioners of New York have never had the courage to inform the public of the number of burglaries and robberies annually committed in the metropolis; but enough is known in a general way for us to be certain that there are hundreds of these crimes committed of which the public is not told. The rule is to keep secret all such affairs when an arrest does not follow the offence, and hardly any police official will venture to claim that the arrest occurs in more than a moiety of the cases. There are hundreds of such crimes every year where the criminal is not detected, and hundreds of thousands of dollars' worth of property stolen of which the police never find a trace. These facts furnish the basis for the common belief that somebody is continually compounding felonies, and that a large part of this stolen property is continually finding its way back to the legitimate owners through means inimical to the best interests of society. The most casual and superficial reader of the daily papers infers as much, when he cannot take up an issue of any one of them without the risk of stumbling upon an advertisement in which some thief is invited to return certain property, "when a suitable reward will be paid and no questions asked." To a deplorable extent some officers of the law have been engaged in this disreputable commerce with thievery, but the bulk of it has been and is done by the private detectives. With them it is natural, for it is their sole purpose to make money, and as they are not sworn officials of the law, they do not feel themselves called upon to cage a thief at every opportunity.

Let me now give some instances to show how private detectives work in their profitable field. In all of the cases cited, names will be suppressed, for the reason that it is intended to arraign a system rather than attack individuals.

Not long since, a person known as a private detective installed himself in the confidence and employment of a large retail house in Broadway, by means of his representations that he knew all the shoplifters and pickpockets, and thus was able to "spot" any of them the moment they entered the shop, and so could save the firm and its patrons thousands of dollars every year. As a matter of fact, he knew none of either criminal class. His presence on the premises therefore did not have the expected effect of preventing depredations. Confidence in his ability to perform as he had promised waned with each successive robbery, and our blatant detective soon saw that he must catch a thief or be himself caught in a palpable false pretence. He was equal to the occasion. By dint of many inquiries among the police, he came to know the persons of two noted female shoplifters, one of whom, by the way, is an exceedingly handsome woman. He made the acquaintance of these outlaws, and, calling upon them at their home, represented himself as on the "cross," and proposed a job in which he should be a partner in the profits in consideration of the assistance he would give in carrying it out. This aid, he averred, would be most effective, as he had "fixed" the clerk at the lace shawl counter, and that person would be conveniently blind at the moment chosen by the thieves to slip the costly articles from the counter into the immense pockets they all have suspended to the waist, under the dress. The women did not rise eagerly to the bait thus presented; on the contrary, they at first absolutely refused, partly through distrust of him and partly from repugnance to stealing when necessity did not drive them. But he was so eloquently persuasive on the absolute safety and great profit of the operation, that they at last consented, and named an hour when they would be at the store to do the job. When the time arrived Mr. Detective had all his preparations made to "spot" and capture them in the act. As he had no legal authority to make an arrest, he detained a policeman who was on post in the vicinity of the store, by his confident assertion that there would be work there presently. True to their promise, the women came, and he, true to his villany, pounced upon them the moment they had slipped several of the lace shawls into their pockets. The policeman was called in, the women given into custody, and, with the stolen property upon their persons, the evidence of guilt was so complete that both were eventually sent to State's Prison. The detective flourished hugely on the credit of that detection, and, not content with receiving the plaudits and presents of his immediate employers, went to all retail dry-goods houses in the street claiming a recompense for caging two such dangerous characters. The truth of the way in which he had caged them soon came out, but it failed to have its proper effect of sending him to keep his victims company at Sing Sing.

The incidents next to be related were developed by a thorough investigation of the rascality they involved, and constitute one of the most curious and characteristic specimens of private detective work ever discovered. A man who was forced to leave Canada because of the authorities pressing him for explanations of certain smuggling transactions, came to New York as a natural refuge, and speedily finding a suitable associate, set up a private detective agency in the neighborhood of Wall street. The two men soon struck a new vein of villany, and followed it with a persistence that was admirable, and a clumsiness that counted largely but safely on the credulity of the business world. One Monday morning, one of these plausible gentlemen waited on the agent of a principal line of ocean steamers sailing between New York and Liverpool, with a marvellous story of contemplated crime of which he had obtained knowledge by the stale device of overhearing a conversation. His revelation was to the effect that he was on board the ship which sailed on the previous Saturday, just before her departure, and happened to overhear a conversation between one of the officers, whom he did not particularly designate, and a man of Jewish appearance, whom he did not know. The purport of their talk was an arrangement for the bringing over of a large quantity of goods, which were to be smuggled on board at Liverpool and to be got ashore at New York, without reference to the customs dues. It will scarcely be credited that the agent, who is one of the shrewdest of the business men of New York, swallowed this chaff without a single grain of allowance; but he did. Dismayed by the prospect of having his vessels made the means of violating the laws, and his fears already seeing ships and cargoes confiscated as a penalty, he asked what should be done with an earnestness that proved the game of the schemer already driven to cover. The detective was fully prepared with an infallible preventive, which was of course the employment of himself and associates to watch and thwart the smugglers. The agent could see no other means of escaping the impending disaster at so cheap a rate; and without the least inquiry as to the character or antecedents of the persons with whom he was dealing, he concluded a bargain whereby they became regular employees at high salaries with the duty of voyaging between New York and Liverpool on the steamers of the company, for the purpose of thwarting the smuggling operations. They were not the men to allow a good thing to pass away from them for lack of effort to retain it, and they were swift to furnish both the agent on this side and the owners in Liverpool with the names of persons whom they had detected in the conspiracy. Some of these purported to be names of residents of Liverpool, and others of New York and Chicago. This game had been played for several months when the suspicions of the owners were aroused, and upon an investigation of the facts so far as it could be had on the other side, they became so doubtful of the good faith of their employees as to order the New York agent to thoroughly sift their antecedents. The result was that the private detectives were themselves speedily under the espionage they pretended to have established upon the smugglers, and were proved by detective Farley, of the New York police, to be as unconscionable liars as ever obtained money by false pretences. Their story from beginning to end was an utter fabrication, concocted for the sole purpose of fleecing the steamship company of a first-class living for many months, besides a large sum in actual money.

Such cases as that just related are of course not common, as the opportunity for the display of the peculiar talent in this peculiar line is seldom offered. It is, moreover, a branch which is soon exhausted; but in the line of felonies compounded there is an unfailing field for exertion. It is difficult, however, to obtain details in any case, as neither party to so questionable a transaction is apt to talk about it afterwards. The information at hand on this point is principally derived from persons calling at police headquarters for aid in the recovery of stolen property, about half of whom, in response to sharp questioning, admit that they have had the matter in charge of private detectives, and have been fleeced. In all such cases money has been paid down in advance, to a quarter of the value of the treasure, in return for which the loser has unredeemed promises to recover the property. In this branch of the business there is no actual compounding of crime, but only a promise that it shall be done; and it is altogether about the meanest work in which private detectives engage. There are, however, some cases of compounding felonies, where the facts are sufficiently full for use.

A firm doing a heavy business in American watches was startled one morning by receiving a letter from a private detective giving his name and agency, in which he stated that he had picked up the enclosure in the street, and upon perusal finding it to be of great importance to the firm, had forwarded it. The firm, coming to the enclosure, read something like this, dated at Elgin, Illinois:

> OLD PAL: I suppose that you have wondered how I got away and where I am things was so hot I had no time to let you know Before. I have one or two small things out this way and have now the best job I have ever been in. There is a big watch movement factory here and I have made every thing with the watchman I have beat it already for a little but Im waiting for some good pal to help me clean it out com on and well make a good haul.
>
> SNOOZER BILL.

No thief ever wrote such a letter as this; but no imposture is too clumsy to answer its purpose when crime is dealing with honesty, and it is not surprising that the firm, seeing ruin coming upon a great enterprise in which they were largely interested, because of these hypothetical burglars, acted precisely as the detective presumed they would, by sending for him and giving the case in sole charge of one who had shown such disinterested devotion to their interests. Having thus received the inch he was swift to take the proverbial ell, and plied the firm with other intercepted letters of Snoozer Bill, until those nervous gentlemen beheld in fancy the enterprising marauders only prevented from carrying off watches, movements, factory and all, by the adroitness, persistence, and courage of their private detective, who all this time did not neglect to make them pay heavily for services they rated as invaluable. After a time, but not until he believed the trick had been exhausted, the detective announced that the burglars were finally foiled, and he was dismissed with plaudits and profit. It is scarcely necessary to add that the burglars existed only in his imagination, that the letters were clumsy creations of his own, and the whole affair from beginning to end a device to obtain money.

The device is a common one with the craft, who rarely fail to frighten merchants out of their senses and money by warnings of thieves at their doors, or intending to be there in the middle watches of some certain night named. The swindle was eminently successful in the case of a large silk house in Philadelphia, which was managed with great skill by the private detectives. One of them went to the house with the story of a conversation he had overheard in a "crib," during which "Stutter Jack," "Glimmer George," and sundry others with similar improbable names, had arranged the preliminaries for "cracking" the house on a night then some time in the future. Soon afterward another private detective called and clinched the nail thus entered, by a story of how he had crept unseen into the pawnshop of a notorious "fence," and had overheard that desperate Stutter Jack arranging with the "fence" to receive the "swag" they were to get from the silk house. He was even prepared to descend into details, and recounted the exact number and style of pieces of silk which were to be stolen and delivered, and the precise proportion of the proceeds which thieves and receiver were to get. The precision and fulness of the information thus obtained, apparently from separate sources, was convincing, and the merchants, in a tremor of fear, fulfilled the expectations of the informers by calling upon them to devise ways and means to thwart the burglarious schemes, not omitting of course to pay handsomely for services rendered and expected. It is to the credit of these skilful operators that they did not rest from their labors with the receipt of all they expected to make out of the transaction, but laid the foundation for similar operations in the future by actually planning a bogus burglary and attempting to commit it by confederates at the appointed time, who were of course frightened away by the preparations made to receive them.

There is one other case to be related where the effort of the private detective to put money in his pocket at the expense of society was lamentably successful. A gentleman who had the misfortune to lose $5,000 in United States bonds by means of a sneak robbery, next encountered the greater mishap of being directed to a detective agency for the recovery of his property. It is but just to his common sense to explain that this new disaster sought him, not he the disaster; for his loss being proclaimed in the newspapers, the private detectives pursued him with ravenous celerity, and by ingenious reasoning soon convinced him that the chances of his ever seeing any of his bonds again were remarkably slight in every way, except through the exertions of the detective, who had no doubt that he could secure the return of the property at a sacrifice of half its value. He did not state in so many words that he knew who had stolen the bonds and then had them in possession, but he strongly implied that such was the case, as a proof of his ability to perform as he had promised. At the first interview nothing was concluded, but the persistent detective returned again and again to the charge, and his terms were finally allowed. His league with the thieves was immediately made manifest by his prompt appearance with the stolen property, which was returned to the owner upon the payment of the stipulated price.

It would be pleasant to know the exact number of these harpies who are feeding upon the community, so that each of us might approximate his chances of escaping the surreptitious consumption of his substance; but there are, unfortunately, no data for making more than a rough estimate. In the city of New York there are a dozen of these "agencies," some of which are of limited capacity, and the several partners comprise the entire working force; but others are of colossal proportions, employing large numbers of "shadows," either casually or permanently. Other cities are equally well furnished; but such centres of commercial activity as New York and Chicago seem to be the chosen resorts of this particular species of birds of prey. In addition to these regulars, there are numerous guerillas, who are by far the most dangerous, because the most unscrupulous and needy. The regular "shadow" has generally a stated salary to depend on, and, appearing as he does in the name of his employer, has some little check upon his actions. Appearances must at least be saved, and the agency which seeks publicity as the basis of a prosperous business, cannot afford those more flagrant operations which have made the term of private detective a synonyme for rogue. On the other hand, the guerilla is always penniless and has nothing in the way of character to lose, so that he is constantly pushed by his necessities to all sorts of desperate devices, and is unrestrained in his pursuit and plucking of his prey by any moral considerations. But for his dread of the penalties of the law, he would be a thief outright.

It must not be supposed, from the general tenor of this article, or from the incidents related, that private detectives are all utterly base. There are probably some of them who endeavor to pursue their calling with all possible honesty; but it is difficult to deny that as an institution they are wholly unnecessary and evil in their influence. The little legitimate detective duty they do would be much more likely to be justly and well done by the regular officers of the law. The tracking of a criminal for gain by a person unauthorized to arrest him when found, breeds indifference to the demands and forms of law, which is calculated to breed contempt for the law itself, and thus lead to the serious demoralization of the community which permits it. In all other branches of their business the private detectives cannot help working evil, for they lead directly and despite them to false witness and all kinds of abominations.

The interests of society plainly demand the suppression of this peculiar industry, and it can be suppressed by nothing but lack of patronage. Every one, therefore, who feels an impulse to pander to his greed by means of this appliance, owes it to the general good to think twice before employing a private detective.

"CIRCULAR" SWINDLERS.

THERE are a dozen adroit rascals in New York who do a prosperous business by acting upon the principle that a large share of the people only need motive and opportunity to become knaves. Of course these roguish cynics offer the coveted chance with the end of making fools instead of knaves of the thousands of people in all parts of the country who listen to their allurements.

No fraud is more transparent, successful, universal in its ramifications, or corrupting in its influence, than that known, for want of a better name, as the circular swindle. Worked from obscure garrets and cellars in New York, it reaches every town and hamlet in the Union, to rob the credulous and tempt the weak-principled into crime. And no fraud ever made more rapid but less unnatural progress. Based upon a scoundrelly belief in the fact that very many men are in too great haste to be rich to scrutinize the means by which the end shall be obtained, it was not long satisfied with the various mean devices to which it first had resort, but speedily reached perfection in this form (I print from a very well executed lithographic letter, which many a simpleton undoubtedly takes to be a written letter prepared for him exclusively):

NEW YORK March 1871.

DEAR SIR; We wish to secure the services of a smart and intelligent Agent in your locality for a business, that cannot fall to yield (without much effort) at least, a profit of $10,000 per year and if shrewdly managed, will return a much larger amount, and this too, without neglecting your regular business. We have been constantly engaged for several months past, in preparing Plates of the $1, $2, $5, $10 U. S. Greenbacks, having completed them, we are now prepared to furnish the bills, of the different denominations, in any quantity desired, above $500. these are without any exception, the finest executed bills, that were ever issued in this Country and cannot be detected, even by the oldest experts, they are correctly numbered, the engraving cannot be excelled, in fact, no expense or labor has been spared, to bring the best talent the country could produce in the art of the engraving and printing, to make our issues, *exactly like the originals*, thus rendering it, just as safe for you to pass them, as if they came from the "*Treasury Department*." We have them put up in packages of $500, $1,000. $5,000, and $10,000. On account of the superior excellence of these bills, as well as the large expense in bringing them to perfection, we shall charge you, 25 cts. on the dollar for them, but in order fairly to start you and to show that we "*mean business*," we will send you a package charging you only 5 cts. on the dollar, *provided* you will pay the balance (20 cts. on the dollar) within 15 Days of receiving the package. You will be required to meet your bills promptly. The first cost to you will be $25 for $500, $50 for $1,000, $100 for $2,000, $250 for $5000, and $500 for $10,000. When you order, be very particular to *send your letter by Express*, for positively we will not fill an order, that reaches us through the Post Office, we have lost large amounts that have been forwarded this way and we will run no risk hereafter.

The Express is sure, safe and expeditious and the money forwarded through it, is at our risk. Seal your order, as you do any letter and mark outside, in large figures, *Value* $500 and it will then be received and forwarded by the Express Co. It is always best, to have a "*Cash remittance*," accompany your order, thus showing good faith on your part. Be very careful to distinctly state, the amount and denominations you wish, also your name and Post Office, with the *County* and *State plainly and clearly written*. You are one of three persons, in your State that we addressed, and with these bills so artistically executed, and the facilities we will give you, you are started at once, upon the highway, to *fortune, and affluence*. You can rest assured of one thing, that you can never be wanting for *funds*, while you are connected with us, and *remain true*. On receipt of your order, we immediately write through the P. Office to your address stating the day we ship your package, and you will always call there before going to the Express. The package is made up in such a way, that no one would ever suspect its nature. *A personal interview* is always desirable, and would better suit us, and might be to our *mutual advantage* as you could then examined the money for yourself, and judge its quality, and the amount you would require.

Fraternally Yours.

JAS. P. BAKER & CO.

No. 150 Broadway N. Y. City.

P. S. We received so many letters; asking for samples, that we have concluded we will, on receipt of $5.00 *by Express;* send sample of our issue. We have also *fractional currency* in 10 c. 15 c. 25 c. and 50 c denominations; fully up to our standard of Bills. *Prompt attention and fair dealing guaranteed.*

No one of these knaves is so poor as to have but one name; and besides being James P. Baker & Co., this fellow is B. B. Walker & Co., 206 Broadway; but he is poor indeed compared with some of his comrades, one of whom begins his lithographic letters thus:

DEAR FRIEND: While conversing with a gentleman from your locality recently, you were named as a shrewd and reliable person and one likely to enter into a business, the nature of which will be explained in this letter. At all events, he said, whether you go in or not, you would keep a still tongue, and would not expose me. He told me that under no circumstances must I inform you who recommended you; and as I claim to be a man of honor, I will never violate a pledge. I have on hand, and am constantly manufacturing large quantities of the best counterfeit money ever produced, in the world.

There are five undivided parts of this sensitive man of honor, which are labelled respectively John F. Hamilton, No. 212 Broadway; Wm. J. Ferguson, 194 Broadway; Robert H. Holland, 142 Fulton street; Thomas W. Price, 89 Nassau street; and Wm. B. Logan, 15 Dutch street. Under each name he offers perfect counterfeits of the $2, $5, and $10 bills and 50 cent stamps in unlimited quantities, and burdens his circular with constant reiterations that he is a man of honor anxious to deal on the square with his customers.

Another of the knaves starts out in this fashion:

BELL & SON,

37 NASSAU STREET, NEW YORK.

MY DEAR SIR: We wish to secure the services of a live gentleman to push the business named in the enclosed circular, and have been informed by a friend who knows you well that you are highly suitable to represent us. As we have had many dealings with that gentleman and know him to be an upright and honorable man, any friend of his will receive our utmost confidence, we therefore feel that there is no risk in confiding to you our secret.

In this particular case he won't require cash in advance, and after making several alluring propositions, he winds up thus:

We know you will serve us faithfully and truly. You cannot afford to deceive us. State the amount and denominations required. When you send the money *please pay the Express charges* and deduct the amount from the principal to pay same. Whatever you do, don't write by mail, as we will not claim or receive any letters from the post office. *Send only by express prepaid!*

Awaiting your early reply,

We are, yours fraternally

BELL & SON.

☞ Take notice that by remitting $25 to us by express and ordering a $2,500 package you will secure the agency for your State.

Please return this letter to remind us.

This gentleman is contented to do business with only the additional names of King & Co., 39 Nassau street; Owen Brothers, 58 Liberty street; and Williams & Co., 196 Broadway.

Another operator, also capable of subdivision, is the one who throws his hook thus baited:

ESTEEMED FRIEND: Being in want of a reliable agent in your State I have selected you in preference to many others, in consequence of your being recommended to me by a gentleman of this city, whose business it is to drum up trade in the country for a large commercial house. I already have 5 agents at different points; but desiring to push my business for the season I have resolved to employ one or two more. I have now on hand about $50,000 in counterfeit $2, $5, and $10 bills. I might as well represent them as genuine, for it would require an expert banker to distinguish them from the notes issued at Washington. They are printed on first-class bank note paper, are of the same size as the genuine, and are correctly numbered. The printing is incomparable. I would not for the world send out a bill that is badly printed.

He gives much excellent advice to his gudgeon to the effect that "When you get the bills ruffle them as to make them look old. Don't pass too much on one man at a time. Put a private marke on the bills, so that, should they come back to you in the course of trade, you will know them. You can carry as much about you as you like, but do not exibit too much. If you follow these instructions I guarantee that you will clear a large sum of good money in a short time. Endeavor to send all communications by Express. Do not under any circumstances send me a letter by mail." This man of careful business habits is variously known as Joseph R. Lee, 82 Nassau street; Horace Madden, 10 Chatham street; George Sommers, 30 Chatham street; Edward F. Dickinson, 36 Maiden Lane; and John B. Forrest, 30 Liberty street.

In addition to these operators doing business under several names, there are a few who, having not yet risen to this preëminence, are content to swindle by a single cognomen. Among them is S. Y. Adando & Co., No. 60 Park Place, whose lithographic letter, covering three large pages, sets forth the manifold excellences of his wares and the extreme reasonableness of his rates. He, too, is "a man of honor," trusting to the "honesty" of his correspondent, and manifests in an extraordinary degree that wholesome dread of the post-office, and great solicitude that money shall be sent only by express, which is prominent in the epistles of all the swindlers. C. E. Benson & Co., No. 176 Broadway, is a shrewder knave than some of the others in many respects, for he boldly puts his letter into type and baits his hook for the most foolish of very tiny gudgeons. After offering a package of $500 for $25, a package of $1,000 for $40, and one of $5,000 for $200, he says:

On receipt of price in registered letter for either of these packages, we will send the goods by mail in registered package which is the only safe way by mail, as there is then no cause for fear whatever, or we will safely pack either size package and send by express, C. O. D. on receipt of a deposit of $2 for No. 1 Package, $4 for No. 2 Package, or $8 for No. 3 Package, the balance to be paid on receipt of package, and mark them in such a way that no one will suspect or know but ourselves. We will give any information desired of us at any time, but we suppose any one knows what to do with money when they get it.

"William Cooper & Co.," who styles himself "dealers in fine stationery, 688 Broadway," has devised yet another method by having all of his thousands of circulars actually written by hand, in which work, up to the time he, or rather his business, suddenly came to grief, he had eight men constantly employed, and had so drilled them that there was no perceptible difference in the chirography of his missives. He also enclosed a printed circular, with the assertion that very few are to be issued, which he begins with this alluring scrap of secret history:

When Congress authorized the present issue of greenbacks, the Treasury Department executed plates of enormous cost and wonderful workmanship, from which the whole amount of currency authorized by Congress was to be printed, and it was ordered at the time, that as soon as the whole amount had been printed the plates, some 100 in number, should be taken from the Treasury Printing Department, conveyed to the Navy-yard and melted. Now it so happened that the plates from which the 1, 2, and 5 dollar bills had been printed were not destroyed. How it was brought about, we, as a matter of prudence, do not state. It is enough to know that the plates are still preserved uninjured, and we trust their whereabouts will never be known except to us.

He then proceeds to offer at fabulously low rates money in any desired quantity, surreptitiously printed from these plates so miraculously saved from the fire. "Rufus Stockton, stationer, wood, steel, and copper engraver," 204 Broadway, is the pioneer title in this fraud, but now is so seldom seen as to be unworthy of further notice.

H. Colter & Co., 195 Broadway, also does business in the usual way and on a small scale. Last, but by no means least, is a rascal who is aware of the rascality of the other fellows, and advises his dupes of the fact thus:

Express all your money to this address. } McNALLY & Co.
229 BROADWAY

DEAR SIR: You no doubt have some reluctance in engaging with us, perhaps you already have received from different parties in New York, who represent things highly colored, with a great mixture of flattery, in respect to the goods they desire to dispose of, and their extreme cheapness, they unaccountably got hold of the way we do business, and as near as possible they try to imitate us; they are flooding the country with circulars, receiving money and sending nothing in return; you can see for yourselves, how can any one sell $1,000 worth of the goods for $10? They can't do it, and more, they don't do it. We have letters every day from parties they have gulled and caught. Now of two evils you can choose the least, we have goods that no one ever has, so far, found fault with. Remember, we do this business with two names. One to write to and one to express all money to; make no mistake in addressing us if you desire to do business and yourself justice. Address by "mail" your letters to

P. MAYBORN & Co., Box 216 Jersey City, N. J.

Thus far I have used my space to present all the names under which this knavery is perpetrated, with enough of the distinguishing traits of each of the circulars to prevent all but those absolutely bent on being robbed from obeying the order of the last quoted, and expressing *all* their money to these rogues. It must next be shown how it is that these men can flood the country with these demoralizing circulars with entire safety. This explanation involves an exposé of a fraud which is so transparent that this exposure ought to be unnecessary. Were there a little more sense and honesty in the people at large, it would be sufficient to say that these circulars are self-evident lies; but this not being the case, it must be shown that these men really do not deal in counterfeit money. In that simple fact is not only their immunity but their profit. To produce an imitation of the United States currency sufficiently exact to have a ready circulation is an operation not only requiring the expenditure of much time, labor, skill, and money, but involving more risk of punishment than most men care to assume. These Cheap Johns of villany have therefore hit upon an expedient which demands no skill, little labor, and less money, besides being perfectly unobnoxious to any crimes act which ever has been or perhaps ever can be devised. When these knaves first began they conducted their business exclusively through the post-office, and at that time they were as grimly jocose with their dupes as now, for they sent as the "counterfeits" the small photographic cards of the greenbacks lately so common, and which could be bought in unlimited quantities for a fraction of a penny each. But the United States Government speedily tired of being partner to this fraud, and without much law to back it up, but with great moral and popular justification, it seized the letters coming to the New York post-office for the counterfeit men, and returned the money contained in them to the senders. But in the end the only effect of this well-meant and resolute attempt to break up the swindle was to put the schemers to the trouble and expense of getting up new lithographs, which bristle with such phrases as this:

☞ DON'T WRITE BY MAIL, SEND ONLY BY EXPRESS, CHARGES PREPAID. ☜

Their own letters, of course, went by mail as before, and being in plain envelopes were unknown and unchecked. By the aid of directories, commercial lists, and advertisements in newspapers, they obtained lists of names of persons in all the important cities and towns, while by some means those of men unknown beyond the narrow confines of obscure hamlets were also on their lists. It was this part of their scheme which involved the most labor and adroitness, for having obtained their lists they had nothing to do but mail their lithographs and sit down with their pockets wide open to catch the golden reflux.

It is impossible to say what proportion of the hundreds of thousands of circulars they issued had the desired effect. Some of the recipients tossed them contemptuously away, others were indignant and instantly mailed them to the New York Superintendent of Police, with the idea that they were putting him on the trail of a hitherto unknown villany, and demanding in most peremptory terms the instant incarceration of the scoundrels who had dared to tempt them. But many read in secret, as commanded, and permitted the golden vision thus skilfully raised to shut out reason and conscience until they at last ventured a little way into the new El Dorado by sending for the smallest quantity of bogus money mentioned in the circular. In the early days of the fraud, when the post-office was the medium of communication between two knaves, the victim knave sent his good money after the bad and waited impatiently for the receipt of his purchase; and he still waits, for the circular swindler could write letters, but he made it a rule never to reply to any. Since the closing of the mails against the business the metropolitan outlaw has still remained superior to fate and his bucolic brother. The business being done by express, two methods are adopted, the first being for the victim to send his money with his order as before, in which case he gets precisely what he did in the mail days. But the more seductive and general way is to have the order come unaccompanied by any money, whereupon the "queer" is "forwarded C. O. D. by express, packed in small boxes so as to defy detection." Every business man can see without further explanation how easily the fraud is managed. The box is duly sent, and on this point the operators fully deserve all their encomiums on themselves for promptitude. When it arrives at its destination the intending knave, who has already cast up a thousand times the profits he is to secure by cheating his friends and neighbors, is equally prompt to demand it, and of course must pay all charges, including the price of the "queer," before delivery. Having obtained his treasure, he steals off to a secret place to examine it, having done which he finds he is the possessor of a small and exceedingly flimsy box filled with saw-dust and little scraps of old iron, to give weight, the whole thing worth upon a liberal calculation perhaps a small fraction of a cent. The remainder of his natural life will probably be spent in pouring forth silent anathemas upon the knaves who have outwitted him. But he must take very good care that his wrath is silent, for there never comes a moment when he can bleat his sorrows in the public ear. He may be as stupid a dolt as ever fell prey to the sharper, but yet has sense enough to know that his is only a case of the biter very savagely bitten, and that so far as intention is concerned he is many degrees more depraved than his city confederate. His mind was fully made up to do all in his power to commit the meanest of all crimes, by uttering counterfeit money; whereas the city rascal had never intended to do anything more or worse than swindle the scoundrel who intended to commit that mean offence. He knows further, that for him to ask the return of his money from the tempter is only to subject himself to derision, for he can make no legal demand, and these fellows have never been known to make any restitution except upon the urgent solicitation of a sheriff or marshal. Therefore the poor bitten rogue must nurse his anguish in secret; his money has gone to the dogs, and he has only to mention the fact to throw his reputation after it.

An average of fifty of these circulars are returned every day to Superintendent Kelso, as they had been for many months to his predecessors in office. They come from all parts of the Union, and in nearly every case the sender, supposing he is dealing with a fraud which is what it purports to be, believes that he is giving the first clue to a nest of counterfeiters which is invaluable to the authorities. Every writer calls upon the Superintendent in the most positive terms to stop the villany and punish the villains; some even going to the length of advising how they may be discovered and entrapped by the law. Very many receive the assertions of the circulars as literal truth, and some are indignant thereat, like the gentleman who writes this:

IUKA, MISS. Dec. 7.

DEAR SIR: I do not feel complimented by this fellow's confidence in the judgment of my "friend." I'll *et* my friend if I learn who it was who recommended me to these scamps. I am very little sorry for the other scamps who bite at these offers. Still, as this fellow says, "*fraternally*," I would be glad to know they—Bell & Son, the unsurpassed rascals—were pecking stone at Sing Sing or Albany. And "fraternally" as tradition teaches some of us the words have been used since Hiram Abiff transferred the cedars of Lebanon to Jerusalem, I would ask your assistance in looking up and *lock*ing up Bell & Son.

Another is solemnly illiterate, but equally in earnest in this fashion:

STAT OF IELENOES

to de anrerale attorete of de sate of New York en cloneng som latters wats i font Pleis do yur doutey and Grab ob saus delings wee Poaybel aeutwest dont want no conterfeit monny out here

YURS TRRLY

A resident of the town of Monticello, Iowa, writes: "If you can get this fellow *Please* hang him without the form of Trial. he has sent some 200 of these things to this Town within the last week of course some will be duped."

A gentleman living at Weston, Mo., endorses a Pierce circular thus: "This infamous communication has just been received by me, and while I have no hopes of your being able to detect the scoundrel, you may be able to give him some trouble, and I hope that you will use it for that purpose. Such infamous things are calculated to cause many inocent persons trouble. Please look after him."

From Yazoo county, Miss., Mr. Kelso had this: "Inclosed you will find a circular from some rascal in your city. This is only one of the many thousands that they are now flooding the South with, several of my neighbors having received similar ones. If you could make any use of this in ferreting out these scoundrels I should feel that I had done a good deed."

Thousands of such letters have been received at police headquarters, but very few like this, written upon the blank space of a Pierce circular sent to a gentleman of Memphis, Tenn.:

Respectfully refered to Mr. Kelso with the suggestion that he grasp the opportunity herein offered of making the 20,000 in a year, as you can retain your position and slide off the "queer" with all possible ease. Mr. P. was mistaken in his offering me his magnificent offer for I have got money enough without going in to this arrangement: still, however, chances like this to make fortunes should not slip, and although I have not the pleasure of your personal acquaintance, still your reputation is known and admired by me, and I therefore freely bestow this fortune of 20,000 on you, hoping you will bear your honors gracefully. I sincerely hope you will accept this for it is given freely, and my heart goes with the gift, and then it is a pity for the money to leave the State.

All of these letters returning circulars go at once to the waste-basket at Mr. Kelso's feet, for the reason that none of them are of the slightest use and tell him nothing that he did not already know. In fact, every intelligent police officer in New York has long known all about these swindlers, except how to baffle them. Their names and haunts are matters of police record; but Kelso, like Kennedy and Jourdan before him, is powerless to interfere with them. They offer indeed to commit a crime, but really commit none except that of obtaining money by trick and device; but no one can afford to come forward and prove it, so they are entirely safe. They absolutely refuse to do business except by express, and therefore the extreme but effective method of placing policemen before their doors to warn away the unwary cannot be adopted in their case, as it has been in those of mock-auctions, panel-houses, and places of similar peril. The United States are equally powerless to interfere; for it is perfectly well known these fellows have no counterfeit money, and their arrest would only be time and trouble thrown away. There is no case upon record where any of these knaves were brought to justice; but there is one where poor hirelings who had no general interest in the fraud beyond their small salaries as clerks were visited by the penalties of the law. A man living in New Jersey to whom one of the circulars of Wm. Cooper & Co. had been sent, being unwilling to trust the treasure therein promised to the uncertainties of express carriage, applied in person at the designated office in New York for a supply of "queer." It is the habit of the knaves when such applications are made, to endeavor if possible to get the applicant to leave his money upon a promise to send the "queer" to his address, but under no circumstances to make any delivery in person. On this occasion Wm. Cooper & Co. was out, and one of his clerks, intending to do a little swindling on private account, took $50 dollars from the Jerseyman and delivered him a box which he opened a few minutes later at his hotel, and found to contain the usual assortment of sawdust. While the smart of the cheat was yet keen, he was not ashamed to rush off to the nearest police station and make public proclamation of his own infamy. Thereupon, a descent was made upon the den by police Captain Hedden, and the eight clerks who happened to be in at the moment were seized with all the contents of the office. The charge of obtaining money by fraudulent practices evaporated in the legal crucible; but it happened that among the rubbish in the place was found a counterfeit $10 bill which nobody there had ever attempted to pass, but its mere presence was so strained at as a pretext and proof that the captives were indicted by a United States Grand Jury. But this case had no prototype and has had no successor, nor does a pure administration of the law demand that it should, for the principal was not reached and the facts were terribly wrenched to obtain the indictment.

Since then, however, various attempts have been made to employ the same means to better purpose. Several persons have called at many of the places from which the circulars purport to issue, with the intent to inveigle the knaves into some clear violation of some law. In many cases the names of the persons appended to the circulars were unknown in the buildings where they claimed to have offices; but in others individuals were found who were or pretended to be the senders of the circulars. In the latter case, an earnest wish to purchase large quantities of the counterfeits upon the spot was expressed, but the person pretending in his lithographs to always have unlimited quantities on hand was at that moment inexplicably out of the article, or he said shortly and plainly that it was dangerous to deal personally in such matters. In either case, he always insisted that his interviewer should leave his money with his name and address, to which latter he would speedily transmit the desired goods. But as the interviewer had no idea of taking or paying for the "queer," these overtures were as fruitless as were all the efforts to inveigle the swindler into an overt act of war against the law. Armed in the impenetrable armor of adroit iniquity, these knaves have foiled all endeavors to even interrupt, much less put an end to, their corrupting practices, and they daily give the lie to weak King Henry's dictum:

> Thrice is he armed that hath his quarrel just
> And he but naked though locked up in steel
> Whose conscience with injustice is corrupted.

It is amazing that by so bald a device as this a dozen men in the garrets of New York can swindle thousands all over the land out of at least $250,000 per annum; but is is true. Let me hope that this plain narration of perfectly well authenticated facts will help to create a public sentiment which will compel every recipient of these counterfeit circulars to promptly cast them into the fire. By the creation of this sentiment, and in no other way can this scandal be removed from the American people, and these hundreds of thousands of dollars saved from these knaves.

Compared with this particular fraud the circular swindles are annoyance rather than dangers. Of late the most virulent and the meanest of these smaller swindles is that of "J. F. Williams & Co., sole manufacturers of aluminum gold jewelry in the United States. Office and show rooms 561 Broadway," whose particular variety is embodied in an advertisement found in nearly all rural newspapers, offering for $3 each their great eureka aluminum gold watches of which they say:

> This Watch we guarantee to be the best and cheapest time-keeper that is now in use in any part of the Globe. The works are in double cases, Ladies' and Gents' size, and are beautifully chased. The cases are made of the metal now so widely known in Europe as Aluminum Gold. It has the *exact color of Gold, which it always retains;* it will stand the test of the strongest acids; no one can tell it from Gold only by weight, the Aluminum Gold being one-fourth lighter. The works are all made by machinery, the same as the well known American Watch. We pack the Watch safely in a small box and send it by mail to any part of the United States on receipt of $3.50; fifty cents for packing and postage. A key is sent free with each Watch. Money should be sent by Post-Office Money order or in a Registered Letter.

The victims of this knavery deserve sympathy rather than censure. To the average uncultured intellect a good time-piece in cases as good as gold is a desirable possibility at $3, and in sending the money to the swindlers who advertise such articles they intend and do no wrong to the community. Thousands do send the money, and either get nothing whatever in return or a small toy watch which can be bought anywhere for five cents. This fact is so perfectly well known that in many cases where the thing is sent by express C. O. D., the express agents kindly tell the consignee the true character of the package, and advise its return to the shipper unopened. Sometimes this sensible advice is acted upon, but instances are not rare where faith has triumphed over reason and the box paid for and taken in spite of the warning. If J. F. Williams & Co. attempted to do a city trade upon the principle that governs their out-of-town business, they would find themselves in jail as a consequence of their first transaction. Protected by the non-residence of their victims, they snap their fingers in the face of the law, and I presume are getting rich very fast. Very similar to their scheme in its purpose and results is that of James T. Barton & Co., 599 Broadway, just instituted, which is called the "Spanish Policy," and seems to be a lottery, offering prizes ranging in value from $25 to $10,000. Circulars are now being sent all over the country, with each one of which are enclosed eighteen checks like this:

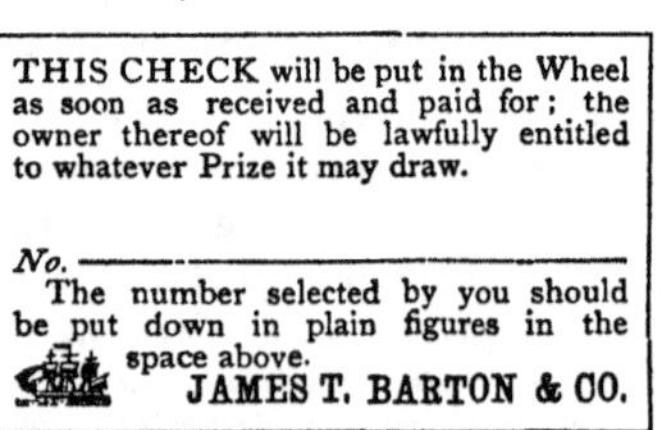
THIS CHECK will be put in the Wheel as soon as received and paid for; the owner thereof will be lawfully entitled to whatever Prize it may draw.

No. ——————————

The number selected by you should be put down in plain figures in the space above.

JAMES T. BARTON & CO.

These checks, it is said, are placed in the wheel, and, we are told, "the drawings take place daily in the large rotunda in rear of our office, at 2 o'clock P. M., in the presence of the purchasers of checks." The laws of New York prohibiting lotteries are rigidly enforced, and if any such drawing took place everybody concerned in it would be immediately prosecuted criminally. But this fact is not generally known, and James T. Barton & Co. are flourishing by reason of large sales of these worthless bits of paper at forty cents each.

There are scores of such schemes as this, differing only in the names attached, but they are unworthy of further description. Out of the more legitimate lotteries has come another swindle, illustrated by such fellows as B. C. Travers, 85 Nassau street, who declare in circular letters that "Fortune knocks once at every man's door," and proceed at once to do the knocking on behalf of Fortune in this most boisterous fashion: "Having long been connected with the Royal Havana Lottery, which draws every Saturday, and knowing that the true way to increase business is to have a nice prize of $1,000 or $2,000 in the hands of some good person who will make it known, I have decided to offer you the chance, and if you will send me $1, the price of a ticket, so that I can account for it as being really sold, I will send you one that will draw a handsome prize in the next drawing after hearing from you. After its receipt I shall expect you to show the money to all your friends, telling them where you bought the ticket, and by that means build up a large business in your section. Answer soon."

Very many do answer soon, and the knaves, who of course buy no tickets in the Havana Lottery or any other, live very cosily on the dollars that flow to them for that purpose.

After the publication of an article upon these swindlers in "The Galaxy," there was an entire change in the names appended to the circulars, which, however, still remained precisely as I have quoted them. Some new devices, however appeared, and none of them more adroit than this:

THE
TISSOT GOLD HUNTING WATCH,
S. L. TISSOT, Manufacturer,
LOCLE, SWITZERLAND.
NORMAN, ADDERSON & CO.,
Sole Agents for the United States,
NO. 7 PINE STREET, NEW YORK.
—o—
Wholesale or Trade Price, $240 *per dozen.*

OFFICE OF
NORMAN, ADDERSON & CO.,
IMPORTERS AND MANUFACTURERS OF
WATCHES, FINE GOLD JEWELRY, &c.,
No. 7 Pine street, New York,

December 15*th*, 1871.

DEAR SIR: As it is now almost one year since we have heard from you, and as we have written twice in the meantime, we have concluded to address you on the subject once more. And should we not hear from you within twenty days, we will consider the watch forfeited, and will dispose of it to our best advantage for ourselves. We would not hurry you in this matter as the watch is ample security for the amount *due*. We must get our accounts all straight so as to settle up our books on the first of the new year. If you wish now to settle the matter, you can send the money by mail or express and we will forward the watch. Please return bill with the money. Or, if it would suit your convenience better, we will send it by express C. O. D. with bill, which you can pay on delivery.

Yours, respectfully,

NORMAN, ADDERSON & CO.

P. S.—We could have sold the watch last June for $90, at which time we notified you by mail and received no answer.

The bill referred to in this case was dated February 27, 1871, and was made up of $3 for repairing a gold watch, $10 for loan on watch, and seventy cents interest, making a total of $13.70. The fraud seems small, but it was this very fact that made it effective. Sent out by hundreds all over the country, these letters produced in the aggregate a very respectable amount for the knaves who mailed them. Many of them of course were unproductive, as the recipients were not caught by the shallow bait, but the majority are hooked. They know of course that they never left a watch to be repaired, and that they never got a loan of $10 upon it, but they suppose that a mistake has been made in addressing the letter, and they cannot resist the temptation to steal by indirection a watch which could have been sold "last June for $90." Many of them therefore hasten to remit the required $13.70, and find that they have themselves been sold at a singularly low rate. If they send the money by mail or express, it is the last act in their transactions with Norman, Adderson & Co. But if they choose the C. O. D. alternative, they promptly receive the package after having paid the bill, and on opening it discover to their intense disgust that it is only stuffed with sawdust.

There is another of these schemes which is somewhat more complex but is of the same general character. The first step in its perpetration is the mailing of letters, offering those addressed the agency of a lottery, the prospectus of which is enclosed. After a time the recipients of these letters receive another, stating that in order to awaken public confidence in the lottery it has been de-mined to present each agent with a gold watch worth two hundred dollars, as a sample of the goods which are to be subjected to the drawing. This offer eliciting proffers to act as agents from many of those addressed, the next step is a third letter, in which it is said that after further consideration the managers have concluded to send a chain also, but for this the nominal price of fifteen dollars each must be charged, and a certificate from a leading house is enclosed that these chains are of a certain number of pennyweights each, and worth a price per pennyweight, which shows them to be double in value the amount charged for them. The preparation of the bait is completed by this plausible letter, and it has been swallowed by thousands in all parts of the country. Those who offer to accept the watch and chain on the terms mentioned, are speedily delighted by its arrival by express C. O. D. Taking their prize to their homes, after paying the fifteen dollars with express charges added, it generally requires some little time to convince them that their gold watch and chain are made of oroide and are worth at least eight dollars. So that they are swindled out of but little more than half of their money. If they expect to recover this amount by confiscating money received for the sale of tickets in the lottery they are again doomed to disappointment, as no tickets are ever sent them, and all efforts to obtain an explanation from their correspondent are unavailing.

This chapter has been entitled "Circular Swindlers," but it would have been, perhaps, more true to have put the title in the singular number. There are, as I have said, some dozen of rascals engaged in fleecing the credulous by these schemes, but they are all base imitators of one man, who may be justly called the shrewdest knave alive. In his fertile brain have originated nearly all the fraudulent schemes of this character with which the country has been afflicted during the last decade. I first knew of him a dozen years ago as the keeper of a gift jewelry store, and it would require the whole of this volume to enumerate the fraudulent affairs in which he has been engaged since that time. Gift jewelry, prize candy, "Milton gold," gift concerts, dollar stores, grand combination lotteries, and circular swindles of every description, have been only a few of his devices for wheedling people out of their money. I have heard of him creating an intense excitement in rural towns by scattering watches and trinkets broadcast from the advertising wagon of a lottery scheme, the tickets for which were sold upon the spot before the astonished people had time to discover that his watches were without works and all his articles made of base metal. I am told, and know enough of the man to believe, that he prides himself upon his fertility in roguery, and counts that month lost in which he does not concoct some new device to part fools and their funds. It must be said to his discredit, however, that he did not originate the sawdust phase of the circular swindle, but he has the consolation of knowing that this most cunning shape which knavery ever took was the work of one who sat at his feet as a pupil until he became a master of his art. For another of his disciples he has only contempt, as he proved a bungler, and thus won the great distinction of being the only circular swindler ever awarded a term in State prison for obtaining money by trick and device. There is no hope that the great master in the art of wheedling will ever meet a like fate, for he is always careful to keep within the letter of the law, or, in default of that, so manages as to make his victims *particeps criminis*, and thus seals their lips as to his transgressions. He is now immensely rich, and if he is as circumspect and fertile in the future as he has been in the past, I see no reason to doubt that he will accumulate one of the largest fortunes ever gathered by human effort. Although known to be a rogue of the first class, it is almost impossible to begrudge this man his bright prospects. In his dealings with his dependents he is more than scrupulously honest, for he is as liberal as he is ready of resource. He has scores of young men in his employ writing the circulars with which the country is flooded, and he pays them so well that rapid penmen can make $60 per week, and his terms to the young women he employs in the stores he opens from time to time, put to shame legitimate tradesmen who starve female labor. It is possible this man may yet be set before the public with the prominence he deserves, and when he is, the good that is in him must be told in mitigation, so far as it will go, of the evil he has done.

"SKINNERS."

OBSERVING Detective Elder looking intently at a man of most respectable appearance, who nodded shortly as he passed us with the quickness of motion peculiar to "the Street," I asked: "Who is that?"

"A Skinner who carries his office in his hat!" was the reply.

When a sharper proves himself a master of his art, always ready to adapt himself to any exigency however suddenly presented, and constantly intriguing with success for illegal gains, without incurring the penalties of any statute of frauds yet devised, he rises to the dignity of a skinner, who is the rankest growth of that rare roguery which dodges the law at every turn, and is nowhere produced in such perfection as in the financial hot-bed of the continent.

Wall street has absorbed more of the twisted intellect which delights in trick and device than any other spot of earth. The place seems to breed indirections as naturally as swamps do miasms; for the line between legitimate operations and achievements which even the moral sense of brokers declares to be crimes is so faint and uncertain that thousands hover constantly on its edge, while hundreds step beyond it without provoking rebuke or punishment. The methods of business which thus merge the devious and straightforward into a mass where one is difficult to distinguish from the other, have so depreciated the standard of honesty that there is little moral difference between the shrewd, driving business man and the scheming, restless scamp.

The knavery which Wall street breeds is known to all the world which has heard of such affairs as the Schuyler frauds, the Ross, Cross, and Van Eeten forgeries, the Harlem corner, the Ketchum crimes, the colossal swindling of Black Friday, and the many great defalcations and embezzlements which the journals have chronicled for a day's sensation. The turpitude revealed by such events as these has been provocative of public philippics without number, and has caused much anxious inquiry for the means of improving the moral condition of the street. The world has been moved to censure and remonstrance by a partial knowledge of the facts, for it has never heard of the numberless transactions which make no noise because of their frequency, and gain only a little "item" report in the newspapers, or are never recorded at all for the public. These lesser affairs, in which the biter is an unknown rogue, who shuns the public honors that wait upon stupendous crimes, and the bitten is not sufficiently injured to fill the whole land with the agony of his depletion, are daily incidents of Wall street life; and only by knowledge of them can a just verdict be rendered in a matter where judgment has been already given against the street, upon the evidence of exceptional cases.

Some general information therefore of the tribe of skinners and their business habits which result in these minor derelictions, will be found to be of interest.

As a rule, the man who carries his office in his hat is not a satisfactory person with whom to have dealings in such immaterial things as stocks and bonds. He will not do at all in that "day game" played in Broad street without interference from the police, who do occasionally pounce upon the gentlemen who seek some show for their money by playing faro in Ann street. In an affair so unsubstantial as gold gambling, the man with his office in his hat would so add to the airiness that "margins" would remain a fleeting show only until the "curbstone broker" had time to get around the next corner; and for the reason perhaps that the members of the New York Gold Exchange know so much themselves, the skinners have rarely attempted to play any of their little games upon them. I have had occasion in these articles to remark upon the wonderful verdancy of people in general, but I do mankind the credit of believing that there are very few people who will pick up a stranger in Wall street of whose local habitation or business standing they have no knowledge whatever, and hand him over some thousands of dollars to wager on the price of gold. The fever of gold gambling has indirectly brought many fish to the skinner's nets by creating an insatiate thirst for speculation in things unseen; but with gold-betting itself he has not often meddled, and the genuine skinner has never done so in person. No one of the class is a member of the Exchange, wherefore he could not himself play in the glittering game, nor could he act for others there. I have therefore not undertaken to obtain any facts as to the operations of skinners in gold, as I was convinced I would be gleaning in a barren field.

Nor has this master workman ever made many attempts to obtain funds by writing another man's name to a check. Forgery as it was practised by the great criminals of the last decade is a lost art. In that dead and gone era when villany was in its swaddling clothes, John Ross astonished and dumfounded Wall street by fleecing it one afternoon of half a million of dollars by means of forged checks, which were such in the true meaning of the words. At an earlier day, and by means of more numerous illustrations, Colonel Cross had achieved a notoriety in the same line which afterwards ripened into fame by his forging his way twice out of prison. But these men, who embodied the highest skill of their day, were forced by their limited knowledge of the capabilities of their calling to go to the banks with checks that had not the least odor of genuineness about them, but were in all respects the handiwork of fraud. Livingston, who obtained $72,000 on a forged check of Cornelius Vandebilt some three years ago, was the last notable case of this species of robbery. Since then the operators in this line have devoted their skill first to obtaining the genuine check of some person or firm having a large bank account, and next to altering it for such sum larger than that for which it was drawn as their necessities may require or their fancy dictate. This was the method of Van Eeten, and all other of the shrewder knaves who have recently become famous as forgers, and it has the great advantage of leaving the lawyers a chance to quibble about the exact character of the offence which has been committed. But it has for the skinners the equally great disadvantage of being an operation requiring time and money for success. From the day when the forger obtains the genuine check by selling the party to be fleeced a bond, asking for a check instead of money, as he desires to make a remittance, many days must elapse before the check will be ready to direct the bank to pay $10,000 instead of $100. The filling up must be erased with chemicals which leave no trace of themselves or the former writing upon the paper, and the blanks must be again filled up for the amount desired in such way as to appear regular and business-like. The skinner has the skill to do this thing or have it done, for he can do anything except obey the primal law and earn his bread by the sweat of his brow; but he has not the time or money required for it. He is a hand-to-mouth knave, who spends as he gets, and generally depends upon the rogueries of each day to pay the expenses thereof. He therefore prefers the swift return and small profit system of conducting his affairs, and will commence and finish a dozen operations during the time the forger is patiently working upon one. There are cases, however, where a skinner who has happened to have a little money to invest has become a special partner in a forgery; but in that event he has only kept sufficient supervision of the matter to protect his own interests, and has by no means neglected his daily harvest of the green things—of things growing so miraculously in Wall street.

If any reader has ever gone into Wall street in pursuit of a stolen United States bond, or to sell an unmarketable security, he can profitably omit a perusal of these pages, if his sole object in reading is the garnering of new facts. In the one case he probably met Detective William G. Elder, or Detective Thomas Sampson, and in the other has had most sorrowful personal experiences, so that nobody can tell him anything new about the skinners. But for the benefit of those who cannot get this positive testimony, which in this case defies the legal axiom, and is the least satisfactory of all, I go on to state that skinners delight most of all in stocks and bonds, and manifest their prowess in connection with these representatives of values in ways more dark and by tricks more vain than any Ah Sin ever mastered. Possessed of rare perceptive powers, great readiness of resource, vast versatility, perfect coolness under all circumstances, attractive appearance, persuasive address, and unlimited shrewdness, these men are gifted with powers that, added to moral force, would rank them among the benefactors of mankind in commerce or finance. But being naturally dishonest, and preferring the oblique path when the straight and narrow way is equally easy of access and more satisfactory in its results, they are among the most finished, plausible, and dangerous of outlaws. Their fertility in roguery is wonderful and perplexing. If one of them is to-day hairy as Esau, to morrow, if an exigency demands it, he appears as a convert to the barber's practice, and the next day reverts to his original faith if the occasion requires another metamorphosis. With all the world before him where to choose his business habitation, he chooses everywhere, so that no man knows where to put a finger on him when he is wanted. With him,

> To have done is to hang
> Quite out of fashion, like a rusty mail
> In monumental mockery,

and he never repeats a fraud precisely as it was done before. In its general aspects it may be like its predecessors, but there is always some distinguishing difference which stamps it as an improved method of roguery. Provided with names in unlimited number, and with cards bearing these several cognomens, each locating his office at a different place, at no one of which is he ever found or known, he is a myth to the law, and only a momentary although terrible reality to his victims.

This perfection of knavery at some time and in some way takes his commission out of nearly every kind of security which is ever offered for sale in Wall street, besides manufacturing some on private account which the street never hears of except through his operations. But so far as he can, and to the extent of the supply, he devotes himself to working back stolen United States bonds into the channels of legitimate business. Coupon bonds are his first preference, as they are of the thief, to whom, after greenbacks, they are the best plunder. Possession being *prima facie* evidence of ownership, the Government has necessarily been compelled to recognize all sales of these bonds as legitimate, as otherwise they would be the least desirable of investments, and money would seek some more satisfactory resting place. But this doctrine, which alone makes these bonds so valuable as a medium of exchange, has the drawback of its application when they get into the hands of thieves. Nearly all of the coupon bonds—probably ninety per cent.—stolen in the United States, begin their journey back to innocent holders in Wall street. The thieves or their agents rarely having the tact or boldness to put them directly upon the market, the skinner obtains his opportunity, which he never neglects. Sometimes he is content with a moderate commission, and, dealing with some broker whose precise status is not the best known fact in the world, he sells the bonds for about ninety—allowing the market rate to be par—and settles with the thief at eighty. The broker who buys has at least an equivocal standing in the street, and generally has little difficulty in disposing of them at the regular price ; and, that accomplished, the bonds are back again where they need not blush for the parties in possession. But this operation is so tame that the skinner never resorts to it when the chance for something better is presented. In some cases he will go to the broker he has selected as his victim, and declare openly that he has stolen coupon bonds and desires to sell them. The price he names is about twenty per cent. under the market. He will give the number of bonds, but never permits them to be seen, much less counted. The broker snapping at this opportunity, an appointment is made for a time and place for the money to be paid and the bonds delivered, both being always certain to be favorable to the sudden disappearance of the skinner. When the parties meet, a package of bonds is exhibited of which the top one is seen to be all regular ; and the money being handed over, the skinner bolts away, leaving the broker to discover that his package contains just one bond, while the remainder of the bulk is made up of blank paper folded to match it. Varied to meet the special details of each case, this fraud has been repeated in the street with a frequency which shows the alarming amount of stolen coupons constantly afloat, and the readiness of unaccredited brokers to assist the thieves in working them back, nor is it often a subject of judicial investigation, as the complainant is not clean-handed, and consequently has no standing in court.

If thieves had more nerve and sense, the skinners would rarely be able to manage this or any other operation in coupons so greatly to their own advantage. It is only by throwing the odor of suspicion upon the bonds, and so conducting the affair as to create a belief among those engaged in it that a very rascally matter is in progress, that the skinner succeeds in so depreciating the property that he can make something out of it. The great army of sneak thieves and bank burglars by whom all of these surreptitious securities are put upon the market are not all dolts, and there are numerous cases where they or their immediate factors have gone boldly upon the market and realized the face of their plunder. One such case occurred not long ago, where the bonds were purchased openly by first-rate houses without suspicion of the way in which they had been obtained ; checks to the amount of $50,000 given, and these latter cashed the same day without question by a leading bank. Unless he has surrendered it to some faro bank, the thief is now enjoying this substantial reward of his enterprise. It is always best to go to leading houses, for if the negotiations are successful in the outset and the bonds purchased, there is no danger of subsequent disaster, as the checks of these firms are guarantees everywhere of the eminent respectability of the whole affair. On the other hand, in dealing with brokers whose standing is not the best, the matter is questioned and scrutinized to the close, and the spoiler is never sure of his booty until he has disappeared around the corner after exchanging his check for the money it demands. And he must in every case undergo this ordeal, for no prudent broker ever thinks of giving money for bonds, but pays for them with a check drawn to order, with the idea that if there is any villany in the thing, it will out before the party holding the check can be identified and get the money. But if he is dealing with a skinner, the broker finds his precaution a broken reed, for the latter never goes to the bank with the check. He goes and buys a small bill with his check, which is unhesitatingly taken, and the difference between its face and his bill given him. The same device for the same purpose is used in many other operations by the skinner, but it is rarely omitted when disposing of a check drawn to order.

In dealing with registered bonds of the United States which have been stolen, the genius of the skinner has greater scope, and he reaches his reward by more devious ways. He first gets his bonds from the thief or receiver, and then meditates profoundly upon the subject of their disposition. He knows that it is utterly impossible to destroy the proprietary rights of the person whose name is upon them, for whether that person be in actual possession or not, by giving the Government a bond of indemnity, he can draw the interest and receive the principal when the bonds mature. Nor will any alteration of the obligations be more than a temporary expedient, for only a moment is required at the United States Sub-Treasury to discover any cheating changes. For these reasons the skinner never attempts to sell registered bonds, although he is always ready to buy them of a thief at twenty cents on the dollar. When he has them, his first task is to prepare them for his purpose by altering the names and numbers. He then establishes himself, either personally or by a confederate, in business, and obtains a financial footing by opening a small account in a bank. There is no one thing so much like charity in its power to cover a multitude of sins as a bank account, and I hardly know what a man may not do who has a balance at his banker's. The skinner in such case becomes a worker of miracles, for no sooner is he known as a customer of the bank than he offers the stolen and altered bonds for hypothecation, and is not refused. He never wishes to sell them, but he never makes the fatal mistake of demanding too little upon them as a loan. In that case the bank would do what would be done in all such cases if these institutions were managed with ordinary prudence—make the trivial examination required to detect the fraud. If the skinner should timidly demand fifty per cent. of the face, he would certainly get nothing; but as he demands ninety, or at the least eighty, his bank is left to meditate upon its folly after he has got his money and withdrawn his account, which are invariably simultaneous events. He has other methods of reaching his end, for he is never so poor as to have but one string to his bow; but he generally adheres to the plan described, with variations in the details to prevent suspicion of his purpose. As an additional safeguard he never attempts any of his games a second time upon the same person. By strict attention to business he manages to deal year after year in the bonds of the United States without anybody but his victims being the wiser, or any body but himself being the richer.

It is not, however, until he gets outside of these bonds, and is put as it were upon his mettle, that the skinner lays any very severe tax upon his resources. These bonds give him a basis of fact for his operations, which are comparatively tame and easy; but when he must create his basis as well, he can feel some pride and interest in his achievements. When he manufactures his securities as well as sells them, he may not make so much money, as in fact he does not; but there is vast satisfaction in swindling somebody with them, as is frequently the case. He adheres in this instance, as always, to strict business rules, and his first precaution is to obtain a confederate who has a room in some garret or cellar, on the door of which he tacks a tin sign bearing the name of some grand consolidated mining or railroad company which is unknown in the street, except through skinning operations. Having a ready reference provided, the skinner watches for his prey with an intuitive perception of the proper person to approach which seldom betrays him into a mistake. The victim is always a new comer or a casual dabbler in stocks, who knows nothing whatever of the wiles of Wall street, and who, having a conviction that he has penetrated into an El Dorado where fortunes are made in an hour, is ready to snap at the first great bargain presented. The skinner knows this individual at a glance, and, easily managing to make his acquaintance, beguiles him with stories of the craft of the street, and advises him to be very careful or he will find himself victimized. Never buy anything on any man's representations, says the skinner, but always demand references and make personal examination into the truth of the statements which have been made. The skinner very probably tells some of his own woful experiences to show that he speaks as one having personal knowledge; but he is always careful to add that he got the advantage of the knaves in the end, and winds up with careless and general remarks, from which his sagacity and prosperity as a dealer in all kinds of known or unknown securities can be inferred. He then invites his friend into some adjacent restaurant or saloon, and while acting as his host does him the favor of showing him a first-class investment by producing bonds of the Grand Consolidated What Not, which he declares to be worth par, but which, owing to the machinations of the street, have been depressed, and are offered at a ruinous discount.

The victim nibbles feverishly at the bait; but suddenly remembering the excellent advice he has just received, astonishes himself by demanding a reference, which is, of course, unhesitatingly given, and he is invited to make the closest inquiry. The address being furnished, he hurries away to the confederate, who, on being questioned, says carelessly that the bonds are not number one, but he will give eighty-five for them. This being at least ten per cent. more than the skinner had demanded, the victim rushes back delighted with the prospect of swindling that unsuspecting gentleman. Both being thus eager for a bargain, it is soon concluded, and the two, as the victim supposes, part company. But the skinner only drops into the background, and keeps his eye upon the other long enough to be assured of his movements after he has discovered the fraud. If he goes away with more of sorrow than of anger in his demeanor after his vain search through the street for the man with whom he had dealt, and for the broker who would give eighty-five, but is always out, the skinner knows it is safe to repeat the operation at the first opportunity; but if the victim hastens at once to the nearest police station, or is seen in conversation with any of the detectives, the skinner is aware that business calls him up town for the remainder of that day; and he appears, if it all, during the next few days, in another round of his favorite characters.

There are literally no bounds to the ingenuity of the skinner when dealing in bogus securities or in the bonds of companies or corporations, public and private, which are not quoted and have only nominal values. He did a good deal in town war debt bonds for a time, but latterly these have been harder to obtain, and he not thinking it worth while to make them outright, his trade in them has almost ceased. There is not space to even enumerate his numberless bond and stock operations, as he has other fields of labor which must be hastily described.

When all other means of swindling fail him he has recourse to the bogus check, which, rightly managed, is an unfailing source of supply. It seems a libel upon the common sense of the mercantile world to believe that the check of a stranger is taken in payment of goods, especially when it is more than the bill, and the difference must be handed over to that stranger in money; but it is an every-day occurrence. There are any number of cases where the skinner has entered a large retail store, purchased goods to a small amount, tendered a check for a few dollars more, and been permitted to walk away with both money and goods. His conduct in these enterprises is always controlled by the special circumstances of each, but in all it is founded on the abounding faith of mankind in the honesty and financial responsibility of the man claiming to have a bank account. Sometimes the skinner is timid and gets only the odd dollars, as he directs the goods to be sent to a house where he is not found and they go back to the owner; at other times he is found, blandly receives the parcel, and disappears with it in some manner the porter is never able to clearly state.

Not long since a skinner, sauntering up-town after a day of ill luck in Wall street, managed to bring down two birds with one stone in a manner that greatly increased the credit of his tribe. Stepping into a leading furnishing store in Broadway, he bought cravats, collars, gloves, and other articles to the amount of $65, and taking out his pocket-book displayed a large roll of bills. But he suddenly remembered that he desired to make other purchases on his way, especially of cigars at a prominent up-town Broadway grocery, and proposed to give a check for $100 for his purchases, as he wished to use that evening a little more money than he had with him. The check was readily accepted, and with his goods and $35 he walked leisurely away. Getting to the grocery, he purchased cigars and liquors to the amount of $75, and desired to pay for them with a check, as he had just paid out all the money he had with him at the furnishing store, which establishment he boldly gave as a reference. He had the goods with the label of the house upon the parcels, his statement was believed and he walked away with another $25 added to his store. In this case he desired the goods sent to his residence, which was done, and being received at the house he had named, they were never afterwards recovered, although upon subsequent investigation, when the checks proved worthless, it was found that he was utterly unknown on the premises. A little shrewder game was played by the fellow who paid for his purchase with a check which was taken without question, as the dealer saw that it was certified. But when it came back bearing the distressing words "No funds," the dealer opened his eyes wide enough to see that the certification was one of the most shallow devices by which a fool and his money had ever been parted. The check purported to be drawn by the secretary of a company, and the certification was by the cashier of the same company, with the word cashier made prominent in a large round hand, while the initials of the company underneath at a hasty glance looked like a mere flourish of the pen. These are only two illustrations out of thousands which might be given showing how the skinners operate in worthless checks.

Another method which the skinner has adopted for making his way in the world, while creditable to his ingenuity, is a great annoyance to the mercantile community. Keeping an eye constantly open for the main chance, he discovers that some quiet firm which is doing a snug business without making any fuss about it, has thereby, and by virtue of years of probity, secured the confidence of a large circle of customers. These are advantages which the skinner could never acquire for himself, and he is therefore forced to appropriate those gathered by others. He prints business cards and circulars bearing the name of the respectable firm, and, although never giving the same location, generally selects the same street. This done, he has his immediate future secured; for he goes out boldly and buys goods on short time in the name, say, of Smith & Co., Water street. Inquiries are of course made by the seller of the Mercantile Agency, where the firm is declared to be, as it is, first class, and the goods are delivered. Sometimes the skinner has them delivered for shipment, and they go off to another city, where they are sold and the proceeds are in his pocket before the cheat is discovered. But oftener he takes the chance of disposing of the goods in New York, in which case the cartman who takes them from the store of the seller dumps them upon some pier, from whence they are taken away by another cartman, and all trace of them is thus lost. In this way many skinners contrive to do a thriving business year after year without detection ; and some of them, even bolder, send circulars through the country and advertise in rural newspapers, by which means they get consignments of produce from farmers, and of course never make a return, nor can they be found when the duped shipper, as he always does at last, comes to the city to hunt up his correspondent. This knavery is so adroitly managed that in many cases the skinner actually pays advances on consignments ; but as it is always only a small per cent. of the value, it will be readily seen that he takes no chance of losing his margins by the operation. By these devices, calculated to deceive men of ordinary prudence and caution, he has done a most thriving trade, and almost undermined public confidence in commercial integrity. Not content with this, he further extracts profit from his bogus character by issuing notes of the business house whose name he has assumed, and readily gets them shaved by the less reputable bill-discounters.

In none of his specialties does the skinner display more ingenuity or reap a greater reward than in his insurance frauds. His simplest method is to constitute himself the agent of a company which has no existence ; but his genius never appears until he appoints himself the president of a first-class company. In this case he must have a confederate in a distant city, where the insuring is done, and he, being fully provided with facsimiles of the blanks of the company, approves the policies by mail, and writes frequent letters of commendation to the agent, which secure that swindler public confidence in the community where the operations are being carried on. If small fires occur, the confederates promptly pay the loss and work the mine they have opened until a large conflagration comes, when they invariably do not. Cases are upon record where as much as $30,000 was made in a few months by skinners working in pairs, and there are numerous instances where smaller amounts have been purloined ; and in no one of these cases was the swindler ever brought to justice. Yet another fraud in this line is when the skinner declares himself an insurance company, and floods the country with his circulars, offering everybody agencies on the most favorable terms. An extensive correspondence is certain to ensue, and the applicants finally discover that to reap the fortunes reserved for the agents of this prosperous company, it is an essential prerequisite that they shall be members of the "National Bureau of Agencies," the entrance fee of which is $50. The bureau is only another skinner, but the whole affair is so adroitly managed that no suspicion of collusion is raised, and very many persons in all parts of the United States, but especially in the West, have paid this $50 at the close of their relations with both company and bureau, for after that payment they never find the faintest trace of either. This swindle has been worked extensively by advertising for agents as well as by circular, and principally in the name of the State Fire and Marine Insurance Company of Boston, with Daniel Mills & Co., at Chicago, as the National Bureau of Agencies. But it has been done in the names of other companies in all parts of the country, and, having been only recently devised, will answer for the plucking of fools for a long time yet, notwithstanding the thorough exposure it has had.

Only a few of the chief means of the skinner for wheedling the unwary have been described, but space will only allow of a brief mention of some of the other more common devices. One of these, which is rarely practised, and never attempted but by the most accomplished of the skinners, is to form a partnership with a reputable broker, and, after a few brilliant days in Wall street, suddenly decamp with the assets of the firm. One such case occurred not long ago, and it was at once one of the most amusing and mournful of financial incidents. The tragical aspect of the case was the ruin of a most worthy broker, who had amassed a small fortune by years of honest dealing; but no one could help laughing, even with this woful result before him, at hearing how implicitly all the statements of the skinner had been believed by his partner and the banks, and how entirely he had been trusted by both. In comparison with these achievements of the skinners, their tricks as bogus employment agents and collectors seem mean and trivial, but they nevertheless derive much substantial solace from them. When, however, they are driven to these resorts, they degenerate into confidence operators, and are unworthy of detailed mention in this *résumé* of the miracles daily wrought by the most insidious, successful, industrious, and adroit of modern rogues.

Improvements in the appliances of the law for the detection and prevention of crime have not kept pace with the improved devices of the criminal to evade them; and it is not therefore surprising that the skinners year after year become more greedy in their depredations upon the public, and rarely suffer the penalties prescribed by the law for their misdeeds. Crime must be proved before it can be punished, and none is so difficult to prove as the obtaining of property by trick and device, or by fraudulent representations, even when committed by tyros; but when done by such adepts as the skinners, it is almost impossible to obtain the needful evidence. The best the law can do is to warn the unwary of their dangers; and this has been done by making Wall street a special field of detective labor. Two of the experienced officers of the Central Detective Office are detailed for duty there every day, and the Board of Brokers have in addition employed Mr. Thomas Sampson, one of the most adroit men in his business, for general police duty. The street also has nearly the whole time of Mr. William G. Elder, well known for many years as one of the most skilful and successful detectives in the country. Many of the leading banks also keep a special officer appointed by the Commissioners of Police constantly on duty in their offices during business hours for their own protection. No harm is done the public, for the banks pay the salaries of the men thus monopolized. The detectives and some of the special officers know many of the skinners by sight, and expel them without much ceremony, and with no legal right, from any business circle in which they are encountered under circumstances warranting a suspicion that they have game afoot. But the fraternity being thicker in Wall street, as one of the detectives informed me, than "fleas on a dog's back," and the detectives few, the work of swindling still goes on quite prosperously. Though the detectives harry them to the extent of their ability, yet the skinners thrive; nor will any amount of police protection which it is possible to extend serve to exterminate them, so long as it is unaided by the prudence of the general public. The day of the skinners has been a long one, and it will last until men with money back it with brains enough to take no man on his own representations, and to avoid the plausible stranger as they would the plague. In law every man is innocent until he is proved guilty; but the neophyte venturing into Wall street must assume every man to be a knave until he proves himself by the most positive testimony to be honest, or he is very sure, by falling among thieves, to be a sorrowful proof that history repeats itself.

"FENCES."

BECAUSE of the rarity of the experience, there is a substantial pleasure in looking over a metropolitan newspaper without seeing an advertisement like this:

> **$50** REWARD.—LOST, ON SATURDAY evening, on board the Plymouth Rock for Long Branch, a Diamond Cluster Pin. The above reward will be paid and no questions asked if returned to N——.

The above is copied *verbatim*, excepting the address. If the advertiser had more honesty and less transparent cunning, he would plainly say what he means, and publicly declare that for the sake of regaining his property he is ready not only to forgive the thief who stole it, but to pay him liberally for his trouble. Or if, as is generally the case, his valuables have already passed beyond the thief, he notifies the "fence" who may have them that he is anxious to negotiate with him on the most liberal terms and without attempting to intrude upon the mysteries of his calling.

Such advertisements as this constitute the only direct evidence which the general public ever gets of the existence and methods of business of the unscrupulous middlemen, without whom thievery would be unprofitable and speedily become a lost art. Known in the dialect of crime as "fences," they have a name as significant as it is pithy, and so appropriate that it has been adopted by Webster in the meaning which outlaws found, and has ceased to be slang. Receivers and traffickers in stolen goods, it is their function to guard the plunder taken by thieves until it can be worked back into the channels of legitimate trade. A professional thief with a great quantity of stolen silks upon his hands is poor indeed. He cannot take them into the open market, for reputable merchants are inquisitive as to whom they are dealing with; he cannot offer them in small lots at a great bargain without awakening suspicion of the means by which he obtained them. He must find some one who is not known as a thief, who has the means of converting his booty into money, and that some one is the receiver. In New York, as in all other great commercial cities, at the present time as in the past, the axiom of the law that "the receiver is as bad as the thief" is daily proved to be strictly true. In fact, it might be shown that the receiver, who is the manufacturer of thieves, is worse than his product. Being in a double sense preyers upon mankind, skulking as they do behind technicalities of the law, so that their crimes rarely receive the punishment they deserve, mean beyond all other classes of outlaws, cheating rogues and honest men alike, ready to turn an infamous penny by dickering with detectives for the return of stolen goods, willing to betray their most intimate associates or the whole brotherhood of crime to secure their own safety, it is evident that there are no criminals more deserving of public attention than these fences, without whom the rogues would be an army without arms.

In no way can the needed light be poured upon these knaves so clearly as by the mention of names and places. In dealing with nearly all the other classes of criminals I have not descended to these details, only because I did not believe it necessary for my purpose; but the fences can be handled effectually in no other way. I must even go back a few years, and resurrect from the grave where he has long mouldered the most successful, adroit, and daring fence known to the police annals of the city. Joe Erich in 1855, and for a few years before, was the most extensive dealer in stolen property on this continent, if not in the world. Located in Maiden Lane, then as now in the business heart of the city, this man was known and sought by all the thieves not only of the city but of the whole country. Buying anything from a penny dip to the most costly cases of silks, to this man came such famous marauders as Jack Spratt, Jack Adams (both dead long ago), Tom Gordon, Tom Kelly, Jim Brady, Bow-legged Moore, Jim Sullivan, Johnny Miller, Jim Painter, Amos Leeds (who was happily killed while blowing a safe), Old Bill Smith, Dick Collard, and Old Jack Cooper, who abandoned the preaching of the Gospel to join these first-class burglars, and became one of the most noted and daring of them all. All of these men were regular customers of Erich, and to him they took the proceeds of the most extensive burglaries committed for a long series of years throughout the country. He became rich enough to defy the law, and although arrested many times was never convicted, and died at last without rendering society an equivalent for his enormous gains, which went as easily as they came, so that he was left poor at last.

While he flourished he did not entirely monopolize the business of conducting the traffic which is constantly going on between thieves and honest men. Even when he was at his prime Ephraim Snow, better known in police annals as "Old Snow," was established at the corner of Allen and Grand streets, where he kept a complete assortment of every variety of stolen goods, which he purchased from the same plunderers who patronized Erich. Less fortunate than that trader, Snow's career ended in disaster, as he was convicted of the crime he was constantly committing, and sentenced to a term of five years' imprisonment. Another of the notable fences of the day was Webber, in Pearl street, who, after a long and prosperous career, was visited one evening by Detective McCord while he was in the act of placing a large lot of household silver in the crucible to be melted into an undistinguishable mass. The first result of the visit was the discovery of the proceeds of twenty-five burglaries in the house of Webber, and its second to send that operator into protracted seclusion in a prison.

These few notable persons are named merely to show that the business of receiving stolen goods is no new thing, and as introducing their more numerous successors. To-day there are scores of fences in New York, and one of the best known among them is Michael Grady, called by his customers and the police "Travelling Mike," who appears to the public as an inoffensive peddler in a particularly bad streak of luck, as he is never seen to make any sales, but who is in fact a "walking fence." With his peddler-box suspended from his shoulder he drops in almost daily upon the pickpockets and house thieves in their haunts, and if they are possessed of any such trifles as watches, pins, jewels, or wearing apparel picked up in their rambles during the previous night, "Travelling Mike" is almost certain to travel off with them without leaving more than a third of their value behind him. A thief is always impatient to turn his plunder into money, but he is doubly so when it is personal property that can be easily identified by the owner; and nobody knows better than "Travelling Mike" that he will snap eagerly at the first offer made by some one known to all the prowling fraternity as one who can be trusted. This walking fence has obtained almost a monopoly of the more portable plunder of such eminent pickpockets and sneaks as Dutch Heinrich, Sheeny Mike, Billy Darrigan, Tom Murphy, "Big Nose Bunker," Tom Biglow, Jim Dolan, Johnny McCarty, "The Doctor," Maurice Harris, Joe Butts, Tim O'Brien, Joe Keyser, Dublin George, and Tommy Moore, all of whom continue to ply their vocation as pickpockets or sneak thieves without much molestation from the law. Heinrich does occasionally get into jail, but he speedily gets out again in some marvellous way not understood by the general public, and immediately resumes the practice of his art. Lately he was sent for by Superintendent Kelso, who told him he must keep off the street cars; but Heinrich answered, "Vell, mustn't a man leeve?" and went off to resume his general transfer business of watches from other people's pockets to his own. Another of these worthies, Joe Butts, lately attempted a daring midday robbery in Broadway, and is in jail, with a pleasant prospect of staying there for some time to come; but as a general thing all these marauders are constantly on hand to contribute to the coffers of "Travelling Mike."

Although he is the only walking fence of any note, Travelling Mike by no means absorbs all of the property stolen in New York. There are many fences whose names, locations, and customers are well known to the police, and who have for years carried on this nefarious business so adroitly that they have scarcely been molested. Among them is "Old Unger," the chosen of the shop-lifters, who keeps in Eldridge street, and to whom Hyman, Nelly Flowers, Mrs. Taylor, Mrs. Palmer, Maggy Erich, Big Sarah Cox, Mrs. Leon, Leon the Kid, Mrs. Coffee, Mother Roach, Nellie Lee, Bill Dums, and other of the more skilful and prosperous outlaws who pilfer stores while pretending to buy, have sold the greater portion of their plunder. Some of these are now, however, doing the State some service; for it does occasionally happen, even in New York, that a professional thief gets into prison. A striking example was afforded lately by Nellie Flowers, whom Detective Farley happened to see riding in a Broadway stage, and, without knowledge of any specific crime she had committed, took her out of the vehicle. It so chanced that the pocket of a gentleman in the stage had been rifled, and there was a probability that Nellie had helped herself to his valuables. There was no positive evidence to change this probability to a certainty, but bad character went a long way with the jury, and the dashing prisoner, who had something of fascination in her personal appearance, was convicted, and is now in Sing Sing prison. Such mishaps as this, however, rarely overtake professional thieves, and no one was more profoundly astonished by the result in this case than the detective who made the arrest.

Another notorious fence is Rosenburg, familiarly known to detectives and thieves as "Rosey," who formerly covered his knavery by the pretence of a jewelry store in the Bowery near Chatham street, but afterward emigrated up that thoroughfare and located himself near Houston street, almost under the shadow of Police Headquarters. I have the authority of Mr. Kelso, the present Superintendent of the New York Police, for saying that Rosey in his day has been a "regular Fagin." In addition to the training of neophytes in the purloining art, he dealt largely with experienced thieves, and counted Scotch Jack, Dave Bartlett, Tony Maguire, Rory Sims, Sukey Backus, George Williams, Phil Brady, Scotch Jimmy, and other first-class cracksmen among his customers. If Rosey had a weakness, it was for fabrics that combined small bulk with large value. He was inordinately fond of silks in a business way, and ready at all times to buy such "swags" on reasonable terms. Goldstein, in Spring street, is another particular person, as he buys chiefly from house thieves such light articles as can be picked up during a hasty visit to a dwelling while the owner is asleep or absent. Once Goldstein got into the trouble which the police call being "got dead to rights," by which they mean being detected in a crime under circumstances which afford sufficient evidence to secure a conviction. Goldstein undertook a speculation in some humau hair which had parted from its rightful owner as well as the original scalp, and he was arrested with full proof of his offence in the hands of the officers; but I never heard that he suffered severely in consequence: these fellows rarely do even when they are "got dead to rights." Very different from Rosenburg and Goldstein is Johnson, in the Bowery near Rivington street, who is said by Mr. Kelso to be probably the most extensive dealer in stolen goods in the country at the present time. He has no specialty, except that he must buy at prices which will pay him a large profit. He is always ready to barter for anything and everything, without the inconvenient formality of inquiring as to the antecedents of his customers. Many of them, however, he knows intimately, and among them are Peppermint Joe, Jim Brady, George Love, Fred Larther, and Charley Eberhardt, first-class burglars; Jack Sheppard, who maintains the traditional glories of his name by being the most daring and expert cart thief alive; Spence Pettis, Jimmy the Kid, Shyster McLaughlin, general sneaks; and many others of less note. From these and chance sneaks who occasionally make illicit forays upon property, Johnson gathers an immense amount of plunder every year, and works it back safely and expeditiously, and with the return of huge profits to himself, into the channels of legitimate trade.

While Johnson may be the most extensive dealer in stolen goods, he is by no means the most artistic fence in New York. He is a mere trader, but William Brandon, in Broadway near Eighth street, is an artist in evil. He proves his superiority over his more grovelling fellows by his location, if by nothing else. While they are content to burrow in side streets or second-class thoroughfares, he boldly establishes himself in the fashionable promenade and business artery of the metropolis. And he declares his higher aims and methods in every other way—in his person, manners, and surroundings. Passing up deserted Broadway on a Sabbath with a friend, we met a carriage containing a party of distinguished appearance. Two were women, two men, and of the latter, one apparently a gentleman of high breeding. He was certainly a fine-looking man, with long, silky auburn beard, clear complexion, a clear eye, and regular features. He was dressed with all the elegance that ample means and good taste can command, and he was evidently on excellent terms with himself and the world, for he chatted gayly but decorously with his companions. "That," said my companion, "is Brandon the fence." There was so much of gentlemanly completeness in the presence of the man that it was difficult to imagine that he had ever stood at the bar of justice charged with the meanest of all the crimes against property. Yet I knew well enough that he was another of those marvellous outlaws who are "got dead to rights" without incurring any of the penalties of the law, and several cases strongly illustrative of the miraculous fact passed through my mind. Almost every detective in the force has had to do with him at one time or another, but he has slipped through the fingers of all of them with equal skill and safety. Once Woolridge had him for $3,000 worth of kid gloves, but there was a defect in the evidence and Brandon beat the law. Once Farley arrested him for receiving some valuable diamonds which had been stolen, and he was held to bail for "examination," but that was the last of the case. At another time

Reilley, another detective, got him for faro checks and other gambling implements, worth $600, stolen by burglars from 720 Broadway; but it was held that such articles are not property, and the receiver got out of the scrape. The same officer took him again for receiving a large lot of silk umbrellas, stolen by burglars from 697 Broadway; but there were no private marks upon the articles, the property could not be proven, and the receiver proved again triumphant.

But it is useless to multiply these citations to prove a fact which cannot be disputed. Brandon does indeed claim to be a dealer in general miscellanies, but he will also admit that he is ready to buy anything under any circumstances if he can make a profit on the transaction. The detectives know, if he does not, that many of the most adroit burglars, pickpockets, and house thieves in the city sell their plunder to him regularly; and they know, if he does not, that he regularly buys and sells whatever they may offer. A gentleman who is anxious to recover his watch without the trouble of attempting to punish the thief who stole it, has only to insert such an advertisement as I have quoted in this article to speedily trace it to Brandon, and regain it on comparatively favorable terms; for the gentlemanly dealer is not a "sheeny," but a devout believer in the fine old maxim of "live and let live." In the prosecution of his business upon these principles he has several times been so unfortunate as to be arraigned before police courts, where he has invariably assumed virtues which he has not, and put on the semblance of injured innocence with remarkable effrontery and success. I have never heard that he has threatened legal proceedings for being called a fence, but I should not be surprised at any time to find him advertising his peculiar industry by such means. Seeming to believe that it is impossible to punish any knave of ordinary adroitness for the crime of dealing in stolen property, he makes no secret of his readiness to buy anything which may be tendered to him, and by his demeanor in his transactions flippantly asks the officers what they can do about it. The police are puzzled for an answer.

Next to Brandon, in the aid and comfort extended to thievery, are the Mandelbaums, located at Rivington and Clinton streets. Here is a family of four brothers, named Wolf, Joel, Hirsch, and David, exclusively engaged in the buying and selling of stolen goods; and nothing shows more strongly the entire safety with which this nefarious business can be carried on than the fact that their being thus engaged is, and has been for years, well known at 300 Mulberry street. It is known there also that Wolf, who is a lawyer and a man of brains, is the general director of the concern, that all of them are adroit knaves, and that their principal customers are such unscrupulous persons as "Black Lena," "Big Mary," Lizzie Stevens, the Pedigers—husband and wife—Mrs. Kleinschmidt, French Louis, Charley Rothschild, Black Joe, Fred Schultz, and Matilda Hildebrand. That some of the Mandelbaums have been "got dead to rights" is a certainty, and that all of them constantly deserve to be in that unpleasant dilemma cannot be questioned. They are of the class that will buy your household plate without a qualm, from the thief who steals it, and within the hour melt it into an undistinguishable mass of silver, and thus place it forever beyond the hope of recovery. They will buy the costly dresses of your wives and daughters at a ridiculously low figure, and in a twinkling so alter them that the fair owners would gaze longingly upon them, but never dare to swear to them. They will ruthlessly tear your diamonds from their settings, and dare you to identify them as your property.

They will offer to sell you pieces of goods stolen from your own store, and if you hint as much, their lawyer comes down upon you with virtuous indignation, and having made you confess that thousands of just such pieces are manufactured every year, wonders how any Christian can find it in his conscience to swear that this particular piece is stolen property. Your trade-mark having been removed, you do not swear, nor do you buy, but you do not recover your own. There is nothing, indeed, in the way of bartering in the plunder of thieves which the Mandelbaums cannot and do not do. In the practice of their arts they have rivals in all who have been mentioned and many besides, some of whom are of considerable note.

"General" Grenthal is of great renown as a fence, and has incurred more perhaps of detective attention than any of his companions; but I cannot find any reason for the fact, unless it be that he trades with all the thieves who have been mentioned, and trace of missing trifles can more often be had through him than in any other way.

There is another receiver entitled to mention, not so much because of the extent or variety of his operations as for the penalty he has paid for what he has done. Known to the police as "Little Alexander," and by no other name, he is entitled to the rare distinction of having "done time," by which phrase the detectives who love to speak in riddles do not mean that he has swindled Time, but that he has served a term in Sing Sing prison.

Besides these professional fences, the more prominent and dangerous of whom have been mentioned, there are many occasional dealers in stolen goods who practically are fences, and yet do not exclusively devote themselves to the pursuit. They are men who do not seek such business, but take it as it comes, and never defeat a good bargain by impertinent inquiries as to the title of the seller. They buy chiefly of beginners in thievery, from dishonest clerks who cheat their employers out of small articles of stock; and the fact that both parties to the transaction are inexperienced in the "ways that are dark" is probably the reason why so many of this class of receivers get before the courts. While it is extremely rare to hear of any one of the great fences who have been named being brought to book, it often happens that chance dealers in purloined property are arraigned before the police magistrates; and it is almost invariable in these cases that the booty is small, and has been obtained from a casual thief. Sometimes, however, it is quite extensive, as when lately a large quantity of kid gloves, which had been stolen a year before by burglars from a large importing house, was found in the shop of a pawnbroker with the original packages unbroken. In this case the booty had undoubtedly been obtained from professional burglars, so that it was in every way an exception to the general rule.

The most usual customers of these casual receivers are clerks, porters, or truckmen, who pilfer from the goods intrusted to their care, or who obtain articles from the business associates of their employers; as, if a clerk should go to a house with which his master is in the habit of dealing, and order a bill on account of his employer, and take the goods to the fence and sell them on his own account. This species of crime is of daily occurrence and of as frequent detection, for it is certain sooner or later to be discovered. When it is, the culprit rarely fails to make an open confession of the whole matter, even to the name of the person who purchased the property from him. It would seem that these are cases which might be prosecuted to conviction of both thief and receiver, but that desirable result is not often achieved.

In addition to these casual receivers there is another class of dealers in stolen goods that may be appropriately called "involuntary fences." There is no pawnbroker and but few jewellers who may not any day become unconsciously, and innocently enough, receivers of stolen goods. Very often it happens that the professional thief tires of the professional fences, and saunters into the shop of a jeweller to offer a stolen watch for sale. In such case he does not betray the flimsiness of his title by either eagerness to sell or readiness to take a suspiciously low price. He pretends indifference, wants something very near the true value of the article, and rarely fails to get it. The jeweller very likely passes the watch on in the course of trade without knowledge of its contraband character, and saves his conscience; but if he does discover it, the watch is passed on with perhaps a little greater speed in order to save his pocket. Pawnbrokers, however, are more frequently the victims of these speculative thieves. There is not a day that many of them are not worried by the visits of detectives searching for stolen property, which in very many cases is found, and taken without regard to the rights of the pawnbroker in the matter. He always clamors for the amount he has advanced upon the article, and if he shows an innocent holdership he sometimes gets it; but his interests are never the first consideration with the detective, who must recover the property to have even a chance of making anything out of the transaction. But he does for that reason become more circumspect in his dealings. Many of them are entirely indifferent as to the character of the persons with whom they traffic, and will make an advance to a known thief as readily as to any one; and others, who would prefer not to have such customers, are too careless or hurried to avoid them.

It may be safely assumed that some of the pledges in the pawnbroker shops of the city are stolen property, and it is more certain that an even greater part of all watches and other light valuable articles bought outright by these brokers are of the same description. The thief usually desires to part company utterly with his plunder for several reasons. First, he never expects to redeem the articles, and he does not desire the record of the transaction which a loan requires to stand upon the books as possible evidence against him; but what is stronger with him than either, he wishes to avoid the danger of having the pawn tickets upon him. It might be supposed that this danger could be destroyed by merely destroying the tickets, and of course it could; but it is one of the strangest peculiarities of crime that the felon never thinks of this simple expedient. Almost invariably pawn tickets representing the booty of several crimes are found upon thieves when arrested. On the day I am writing a noted depredator was arraigned before one of the police courts, on whose person no less than twenty-seven of these tell-tale bits of paper had been found, and it has already been ascertained that they represent as many different larcenies. Great bond robbers are not free from the weakness, and the fatality with which all grades of criminals cling to these scraps of paper, which are utterly worthless to them, is as inexplicable as it is amusing to the detectives. It is nothing marvellous therefore that the thief, who is undoubtedly aware of his idiosyncrasy, is always anxious to sell rather than pledge when he resorts to the pawnbroker or jeweller, as he often does in preference to the fence. These facts are stated to show that the occasional and involuntary receivers of stolen goods have no lack of temptation, nor do these dealers evince much less of conscience than some persons who claim to be beyond reproach. Not long since I heard such a man boasting of an exploit of which almost any man living under the three golden balls would have been ashamed. This man was aware that a watch of a certain number had been stolen and a reward of $100 offered for its recovery. He happened to be in the shop of a pawnbroker when this watch was offered for sale, and instead of arresting the person offering it he insisted on the privilege of buying it, which being accorded by the pawnbroker, he gave $50 for it, returned it to the owner, and pocketed the reward. This he called smartness, and a man claiming to be honest having such ideas, it is not singular that thieves encounter so little difficulty in turning their plunder into money.

Receivers of all classes do a large business in New York; but it is impossible to say what is the value of the property which annually passes through their hands. In the last report of the Police Commissioners it is stated that during the year 1870 the amount of property lost was $1,151,325 50, of which $919,004 98 was recovered, leaving a total loss of $232,320 52. I have had occasion to show in prior articles that the statistical system of the Commissioners is extremely faulty, and especially that it does not present a true exhibit of the amount of property annually passing into the hands of thieves; but these figures are of more value in estimating the business of fences. Although a compilation is made together of property both lost and stolen, the figures represent the latter chiefly, and it is certain that of this nearly all, both of that recovered and that which is represented as a total loss, passed through the hands of the fences. It is equally certain that it is only a small part of the plunder which was devoured by those beasts of prey. I very much doubt the accuracy of the police figures for 1870, as in 1868 the amount of property lost by the same showing was $4,755,077 83, and the decrease to less than one-quarter that amount in 1870 is unnatural, even admitting that crime is decreasing in the city, when the reverse is the truth. I claim that the reports of the Commissioners for a number of years, with other facts in the exhibit for 1870, show that the property stolen in that year was at least thrice that reported as lost, and that from all sources the fences of New York do a business of five million dollars per annum in the real value of the goods handled. Of course the amount of money changing hands is much less than this, for no fence was ever induced to pay more than half price for stolen property; and every one who buys from him insists on having at least a third of the market rate as a margin for the extra risks incurred. As this is a very important fact, it is worth a general illustration. A burglar breaks into a store and takes away with him silks valued at $4,000 by the owner. When the burglar disposes of these goods to the fence, the utmost he can possibly get for them is $2,000; and when the fence in his turn disposes of them, he does not even demand more than $3,000. Property therefore depreciates at least one-fourth by criminal custody, and goods worth $5,000,000 in the hands of the legitimate owners become worth only $3,750,000 by surreptitious exchange. Even this amount seems large, but it is divided among so many fences that it leaves comparatively only a small portion to each; and no fact is better known than that these fences are generally poor men. Their receipts are often large, but so are their expenses. They are continually getting into legal difficulties requiring large outlays to lawyers and the sharpers who infest the lower grade of our criminal courts, beyond which the cases of receivers rarely go. But their chief loss is perhaps in being made to disgorge stolen property found in their possession, for there were only one hundred and sixty-three arrests in the last year of receivers, and very few even of that small number were ever brought to trial. One way or another the funds of the fences go as easily as they come, and they are generally poor. None of them ever accumulate, and when they die they are buried by the charity of their associates. Like all other classes of outlaws, their experience proves that the way of the transgressor is hard.

But their financial embarrassments do not arise from any difficulties they encounter in working off their illicit stock in trade. They know the deplorable fact that there are many men engaged in business which seems legitimate who are ready at any time to dabble in anything that promises a profit. It was on the day of this writing that a striking illustration occurred in the Tombs Police Court. A merchant in Warren street, being met by one of his customers with the assertion that a certain quality of sewing silk could be bought at less than his offering, was positive to the contrary, for there was none in market except what he put there. But the customer was positive, and upon investigation a man was found in Broome street selling such silk at less than half price, but it proved to have been stolen from the Warren street merchant eight months before. Such cases are constantly coming up, and in sufficient number to prove both the readiness of a large class of business men to buy anything which can be sold at a bargain, and the vast amount of stolen property which is always being passed from hand to hand in this city. No fence of experience ever has the slightest difficulty in selling his plunder, and his chief concern is to prevent its being wrested from him by the joint efforts of the thieves and police before he has had sufficient time to dispose of it. This is one of the principal dangers of the fences, and many flagrant cases of collusion between the police and plunderers to wrest stolen goods from the receivers have been suspected, and one lately was clearly proven by circumstantial evidence. The first object of the detective police being to recover the property for the sake of the emolument it will bring, it is only because of their adroitness that criminal collusion between them and the thieves is not proven as often as hinted. As it is, one detective can seldom bring a case upon which he is working to the happy consummation of recovering the property, without his fellows declaring that it has been "a dead give-away," whereby they mean to say that no skill has been displayed in the matter, because the detective has been guided from the outset by the thief who stole the plunder. I do not say that these things are true, but I do aver that they are often alleged.

The traffic in stolen goods has gone on almost unchecked in New York, and will probably, to the end of the chapter. At a first glance it appears easy to exterminate the crime by the punishment of the offenders. The possession of the property is the gravamen of the offence, and nothing is so easily established as a fact so palpable as this. But after the property is found in possession of a fence there are two great difficulties in the way of punishing him for having it. First, it is to the interest of everybody that the case shall not go to court; the owner wants his property, the policeman his reward, and the fence immunity. Second, should the two first decide to prefer the interests of society rather than their own, and prosecute the fence, they are met by the almost insuperable obstacle of legally proving the property found to be identical with that which was lost, the fence has so changed its appearance. Because of these two facts, dealing in stolen goods has become, and threatens to permanently remain, one of the leading industries of the metropolis.

FARO-GAMBLERS.

"WHO'S payin'? I'm dead broke!"

"What! Cleaned out?"

"You bet. But if that dealer hadn't railroaded, I'd a got square copperin' the ace."

The words being spoken at two o'clock in the morning in a basement coffee saloon which had the one merit of cheapness, and the speakers being men of generally mildewed appearance, with moustaches surprisingly huge and hats suspiciously glossy, I was aware that I had been made acquainted with one of the vexations of grovelling gambling life, at no greater cost than some execrable refreshments and the temporary companionship at a ghostly hour of three accomplished pickpockets, one burglar of excellent reputation in his profession, a dilapidated skinner, six abandoned women, and four victims of the uncertainties of faro.

The last were types of a class to be met in certain localities and at certain hours, with such frequency as to prove that it is respectable in numbers if nothing else. At any of the later hours of the night, in any one of the cheap eating shops in or near Broadway, from Spring street north to Tenth street, can be found one or more of the shabby-genteel men who bear unmistakable evidence in their speech, manner, and appearance of long and generally disastrous fighting with the tiger. These are the *canaille* of gamblers, who hang precariously on the edge of a terrible fascination, and manage to supply the necessities of life in a cheap way, from chance success in small bets and by a few dollars picked up by guiding more profitable customers to the houses where they are known. Strictly speaking, more "cappers" than gamblers, they are not only at the bottom of the profession, but their right to the proud title of "sporting men" is stoutly denied by their more prosperous and reputable brethren of the green cloth. Improvident, unclean in habits and language, unscrupulous, they are the natural products of sporting life, but which the faro banks nevertheless strive, although in vain, to shake off. Every house has several of these forlorn attachés, who play when they have money, and introduce a desirable stranger when they can, but are constant in their attendance upon the banquets daily spread in these houses, and are thus obliged to take the chances as to lodgings and raiment only, save when their hospitality has been worn threadbare, and they are then found in the places where I heard one of them declare the emptiness of his pockets in such emphatic manner.

Very different in most respects is another class of gamblers who can be seen any fine afternoon decorating Broadway with the splendor of their apparel, for as a rule the sporting fraternity is unexcelled in elegance of raiment. If you meet in Broadway a man who lounges listlessly onward as though he had no well-defined object in life, and whose garments are cut in the latest style and of the finest material, you may wager he is a gambler in good luck, provided his silk hat is in the highest possible state of polish and his watch chain unusually heavy. Very elegant in appearance, very quiet and gentlemanly in their demeanor, are these professional sports of the better class at all times and in all places. I have met men eminent in science, literature, art, politics, and the ast in great numbers, in faro resorts, no one of whom could exceed in good breeding the polished proprietors, nor even some of the professional gambler who were present. Generally they are men of fair intelligence and education who can converse agreeably upon current topics; and I have met some few who were possessed of the highest intellectual powers, which had been most liberally cultivated. One whom I knew, but who is now dead, was the son of a Portuguese nobleman, exiled for political reasons, who, with the finish of a courtier, had a mind of great originative power, which had been trained and stored in the best universities of Europe. This man, who was capable of outstripping his fellows in almost any field of human effort, was the keeper of an ordinary faro bank; and although an exception perhaps, men but little less than he was in gifts, acquirements, and opportunities, can be found in almost every first-class gambling resort, trusting to the turn of a card for the means of life. They are men who are so convinced of the emptiness of life that they are incapable of making an effort for any of its prizes, and are content to take such pot-luck with the world as their perfect mastery of the science of chances in card-playing may give. Scorning equally to take a dollar by false play or to introduce a novice to their method of living, there are many worse men to be met, and in much more reputable places, than these professional gamblers, who wrong only themselves. A public danger as they are in the example they set, it is impossible not to deal more in sorrow than in anger with men who do evil so suavely, and who tacitly admit, by every act of their lives, that they are fully aware of the wrong they are doing themselves and the community.

Another class of men who live by the cards are not entitled to any such consideration. Coarse-featured, moustache bristly, hair close-shaven like a convict's, apparel obtrusively gaudy and loaded with massive ornaments pretending to be of gold and precious stones, these are men to be shunned as the sharks which their appearance and their every act proclaim them to be. They are the proprietors or enticers on commission of the third-rate dens, where a "square" game is never played even by accident. Faro failing to return a profit, these fellows are ready to try anything else, from a game of poker to downright robbery, as a means of obtaining money without honest labor, which they abhor as the lowest estate of man. Any one can make a living by work, they say, but it requires a smart man to get it without; and they are so bloated with a sense of their exceeding shrewdness, that they sometimes try their hand at some one of the confidence operations in which the skinners are adepts, and almost invariably do it so clumsily that failure is the result. Their chief occupation and main reliance for a livelihood, when they are not the owners of a small den, is as "ropers in"; and it is surprising, considering how uncouth they are in appearance and address, that they are so successful in enticing strangers into the holes where they can be fleeced. These strangers thus inveigled come under the name of occasional players, whether guided by the better class of ropers into the first-class saloons, or by these viler ones into the low cribs; and whether in the one or the other, they are the vivification of all gambling. So long as one sport wins or loses from or to another, no harm is done the community at large, but no good is done the gamblers. The occasional players furnish the means to replenish the faro banks, or they would soon be empty; and the strangers who play not more than two or three times in their lives are the meat upon which this vice has grown so great.

It is not singular that the novice is so apt to try his luck when he has once been induced to enter the gambling room. The universal American game is "faro," and it looks so simple, so safe, so entirely fair, that the chances appear in favor of rather than against the outside player. There is, first, the large massive table covered with green cloth, and on it, occupying less than half its surface, is the "lay-out," which is a full suit of cards, from the ace to the king, painted in a parallelogram. Then there is the dealing box, into which the cards are put face upward, and the whole game consists in guessing what card will be reached as they are drawn from the box. All being ready, the players make their bets by placing upon a card in the lay-out the amount they desire to risk upon it, and the game can be best described by supposing that one of these is sanguine the queen will win. He therefore puts on the card the small round pieces of ivory called "checks," which he has purchased of the dealer, and each of which represents a certain sum, ranging all the way from twenty-five cents to one hundred dollars. The first card, having been exposed before the game opens, is "dead," and does not count. If the second should be a queen, the supposed player loses; but if the third, he wins. The same rule holds good through the seventeen turns in each deal, the dealer winning on each alternate card beginning with the second. But when only four cards remain in the box, the game assumes a new phase as the last turn is called. The first and fourth card being "dead," only the second and third are open to speculation, and the chances are considered so greatly against the player that the dealer pays four for one on this turn. All this appears very simple to the tyro, and he cannot be made to understand that the bank has any advantage over him in guessing the order in which the cards in the box will be reached. He is fully prepared to believe that the only chance against him is the "splits," as the bank takes half of whatever may be bet upon the card when two of the same suit appear on the "turn," and gives him nothing. Convinced, as the great majority of people are that there is only this risk against them, it is not strange that faro has become the most popular and universal of games of chance.

It is made more alluring by its surroundings. Nowhere has sumptuous elegance been attained in such perfection as in the first-class gambling saloons of New York. Generally each has a suite of rooms, the largest of which is devoted to faro, with perhaps a roulette wheel in one corner, while others are sacred to short card games, and one is always exclusively used as a banqueting hall. All are furnished without regard to cost, but there is never anything in any of them to offend the most fastidious taste, although there may be sometimes a grim humor in some of the decorations, as is the case in one house where a magnificent oil painting of a tiger is suspended to the wall immediately over the table, so that none of the players can look up without meeting the glaring eye of the beast which is held to be the presiding deity of the game. But such suggestions as this are rare, as in general there is nothing anywhere but the faro table to declare the uses of the place; take that away, and the visitor would imagine himself in the private parlors of a gentleman whose great wealth was fortunately equalled by his refined taste. This delusion would be strengthened by a seat at the banquet, where the viands of all possible varieties are of the best quality, and are served with a finished elegance in the plate and all table appointments, including the waiters, which is not exceeded even in the most select houses. At the table and on the sideboard in the saloon are liquors of such excellent quality that they would have angered old blear-eyed, besotted Silenus, as wanting in the fire he demanded in his drams, but although freely offered they are never pressed upon the visitor, and it is possible for a man to frequent these saloons for years without acquiring a taste for liquor. There is, in fact, very little drinking in them, and none at all of that fast and furious potation which hurries so many thousands of Americans to physical and mental ruin. No sight is rarer in a gaming-house than to see a man maudlin drunk, and still more rare is it to find one under the influence of liquor engaged in heavy betting. An intoxicated man is never allowed to profane the place, and if he appears in the person of a valuable patron is quietly led away, to be put to bed in some remote room; but if he comes as an unknown casual, he is put into the street with little ceremony, but no violence.

What has been said of the appointments of faro houses applies of course only to the first-class and most prosperous establishments. The places next in order ape them in everything, but are far below them in all. A second-class house has sometimes even more of glitter than its rival, but it is easy to see that it is pinchbeck grandeur. There is an entire absence too of the refined taste which presided over the decoration and furnishing of the better houses. The rooms are glaringly painted, filled with odds and ends of furniture of all ages and patterns, so that they look not unlike the wards of a hospital for superannuated and diseased household goods turned over in their old age to the auctioneer's hammer. The suppers and liquors, however, most plainly proclaim the lower caste of the place. While the variety in both is abundant, the first are execrably cooked and served, and the quality of the latter would not be strange to the most experienced patron of the ordinary Broadway saloons, which are proverbial for furnishing every kind of beverage except good. But if the second grade houses are bad in these respects, there are some below them which are much worse. If a man can digest the so-called game suppers and survive any considerable drinking of the liquids which are offered as pure whiskey and brandy in the lowest class of faro-houses, he ought to be able to insure his life upon the most favorable terms. And the appointments of these houses are in keeping with their entertainment. The chairs, sofas, and carpets were of the most tawdry description when new, but are ragged with long and ill usage; the gambling-checks, which range in price from twenty-five cents to one dollar, are grimed and dented with much handling; the faro-table, which elsewhere is enticing in its newness and cleanliness, here is old and smeared with grease; the dealing-box, which in first-class houses is of pure and polished silver, in the second-class of German silver, but equally polished, here is of pewter and dingy. So in all the minutiæ of the place it is repulsively suggestive of squalid and unprosperous vice, and if by any chance a gentleman enters, he leaves at once to lose his money under more elegant or at least cleaner auspices.

Provided a "square" game is dealt, the actual playing of faro is precisely the same whether thousands are wagered in the elegance of Twenty-fourth street, or as many pennies in the squalor of the Bowery. The players being seated around three sides of the table, where there is room for six or eight, the dealer takes up the other side, with the marker of the game generally at his elbow. This marker has the cue-box, a glance at which at any time will show the players which cards of each suit are out and which yet remain in the box; and it is a knowledge eagerly sought by the bettors, who are to a great extent guided by it. There is rarely a word spoken during the progress of a deal, for faro is the most quiet, and in that respect the most gentlemanly of all games. A glance at the cue-box tells the player the condition of the dealing-box, and he silently places his wager in the shape of checks upon his chosen card or cards, with a copper upon them if he desires to bet upon the side of the bank, as he is at liberty to do. After each turn the dealer glances over the board, and without a word picks up the checks he has won, or adds the same number to those already upon the cards in the cases where he has lost. Any player is free to cease playing at any moment, and at the close of a deal can obtain the money for whatever number of checks he may possess by handing them in to the dealer. From this operation, suggestive of a closed career, has come one of the most common of modern slang phrases, "handing in his checks," as a synonyme for death; and there is something of a grotesque humor in the metaphor, when the circumstances which gave it birth are fully considered. There is something funereal in the gravity and decorum of the faro room, and there is a deal of the utter *abandon* of death in the staid recklessness with which an infatuated player stakes his last dollar on the turn of a card.

Even where the game is not "square," it is usually marked by the same solemn propriety during its progress, for it is not often the victim discovers that he has been cheated until long after the close of the operation. The frauds of faro, once known, are so transparent that it is amazing that they are not discovered at the moment their preparation is attempted. The most common is that of the sanded cards, by which is meant cards with the surface roughened, so that the two being handled in a certain way will adhere and appear as one. The dealer, intending to make assurance doubly sure, and to be certain that the players shall lay down and take up their money only at his pleasure, arranges the cards before beginning the deal so that he knows precisely the order in which they will come out. During the progress of the deal he is therefore able to baffle chance by pulling out one card or two, as the bets upon the table may demand. If the patron to be fleeced has wagered on the ace, the dealer easily makes that card win or lose, to serve his purpose; and in these "skin games," where everybody but the goose who is being plucked is in the confederacy of roguery, nobody keeps tally of the turns, and the victim at the close of the deal is ignorant whether there have been seventeen turns or half that number. Yet the most superficial knowledge of the game and the slightest practice ought to save any one from a swindle that is daily practised, and is but little less clumsy and transparent than the next most ordinary fraud of dealing from a pack with more than the fifty-two cards, where the presence of the dishonest supernumeraries immensely increases the chances against the player. Of course a little observation would reveal the superfluous knave, but the cheat is usually practised upon men who hardly know one card from another, and has therefore been successful far beyond its merits. Even if the dupe should discover his true position, he has wit enough as a rule to do nothing more than cease playing upon the first plausible pretext, and go quietly out of the house. There is hardly any position in which a man can be placed which is more trying to the nerves than to find himself alone in a "skin" house, as the dens where cheating games are played are called, with a terse truthfulness that is in itself quite appalling. Surrounded by the ruffians of the gambling fraternity, who watch his every movement with suspicious greed, he is not conscious of his peril until he finds that he is being cheated, and betrays the consciousness by some word or look. Then he feels himself walled up from sympathy and safety by the merciless gamesters around him, and nothing is further from his thoughts than to demand the return of his money. All that he asks is a chance to breathe the free air of the streets again, and that is all his despoilers will allow. A patrolman pacing his beat in the small hours of a sleety morning was accosted by a pallid stranger, who, pointing to the lighted second-floor windows of a well-known "skin" house, asked "Stranger, what's that?" "Faro," was the answer; but the stranger said, "No, sir; it's hell! I've been there! The devils will be out presently; please don't let 'em follow me." And having, as he thought, established a strong rear-guard in the policeman, the victim retreated hastily but in good order. Such horrors as this man had evidently met face to face are nightly encountered in the great city, where the skin game is played in scores of dens that wear a charm against the penalties of the law in the terror they create in those who have been cheated in them.

Faro houses in New York have rarely exceeded one hundred in number, except during the latter part of the war, when speculation going mad in Wall street stalked over the land, demoralizing and ruining thousands. In those feverish times faro-playing naturally increased with stock-gambling, and the faro houses multiplied until they vibrated between one hundred and twenty and one hundred and thirty in number. Of late years, however, they have steadily decreased, and during the year 1871, when the public excitement upon the subject oft caused the sensational statement that the city contains six hundred of them, ninety-two was the largest number open at any time. The number seems small in comparison with the size of the city, which, besides the large resident reckless population, contains tens of thousands of strangers anxious not to miss any of the sensations of the metropolis. Yet these faro banks not only are enough to do all the business presented and enticed to them, but some have a very precarious life owing to the lack of custom. The first and second class houses are under very heavy expenses, a principal item of which takes the shape of rent. They must be and are located in the principal thoroughfares, near the leading hotels, with the exception of those anomalous institutions known as "day games," which are found in Ann, Fulton, and Chambers streets, for the accommodation of business men, many of whom have acquired the bad habit of seeking solace for the vexations of legitimate transactions in the delights of faro. A seizure was made of these places lately, upon the ground that they are of all the gambling establishments in the city the most dangerous to the public. It is not necessary to endorse this statement in order to justify the attempt to suppress day gambling; but if activity in this direction is intended to excuse the toleration of all other houses, it will result in more of evil than good. The night houses into which strangers are inveigled and robbed, which are the resorts of young men of fortune, who here take the first steps in a downward road which leads them and their families to shame and ruin, are worthy of at least equal attention. Besides being more frequented, these night houses have a much greater number of hours for play. The day houses are only in full operation four or five hours per day; but in the night houses a game can be had during the afternoon and at any hour of the night, while the average of play, take them altogether, is fully twelve hours in each twenty-four. The night houses, therefore, which can be found in upper Broadway and the cross-streets near the large hotels, do the most faro-playing, and are necessarily greater evils than places which are only accessible during a few hours, and then only to a single class. In the absorption and waste of capital, the half score of day houses cannot be compared to those where most of the play is at night.

I have endeavored, but without the success I hoped and desired, to get accurate statistics upon this point, and am therefore forced to use approximate figures, which are, however, very near the exact truth. The faro banks of New York have as capital a little less than one million of dollars, which is very unequally divided, as the ninety-two houses vary from $2,000 to $50,000 each, although only three or four have the latter amount, and the average banking capital is about $10,000. It is impossible to say what amount of money changes hands upon this basis, but I have learned that the average yearly winnings of all the banks taken together is about fifty per cent, exclusive of the capital required to keep up the establishments, so that every year these gamblers absorb about $500,000, and the actual profits are more than 100 per cent.

These figures are conclusive that the way of the transgressor is hard. Yet it is the uncertainty of faro that constitutes its fascination, and makes it possible for the houses to have so large an average of profit. As against a single player the bank is estimated to have an advantage of but fifteen per cent. in the chances, but as against all of its patrons its odds are almost incalculable. I have seen a game where one man would win steadily through several deals, while the several other players as steadily lost, and was told by experienced professionals that I was witnessing an event of constant and expected occurrence. But I was also warned not to judge of ultimate results by the one lucky man, as my kindly mentor assured me that at some time that individual would lose back to that bank, or some other, every dollar of his winnings. In the long run the bank must always win. It has been said that no Frenchman can avoid death, or the Cross of the Legion of Honor, and gamblers have a saying as caustic and more true, that a "Stormer is sure to be a piker." The first term interpreted into English, means one who has an extraordinary run of good luck by which he has pocketed thousands, while a "piker" is a tolerated collapse who makes a stray bet when he can beg or borrow a "check."

These ups and downs are the safeguards of the banks and the ruin of the players. No man would play long or heavily if constantly a loser from the start, but buoyed by occasional gains, the fangs of the game are fastened into his very nature. There are exceptions, of course, of which I have seen some, and heard of others; but the rule is that a beginner becomes a confirmed player and ends in bankruptcy. No vice has blighted so many lives, has illustrated so many epics of anguish, or has cost the productive industry of the nation so many millions of money, as faro gambling. There is scarcely a business man who cannot point out some hulk floating in the streets covered with the mire of poverty, who once had fate behind him, but, forsaking trade for faro, became what he is; and the liberal professions—but especially the law—can furnish in proportion even a greater number of these warning examples. There is scarcely a lady in good society who cannot tell of some refined and elegant woman, once the pride of her circle, now living in penury and neglect, whose fortune has been wrecked by her husband on that fatal table. There are hundreds of orphans wailing for bread, whose guardians have sunk their portions in the maelstrom of faro. Trust funds, public and private, have been piled upon the green cloth, to disappear in the insatiable drawer of the dealer. And all this misery, shame, and loss has been inflicted upon the country because faro honestly played is a game of pure chance, and sometimes favors the unfortunate who meddles with it.

It is scarcely necessary to prove these general truths by the recital of special cases, for every reader of the daily newspapers can recall the heart-rending history of some victim of this deadly fascination. It is not often that the splendors of the gambling saloons are dabbled with blood, but the stains are scarcely yet removed from a day house where an infatuated youth balanced accounts with the despiteful ace by blowing out his brains beside the gambling table. If such tragedies were more common, there would be fewer victims of the game; for that revelation of the innermost secrets of faro life did more to startle the devotees of the game into abstinence than anything which could be said or done concerning the vice. The experience of all the years during which faro has flourished in New York is convincing that moral force is powerless against the game, and that the law which has been made for its suppression cannot, or at least will not be enforced. The penalties of the statute which was enacted in 1851, are sufficiently severe if they could be inflicted upon even a moiety of the houses, to entirely suppress the game. But it is a suggestive fact that there has never been but one conviction for the offence of gambling in the city of New York. The statute specifically enacts that "if any person for gambling purposes shall keep or exhibit any gambling table, device or apparatus, or if any person or persons shall be guilty of dealing 'faro,' or banking for others to deal 'faro,' or acting as 'look-out,' or gamekeeper for the game of 'faro,' shall be taken and held as a common gambler, and upon conviction thereof shall be sentenced to not less than ten days hard labor in the Penitentiary, or not more than two years hard labor in the State Prison, and be fined in any sum not more than one thousand dollars." It is made a misdemeanor punishable by fine, for any person to persuade another to enter a gambling room, or for the owner or lessee of any premises to permit gambling therein, and it is "the duty of all sheriffs, police-officers, constables, and prosecuting or district attorneys to inform against and prosecute all persons whom they shall have credible reason to believe are offenders;" and it is a misdemeanor punishable by a fine of not more than five hundred dollars for any of these officials to neglect this duty.

Armed with these great powers, it would seem to be no very difficult task for the people to successfully battle with "faro"; yet this stringent law, which the casual reader would suppose a most effective piece of correctional mechanism, has been inoperative from its enactment. Many attempts have been made to enforce it, some of which had an honest intent to accomplish its purpose, while others had no better design than to blackmail the gamblers; but both ended in ignominious failure. The seizures of the houses and implements of the game permitted by the law, have been successfully made many times, and the supposed principals have as often been held for trial in the Court of General Sessions by the police magistrates, but with the single exception of the complaint against Pat Hearn, no case has ever gone to a conviction. The abnormal result in Hearn's case ought to have encouraged the authorities to use all possible means to secure a like conclusion in others, as it for the time entirely suppressed faro gambling in New York. But it has never had a companion, and faro as a consequence has had a long career of uninterrupted prosperity. Various district attorneys have attempted to explain why an effective remedy for a gigantic evil has been so seldom used, by the excuse that in all the cases the proof is so defective that a conviction could not be had, and no good could be effected by bringing them to trial. To the general mind it would appear a not impossible task to obtain the necessary evidence at least once a year against some one of the ninety faro houses, and by the condign punishment of the conductors of that one, cause all their fellows to flee from the wrath to come.

For thirty years there has been a strong conviction in the public mind that the community can be saved from the dangers and losses of faro by punitive law alone, and admirable appliances to this end having long ago been provided, a day must soon come when the people will demand of their servants that the law shall be enforced against those glittering, fascinating hells, where

> Some men creep in skittish fortune's hall,
> While others play the idiots in her eyes.

Whenever these servants conclude to enforce the law, they will do well to commence operations with the establishment of "Big Murray," lately opened in Eighth street just east of Broadway. For comprehensive gambling this house is unequalled in New York, and probably not surpassed anywhere. It is a large five story and basement structure, is fitted up from cellar to garret with great splendor, and every possible device to make money change hands without giving its value in return can be found within its walls. Separate apartments are devoted to "faro," "roulette," "rouge et noir," "poker," and even the vulgar game of "keno" has its place. Murray boasts of his "influence," and has certainly thus far escaped molestation by the police. There are ugly stories afloat to account for this immunity, which may be as untrue as they are scandalous if true. It is only certain that all these games are carried on nightly under the one roof with the full knowledge of the police, who cannot be supposed to be ignorant of a fact which is of common notoriety. Another house which has been long established in official favor, is No. 818 Broadway, known as the "Combination Game," from the fact that it has several proprietors, each one of whom is a professional gambler of some note. It is a handsome four story and basement brown-stone edifice in the most public portion of Broadway, and is furnished throughout with tasteful elegance. "Faro" is the principal occupation of its frequenters, although, as in all first-class houses, there are conveniences for "roulette" and all short card games. There have been two or three pretended attempts by the authorities to close the house during the past three years, the last of which was plainly incited by a political pique against the celebrated John Morrissey, one of the reputed owners. But the raids made upon the house always had the appearance of being intended merely as momentary annoyances, and were certainly never anything else in fact, as the house was always in working order again within two or three days after these raids, and was allowed to go on again for many months without interference. These are only two of the many leading gambling dens in the city, which are so well known that their location is a matter of common knowledge. Any patrolman of the Twenty-ninth Precinct can, and most of them will, direct the inquiring stranger to the almost as extensive and equally alluring houses in the same neighborhood, known as Ransom's and Chamberlain's; and the dens of lower grade so numerous in Broadway from Bleecker to Tenth street, of which that of Harvey Youngs is a fair sample, are as well known to the police and public. These are a few of the many places which occur to me without special investigation, and what is so generally known must be within the knowledge of the police. Ignorance of the location of the houses where the crime of gambling is constantly committed cannot therefore be pleaded, and the police have always sought for some other excuse for their inactivity. The one most generally advanced is the difficulty of obtaining legal evidence of some specific act of gambling, and the officials who use it do not seem to be aware that it is only a most conclusive proof of their own stupidity or insincerity.

LOTTERY GAMBLERS.

BY the laws of New York all lotteries are declared to be common and public nuisances, and all persons keeping an office for the sale of lottery tickets, or in any way aiding and abetting in the sale of such tickets, are made liable to fine and imprisonment. Lawmakers have seldom descended to such detail as they have in the statutes of the State of New York against lotteries and gambling, which are laboriously and carefully drawn to make violations of them impossible.

While these statutes have stared the administrators of the law in the face for more than a generation of human life, no offence has been so habitually and openly committed in the city of New York as dealing in lottery tickets. There is scarcely a street in the whole city, from the Battery to Harlem Bridge, where the shops of the lottery dealers cannot be found. In the lowest slums and in the most respectable quarters, in the midst of dwellings and among the great financial institutions, it is equally impossible to avoid the shops, concealed under the thinnest possible of disguises, where tickets are sold in the regular lotteries, which are just now the Havana, the Kentucky State, and the Paducah, and where also you may play policy in any way and for any amount you may choose.

It is true there is no inscription on any of these shops proclaiming the precise character of the business carried on within, but the legend they do bear has long been so generally understood that the words "Exchange Office" have come to be synonymous with lottery office when found upon a street window under circumstances now to be detailed. In every case where the words given are seen upon a street window, and the curious upon entering the street door sees a close partition four or five feet in front of him in which there is a door, the upper part of which is of frosted glass, he has but to open and pass through this door and state his desire to purchase a "Havana," "Kentucky," or "Paducah" to have those of the day spread out before him on the counter without question or remark. The visitor, looking about him, will notice that the inner office is at least thrice the size of the outer one, and if he tarries will see that no business whatever is transacted in the latter. Once in a while some bucolic person will enter and ask to buy gold or exchange; but the man who steps from the inner shop, with a tinge of contempt for the excessive verdancy of his customer in his tone, will answer shortly to the effect that he cannot accommodate him, and hurry back to his proper post behind the partition. Noticing these things, you become convinced of what you before suspected, that it is the sole business of all these shops to vend lottery tickets or take plays upon "policy."

If the visitor lingers long enough, and merely keeps his eyes open, or does better and avoids suspicion by visits on successive days when he makes purchases to small amounts of both tickets and policy slips, he will very soon come to understand the general workings of the little game he is observing. Having obtained my knowledge of the swindle by the latter method, I must insist on the *small* amounts to any reader who may be incited to follow my example, and give as a reason that he has about one chance in ninety thousand to get his money back.

The price of a full Havana lottery ticket is thirty-two dollars, but it is divided into tenth and twentieth parts, each purchasable at a proportionate price. The domestic article comes cheaper, as the price of tickets in the most expensive "schemes" is but ten dollars, and you can get half or quarter tickets for a proportionate sum. Usually, however, the cost of wholes is but five dollars, and there are some drawings every week when the price is but two dollars and fifty cents, and once each week when it is but one dollar, on which occasion you can try your luck for the fourth of five thousand dollars at a cost of only twenty-five cents, less a discount of fifteen per cent. if you take the precaution to purchase of a large dealer. When you have obtained your ticket, whatever may be its cost or chances, it will have three numbers printed in the corner and across the face, and will have a promise to pay whatever prize may be drawn to these numbers forty days after the drawing, which is particularly specified as to its date and the number of its class.

To the thousands who constantly have one or more of such bits of oblong paper in their pockets there seems to be a strange fascination in the possession. Both sexes, all ages, from childhood to the decrepitude of years, all grades and races of mankind, indulge in the possibilities represented by these scraps, so that there is no vice more generally practised than that of gambling in lotteries. It is perhaps less dangerous to its votaries and not so inimical to the public good as faro-gambling, but it is sufficiently hurtful in both respects to make it worth while to have the laws against it enforced. While a few of the very poor and some of the extremely rich take its chances, the great mass of its devotees are from the middle classes, who are sufficiently refined to yearn for something more than the comforts of life, and hence crowd the dubious path which seems to offer the chance of leading to sudden wealth. These are mostly young men who have been well reared, and, marrying upon slender means, find themselves every year staggering more and more under the augmenting burdens of an increasing family. Nothing is more natural than that they should seek by every possible means to avert the descent in social condition which is the inevitable corollary of such circumstances. The man who has been well housed, well dressed, well fed, and surrounded in his home with some of the appliances of refined life, is appalled when he finds at the end of the year that he has exceeded his income and must curtail his expenses. The horrors of the tenements or the shabby gentility of lodgings staring him in the face, he kicks against his fate with something of desperation in the effort. The man of nerve finding himself in this condition seeks to better himself by legitimate operations, and tries desperate ventures which make or break him with bewildering rapidity. But the weak man, who has nothing in his nature wherewith he can buffet fortune, broods over his misfortunes until at last the happy thought strikes him and he hastens off to buy a lottery ticket. When his ticket proves a blank, as it is sure to do, he clutches at the delusion of better luck next time, and he buys again and again, until his substance is all gone and he has sadly illustrated the inspired truth: "Unto every one that hath shall be given, but from him that hath not shall be taken away even that which he hath." Side by side with these ne'er-do-weels are other buyers of a totally different stamp. There are hundreds of men who constantly but carefully invest in the delusive bits of paper and give to

—airy nothings
A local habitation and a name,

from their reveries based upon the mere possession. Slowly but steadily accumulating by their regular avocations, they are in haste to be rich, and are impelled to lotteries by the same cause which, acting in a different way, drives others into Wall street gambling, and still others into opening a bank with a crowbar. They buy nearly every day, always twice or thrice in each week, but rarely invest sums large enough to pinch them by the loss. They are incorrigible believers in the proverb that "it is a long lane which has no turn," and they confidently believe that each ticket will bring them to that turn. They constantly harbor and often cite the case of the man who commenced buying lottery tickets when a mere boy and kept it up year after year until at last he secured a $30,000 prize, whereupon, remarking sententiously that "lightning never strikes the same tree twice," he at once and forever abandoned the practice. They all intend to imitate him.

These are only generalizations of lottery buyers, who may be classified in regard to special characteristics in much more numerous subdivisions. There is the man who once secured a small prize, and has since spent twenty fold its amount in the vain hope of obtaining a successor of more respectable proportions. There is the man who knows a man who heard a fellow talking of another fellow he once knew who had drawn a "capital," and he cites the misty tradition as a certain sign that he is sure to have the same luck. There is the man who saw the new moon over his right shoulder the previous evening, and augurs from the accident that he is to have a good run of luck. There is the man who wooes the goddess Fortune in dashing haphazard style, and pulling out the first ticket he happens to get his fingers on, resolutely turns his eyes ceilingward so that he can thrust it into his pocket without seeing what numbers it bears; he has an unfaltering belief that this way of doing the thing is vastly superior to any other, and is certain to bring a prize sooner or later. There is the man who is an exact opposite, and makes the selection of his ticket a matter of close calculation of chances by looking over the drawings for a number of days to get precise information as to what numbers have been drawn, and from this shadowy foundation divine what ones will be drawn. He is a devout believer in the solemnly uttered axiom of the lottery dealer that during the year each number is drawn an equal number of times; and if any one has not been drawn for several days, he begins to purchase tickets bearing it with an unquestioning faith that is amusing to an unbeliever. There is another man, however, whose faith in his powers of divination is as amazing as the case cited is amusing; and this is the individual who is certain that a selected combination of numbers is sure to be drawn, and who rushes in frenzied haste from one office to another looking for the ticket bearing it, and, inconsolable if he does not find it, nevertheless does not let fortune give him the slip altogether, but plays the numbers in that delusive game called policy, which is to be described. This sort of buyer can never be mistaken. He is the person who rushes into an office, eagerly calls for the "Kentuckys," hastily looks over the tickets, departs as hurriedly as he came, and of whom the man behind the counter remarks, before he is fairly out of ear-shot, "One of the sharps—he's goin' for a sure thing."

These, however, are but mild types of a superstitious credulity that would be incredible to any one not familiar with the interior of a lottery office. In each one of these of the lower grades is kept a small volume which has the alluring title, "Wheel of Fortune," and no other book has been so eagerly and devoutly read by so many thousands. It is the book of the dreamers, and pretends to give the numbers which represent not only every possible phase of rational action, but all imaginable phantasma of troubled sleep. There is nothing man or woman can do or omit to do, nothing they can conjure up in the slumber of indigestion, but the "Wheel of Fortune" has the numbers which will play for it. If a man reading Darwin goes to bed and dreams his grandfather was an ape, the book tells him what numbers he must choose to win a prize. If a late and heavy supper produces a sense of suffocation that leads the slumberer to take the principal part in a hanging scene, the book tells him how to make his nightmare pay a handsome sum. There is a general but entirely erroneous idea that this lowest manifestation of superstition is confined to negroes. It is true that that impressionable race are almost invariably its victims, but I have seen hundreds of white men consult the oracle and unflinchingly act upon its suggestions. Nor have these men always or even generally been, judging from their appearance, of the ignorant or debased class. Persons of fair education, of average intellectual gifts, and of tolerable judgment in ordinary affairs, have been the victims of this delusion. I have never observed any one case long enough to know the fact positively, but I have been told and can readily believe, that once fairly seized by this delusion the victims never afterwards escape from it. Although every day of every year the oracle is proved a sham, they cling to it year after year, and pin their faith to it so long as they can scrape together the pitiful sum necessary to purchase the ticket it indicates as sure to win.

Among these victims can be found the pitiful and warning examples of the lottery mania. No long-established office is free from the wreck of a former patron who has grown prematurely old, and whose mere appearance plaintively illustrates the truth that hope deferred maketh the heart sick. This is a man who bought lottery tickets until he spent his last cent, and, though unable longer to feed his delusion, yet cannot quit the scene of his many disappointments. He finds his only solace in life to be gazing upon the daily drawing, and imagining what millions he might have had if he had only had the money to buy those three numbers which he knew beforehand were sure to head the list in this identical drawing. I have seen scores of such creatures who eke out their miserable lives by begging for food and raiment, and by doing odd jobs of work manage to obtain shelter and to save the few pennies required to again tempt outrageous fortune. One whom I saw every time I entered a small office on a side street I was told had been a patron for years of several shops, and a lounger in the one in which I saw him for months. His gaunt face with its sharp angles, and his coarse, patched clothing, told of extreme poverty, yet this man had once been possessed of a competence. He had never been addicted to dissipation, had been abstemious in all his habits, to the extent that he had denied himself many of the comforts of life even when he had ample means to obtain them; yet he was a pauper, and made such by his own weakness. All that he possessed had gone into the tills of the lottery dealers, where it had produced nothing but gorgeous phantasms of sudden wealth which were never to be realized. But this old man was still sanguine that he was to clutch the purse of Fortunatus, and that some day a stray penny luckily invested was to return to him in a few hours multiplied a hundred fold, and this product being reinvested was to yield a like quick and large return, until in a few days he was to be a moneyed power in the land. And meantime he filled the air with his magnificent castles. His shabby raiment became the most costly vestments, his squalid lodging expanded into a grand palace, and his coarse food begged at area doors became dainty viands. This old man was a perfect type of the lottery buyer, and illustrated very sharply the evil effects of the mania. No experience could wean him from his delusion At the end of years of disappointment, when he was bankrupt alike in friends and substance, he was certain as he had ever been that to-morrow, or possibly the next day, but surely before the end of the week, he should get back all he had ever spent, increased many fold. Once I saw a poor twittering bird jumping nervously, and with every mark of intense fear, along the limb of a tree toward the head of a huge black snake, which was coiled and motionless a few feet away. I do not assert that the reptile was "charming" the bird, for the possibility of the achievement is denied in respectable quarters, nor do I know how the bird would have fared in the end, for a lucky cast of a stone brought the snake to the ground and speedy death; but I do know that I never saw that poor old man drawn by a fascination he could not resist to the lottery wheel, but I thought of the twittering bird hopping toward the terrible eye of the huge serpent.

This old man has been cited only as an example and not as an unusual incident of lottery scenes. There are hundreds like him, and no one among them can be made to understand the enormous chances against him in the desperate game he is playing. It is useless to tell him that his one ticket has but one combination out of 78,000, and that he has therefore just 77,999 chances against him for the capital prize, which is the one he is constantly expecting to win. Pages of explanation would not clearly show the character of these lottery schemes, but a general idea of them may be had by a knowledge that the drawing is thirteen numbers out of seventy-eight, that the first three constitute the capital prize, the second three the next largest prize, and after the regular order is exhausted that the first, third, and fourth drawn, and others taken on the same principle, constitute the smaller three-number prizes. The two-number prizes are made up in the same way; and finally come the single-number prizes, which are the sums paid for the tickets less fifteen per cent., and one of which is accorded to every ticket having on it any one of the drawn numbers without reference to its place in the drawing.

It is necessary to add that the Kentucky lottery is drawn twice each day by commissioners at Covington, Kentucky, and is duly authorized by that State. I witnessed a drawing several years ago, and found it to all appearances a marvellously proper proceeding, but painfully tedious. The wheel was of glass, and stood where all the spectators could see that at the commencement of the operation it was absolutely empty. As the first step, one of the commissioners picked up the numbers from one to seventy-eight successively, and having held them up to the view of the audience, which on that occasion was composed of a small negro boy and myself, rolled up the pasteboards on which the numbers were printed, and, putting each one in a small brass tube open at both ends, dropped it into the wheel. When all the numbers had been thus disposed of, the aperture in the wheel was closed and locked, after which another commissioner turned the wheel rapidly several times in both directions so as to mix the numbers thoroughly. A blind boy whose arms were bare to the shoulder was then led up to the wheel, and, the aperture having been opened, thrust in his hand, took out one of the brass tubes, and handed it to one of the three commissioners. This official took out the pasteboard, and having displayed the number upon it called it out to a clerk, who wrote it down and bellowed it in his turn to a telegraph operator standing at his instrument in a remote corner of the room. All this having been done, the wheel was again closed and turned twice around. This operation, with the one before described, was repeated until all of the thirteen numbers of the scheme had been drawn, and the proceedings were then concluded by the commissioners signing a certificate, stating the time and place of the drawing, the numbers placed in the wheel, what ones were drawn, and the order in which they were drawn. The certificate is a printed form, and copies of it can be found in every office in New York where the tickets of the lottery are sold.

Anything more fair than the drawing it was impossible to imagine, and I am forced to the conclusion that the fraud of the thing is in the scheme itself, and not in its practical operation. The numbers drawn are telegraphed simultaneously to all the large cities to an agent of the managers, by whom they are printed in certificates like that given and distributed to all the offices, so that the results of the drawings are found in these places at noon and at five o'clock in the afternoon of each day, or an hour after each drawing. It is therefore not probable that any frauds are attempted in the publication of the drawn numbers, as the drawing follows so quickly on the closing of the books that neither the agents nor the dealers can tell what tickets have been sold, and it is impossible to guard against the selling of a prize by fraudulently altering the numbers; and the risk is so small that it is not worth while to avoid it by cheating. As to the risk of each of the three-number prizes, the managers have nearly a hundred thousand chances to one against each of their customers, and hold almost equally tremendous odds against them for the two-number prizes. For the single-number prizes, which are merely nominal in amount, the chances are more nearly equal, and the deluded buyers are lured on to additional purchases by securing one of these trifles. The argument they use to satisfy themselves is, that having got their money back they are making these further ventures with the money of the managers; for they do not remember that the fifteen per cent. is deducted from each prize, no matter how small, and that they are doomed to lose that amount in any event. While the securing of either of the large prizes is a possible event, there is nothing so improbable. I have never heard of but one well-authenticated case where the capital in the Kentucky was sold in New York, and the sale of the smaller prizes is so infrequent that the fact is blazoned upon the certificates for weeks afterward. It often happens of course that prize tickets are returned unsold by the dealers, and this circumstance also attains the dignity of large type on the certificates, for the purpose I suppose of convincing the patrons that they have failed to take fortune at the flood by neglecting to buy all attainable tickets.

Before proceeding to mention the other lotteries, I must expose the game of "policy," which depends for its results upon the drawings of the Kentucky or some other combination lottery. No game is more generally played, none presents such enormous odds against the player, and none is so peculiar in its technical terms. The principal of the latter are "saddle," "gig," "flat gig," and "horse," each of which has a distinctive meaning, easy of attainment by the player, but difficult to convey to the reader. A player has a "saddle" when any two of the numbers he selects are drawn, a "gig" when three of his numbers come out, and a "horse" when the four appear; but he has a better chance to acquire Dexter, or any other carefully-guarded steed, than he has to attain this highly apocryphal animal. A "flat gig" is three numbers played for all three to be drawn, and gets its name, I presume, from the fact that it is played by nobody but fools, who are known in the dialect common to detectives and thieves as "flats." Yet no phase of "policy" is more common, and there are thousands who trust to luck so implicitly that they will persist in playing the gig flat, when by also playing for the saddles, of which there are three in the gig, they might increase their chances of winning something to a prodigious extent. Lest the general reader may be unable to fathom this mystery, I will illustrate it by supposing that the player selects 7—18—25, and plays them for the flat gig. To win anything, all the numbers must be drawn; but suppose he also saddles the numbers, he will win proportionately if either 7—18, 7—25, or 25—18 happen to come from the wheel. He may again increase his chances by also playing for the single numbers; and if he should play each of them say for one dollar, the saddles for fifty cents each, and the gig for twenty-five cents only, he would be indulging in a tolerably sensible gambling operation.

I once met a gorgeous youth in a policy office, who took me into his confidence so far as to inform me that by adhering to this system and never changing his numbers he had made a very comfortable living, but I didn't believe him. I admit, however, that a player of iron nerve and inexhaustible purse might in the end beat the bankers of the game with this system by simply doubling his ventures every time he lost, and never omitting a single drawing in his play; but I never heard of anybody doing it, and do not believe it ever can be done.

The game is so entirely safe for the bankers that immense odds are given the players, in promises at least. For single numbers they pay four dollars for one; for saddles, forty for one; for gigs, three hundred for one; and for horses, about five hundred for one. If the player undertakes to name the first number to be drawn at any lottery, the policy bankers agree to pay him, if he succeeds, one thousand dollars for the one he pays them; but, as may be imagined, they are rarely called upon to redeem their promises. But this play is unusual, as even the most sanguine of players have little faith in their ability to select at nine o'clock in the morning the number that a blind youth will pick first out of seventy-eight two hours later. They are as able to do it as to do any of the other things they confidently expect to perform, but they cannot be made to believe so. The policy-players are the most radical of fatalists as a general rule. To a greater extent even than lottery-buyers they depend upon the signs and portents found in dreams, or in the most trivial accidents or incidents of their waking hours, to determine their play. The "Wheel of Fortune" stands them in good stead, and few of the habitual players make a venture without consulting that oracle. Negroes are the most constant of policy-players, but hardly the most profitable to the bankers, as their investments are usually very small. They generally confine such operations within twenty-five cents, which they judiciously divide between the "saddles" and "gigs," as five cents is usually their limit as to the latter. Every day the policy shops in Thompson and Sullivan streets are crowded with negroes of both sexes, and it is a common thing for the "book" of the dealer not to exceed five dollars for every drawing when he is apparently doing an immense business. While few of his customers exceed the amount I have named, many of them play one cent on saddles and three cents on gigs, and revel until the drawing arrives in the anticipation of getting forty cents or nine dollars by the venture. As the hour approaches when the return of the drawing is expected, these players gather in great force at the various shops, and the probabilities are eagerly discussed. If, as often happens, any number has not been out for several days, there are a good many cents bet on its appearance, and the excitement is intense. Sometimes a mania seizes the entire fraternity of colored players to play some particular "flat gig," which is generally 4—11—44, and the numbers being sure to be drawn only after everybody has been tired out and quit betting on them, their appearance evokes a storm that is comical in its intensity when its occasion is remembered.

But no class of players is free from the infatuation which the game produces. The most open kind of gambling practised in New York, policy is also the most hurtful in its general effects. It absorbs a vast capital, and every day takes bread from the mouths of hungry children. It beggars the rich and converts poverty into pauperism. It propagates slothfulness and idleness, and next to the rum shops does more than any other agency in the metropolis to fill its almshouses. Having scores of customers where one is a buyer of the lottery tickets, the evil engendered by policy-playing is by far the more serious of the two. There is no possibility of giving the exact sum of money which is annually entombed in policy or lottery, but an approximation can be made which will show a total large enough to deserve attention. Lottery and policy are almost inseparable companions, and there are few offices, except those selling the Havana exclusively, that do not deal in both tickets and policy slips. The number of such offices fluctuates greatly in the city of New York, but the average has been three hundred and fifty during the past two years. These must all average a business of at least ten dollars per day in receipts to much more than pay current expenses, and I have no doubt that the average is much larger, as there are few shops which have less, and there are many where the business is many times greater. But keeping within safe bounds, it is easy to calculate that these offices must withdraw from productive industry in the city of New York alone three thousand five hundred dollars per day, or a little more than one million of dollars per annum, I am aware that the United States Internal Revenue Service might be supposed to have some statistics of lotteries for the purposes of taxation, but they are necessarily so imperfect that I am convinced that my estimates, founded upon observation of the shops, are equally valuable. However great may be the amount annually sucked up by these swindles, it is certain that it is no less than I have stated. It is more difficult to be precise as to the number of persons from whom this vast sum is drawn. There are thousands of casual dabblers in the possibilities of the wheel, who buy half a dozen lottery tickets or policy slips perhaps in the course of a year, and there are thousands of occasional buyers who venture into the uncertainties once or twice per week. There are other thousands who are habitual buyers so long as they have the means; and it is perhaps safe to say that there are thirty thousand different persons who every year contribute to the lottery leeches. This would seem to give an average of only about thirty dollars per annum as the contribution of each person; but it is a deceptive calculation, because of the great disproportion between the expenditures of the different classes named. Some of the casual buyers spend only a dollar or two, many of the occasional not more than five dollars, and the bulk of the annual amount is handed over by the habituals. It must be remembered that I am speaking now only of the Kentucky and other three-number lotteries, which are the only ones which have policy for an ally. The Havana and special schemes yet to be mentioned absorb as much more of the capital of the country.

There is a great difference between the schemes which have been described and the Royal Havana Lottery of Cuba. The former are formed of three-number combinations, are drawn twice each day, and in the days of wildcat banks, whatever may be the fact now, paid their prizes in depreciated paper money. The Havana, on the other hand, is a single-number lottery, is drawn only once in every seventeen days, and pays all prizes in gold. As a lottery it is respectable, but although openly advertised by three firms in Wall and Broad streets calling themselves bankers, it is nothing but a lottery I am not familiar with its working, but have been assured on good authority that it is honorably managed. There is no better chance, however, for the patrons to get prizes than in the other schemes, and I need cite no stronger proof of the truth of this assertion, than the fact that a tenth of the extra capital prize of $200,000 gold sold in this city in April of 1871, was advertised by one of the bankers alluded to for nearly a year afterward. But while the Havana is tolerable as compared with the Kentucky, there are some special schemes which are much worse than the latter, as they are usually barefaced swindles, organized and managed with the sole purpose of cheating. There is always one or more of these enterprises before the public, openly advertised and never interfered with. They usually take the shape of gift concerts, and always pretend to be for the benefit of some charity or legitimate industrial enterprise. Some of them are on the most gigantic scale, and permeate the whole country, while others are petty frauds and intended to swindle only the metropolis. The Chicago fire has been the excuse for several, and the exhaustion of the South by the war gave birth to scores, of which some are yet in existence, appealing by huge placards on their offices to the credulity of the people, to at once enrich themselves and benefit their brethren of the South, by purchasing tickets in the Monster Gift Concert for the benefit of some named locality. It is the leading peculiarity of these concerts that they are postponed from time to time, and usually never are given. Some, however, have occurred, and pretence has been made of distributing the announced prizes, but none of the ticket-holders were much the richer for the operation. Some of these enterprises are, however, such outrageous frauds that the police are forced to close them summarily. The last of these was a grand distribution of "elegant" furniture and "splendid" paintings, which was opened in an immense store on Broadway, and to which the public was attracted by a band of music and huge posters. About half the articles in the place bore placards announcing the name of the lucky individuals who had drawn them. The proprietors seemed to violate the law by having a drawing on the premises, but the wheel, being seized by the police and examined, was found to contain nothing but blanks. The managers were able to show that there was no chance whatever in their operations, but the public also got a knowledge of the interesting fact, and although the swindlers escaped the penalties of the law, they were forced by a lack of customers to hastily abandon their enterprise.

This was the only effort made of late years to interfere with any of these special schemes, and only once within the last five years has any attempt been made by the police to enforce the law against the regular lotteries. In the summer of 1870 a raid was made simultaneously on all the offices in the city. Like all such affairs, the raid was barren of the result which it was claimed it was intended to secure. All the lottery dealers were required to give bail for trial; few of them were ever tried, none were ever punished. The offices, it was grandly announced, had been effectually closed by the energetic action of the police, and they remained closed exactly one day. The next day after the raid they were again in operation as usual, and have remained so until the present day. If there was any earnest desire to put a stop to this traffic, nothing could be more easy of accomplishment. The necessary proof of the violation of the law against lotteries could be obtained any day against any of these dealers, and it would only require a little persistency to utterly extirpate them. The spasmodic raids do so little good that it is difficult to believe that they are intended to accomplish any.

TENEMENT LIFE.

AS we stopped in Cherry street at the entrance to Gotham Court, and Detective Finn dug a tunnel of light with his bullseye lantern into the foulness and blackness of that smirch on civilization, a score or more of boys who had been congregated at the edge of the court suddenly plunged back into the obscurity, and we heard the splash of their feet in the foul collections of the pavements.

"This bullseye is an old acquaintance here," said the detective, "and as its coming most always means 'somebody wanted,' you see how they hide. Though why they should object to go to jail is more than I know; I'd rather stay in the worst dungeon in town than here. Come this way and I'll show you why."

Carefully keeping in the little track of light cut into the darkness by the lantern, I followed the speaker, who turned into the first door on the right, and I found myself in an entry about four feet by six, with steep, rough, rickety stairs leading upward in the foreground, and their counterparts at the rear giving access to as successful a manufactory of disease and death as any city on earth can show. Coming to the first of these stairs, I was peremptorily halted by the foul stenches rising from below; but Finn, who had reached the bottom, threw back the relentless light upon the descending way and urged me on. Every step oozed with moisture and was covered sole deep with unmentionable filth; but I ventured on, and reaching my conductor stood in a vault some twelve feet wide and two hundred long, which extended under the whole of West Gotham Court. The walls of rough stone dripped with slimy exudations, while the pavements yielded to the slightest pressure of the feet a suffocating odor compounded of bilge-water and sulphuretted hydrogen. Upon one side of this elongated cave of horrors were ranged a hundred closets, every one of which reeked with this filth, mixed with that slimy moisture which was everywhere as a proof that the waters of the neighboring East River penetrated, and lingered here to foul instead of purify.

"What do you think of this?" said Finn, throwing the light of his lantern hither and thither so that every horror might be dragged from the darkness that all seemed to covet. "All the thousands living in the barracks must come here, and just think of all the young ones above that never did any harm having to take in this stuff;" and the detective struck out spitefully at the noxious air. As he did so, the gurgling of water at the Cherry street end of the vault caught his ear, and penetrating thither, he peered curiously about.

"I say, Tom," he called back to his companion, who had remained with me in the darkness, "here's a big break in the Croton main." But a moment later, in an affrighted voice: "No, it ain't. It's the sewer! I never knew of this opening into it before. Paugh! how it smells. That's nothing up where you are. I'll bet on the undertaker having more jobs in the house than ever."

By this time I began to feel sick and faint in that tainted air, and would have rushed up the stairs if I could have seen them. But Finn was exploring that sewer horror with his lantern. As I came down I had seen a pool of stagnant, green-coated water somewhere near the foot of the stairs, and, being afraid to stir in the thick darkness, was forced to call my guide, and, frankly state the urgent necessity for an immediate return above. The matter-of-fact policeman came up, and cast the liberating light upon the stairs, but rebuked me as I eagerly took in the comparatively purer atmosphere from above. "You can't stand it five minutes; how do you suppose they do, year in and year out?" "Even they don't stand it many years, I should think," was my involuntary reply.

As we stepped out into the court again, the glare of the bullseye dragged a strange face out of the darkness. It was that of a youth of eighteen or twenty years, ruddy, puffed, with the corners of the mouth grotesquely twisted. The detective greeted the person owning this face with the fervor of old acquaintanceship: "Eh, Buster! What's up?" "Hello, Jimmy Finn! What yez doin' here?" "Never mind, Buster. What's up?" "Why, Jimmy, didn't yez know I lodges here now?" "No, I didn't. Where? Who with?" "Beyant, wid the Pensioner." "Go on. Show me where you lodge." "Sure, Jimmy, it isn't me as would lie to yez."

But I had expressed a desire to penetrate into some of these kennels for crushed humanity; and Finn, with the happy acumen of his tribe, seizing the first plausible pretext, was relentless, and insisted on doubting the word of the Buster. That unfortunate with the puffy face, who seemed to know his man too well to protract resistance, puffed ahead of us up the black, oozy court, with myriads of windows made ghastly by the pale flicker of kerosene lamps in tiers above us, until he came to the last door but one upon the left side of the court, over which the letter S was sprawled upon the coping stone. The bullseye had been darkened, and when the Buster plunged through the doorway he was lost to sight in the impenetrable darkness beyond. We heard him though, stumbling against stairs that creaked dismally, and the slide being drawn back, the friendly light made clear the way for him and us. There was an entry precisely like the one we had entered before, with a flight of narrow, almost perpendicular stairs, with so sharp a twist in them that we could see only half up. The banisters in sight had precisely three uprights, and looked as if the whole thing would crumble at a touch; while the stairs were so smooth and thin with the treading of innumerable feet that they almost refused a foothold. Following the Buster, who grappled with the steep and dangerous ascent with the daring born of habit, I somehow got up stairs, wondering how any one ever got down in the dark without breaking his neck. Thinking it possible there might be a light sometimes to guide the pauper hosts from their hazardous heights to the stability of the street, I inquired as to the fact, only to meet the contempt of the Buster for the gross ignorance that could dictate such a question. "A light for the stairs! Who'd give it? Sweeney? Not much! Or the tenants? Skasely! Them's too poor!" While he muttered, the Buster had pawed his way up stairs with surprising agility, until he reached a door on the third landing. Turning triumphantly to the detective, he announced: "Here's where I lodges, Jimmy! You knows I wouldn't lie to yez."

"We'll see whether you would or no," said Finn, tapping on the door. Being told to come in, he opened it; and on this trivial but dexterous pretext we invaded the sanctity of a home.

No tale is so good as one plainly told, and I tell precisely what I saw. This home was composed, in the parlance of the place, of a "room and bedroom." The room was about twelve feet square, and eight feet from floor to ceiling. It had two windows opening upon the court, and a large fireplace filled with a cooking stove. In the way of additional furniture, it had a common deal table, three broken wooden chairs, a few dishes and cooking utensils, and two "shakedowns, as the piles of straw stuffed into bed-ticks are called; but it had nothing whatever beyond these articles. There was not even the remnant of a bedstead; not a cheap print, so common in the hovels of the poor, to relieve the blankness of the rough, whitewashed walls. The bedroom, which was little more than half the size of the other, was that outrage of capital upon poverty known as a "dark room," by which is meant that it had no window opening to the outer air; and this closet had no furniture whatever except two "shakedowns."

In the contracted space of these two rooms, and supplied with these scanty appliances for comfort, nine human beings were stowed. First there was the "Pensioner," a man of about thirty-five years, next his wife, then their three children, a woman lodger with two children, and the "Buster," the latter paying fifteen cents per night for his shelter; but I did not learn the amount paid by the woman for the accommodation of herself and children. The Buster, having been indignant at my inquiry as to the light upon the stairs, was now made merry by Finn supposing he had a regular bed and bedstead for the money. "Indade, he has not, but a 'shakedown' like the rest of us," said the woman; but the Buster rebuked this assumption of an impossible prosperity by promptly exclaiming, "Whist! ye knows I stretch on the boords without any shakedown whatsumdever."

Finn was of opinion the bed was hard but healthy, and fixing his eyes on the Buster's flabby face thought it possible he had any desirable number of "square meals" per day; but that individual limited his acquirements in that way for the day then closed to four. Finn then touching on the number of drinks, the Buster, being driven into conjecture and a corner by the problem, was thrust out of the foreground of our investigations.

By various wily tricks of his trade, Detective Finn managed to get a deal of information out of the Pensioner without seeming to be either inquisitive or intrusive, or even without rubbing the coat of his poverty the wrong way. From this source I learned that five dollars per month was paid as rent for these two third-floor rooms, and that everybody concerned deemed them dirt cheap at the price. Light was obtained from kerosene lamps at the expense of the tenant, and water had to be carried from the court below, while all refuse matter not emptied into the court itself had to be taken to the foul vaults beneath it. The rooms, having all these drawbacks and being destitute of the commonest appliances for comfort or decency, did not appear to be in the highest degree eligible; yet the Pensioner considered himself fortunate in having secured them. His experience in living must have been very doleful, for he declared that he had seen worse places. In itself, and so far as the landlord was concerned, I doubted him; but I had myself seen fouler places than these two rooms, which had been made so by the tenants. All that cleanliness could do to make the kennel of the Pensioner habitable had been done, and I looked with more respect upon the uncouth woman who had scoured the rough floor white, than I ever had upon a gaudily attired dame sweeping Broadway with her silken trail. The thrift that had so little for its nourishment had not been expended wholly upon the floor, for I noticed that the two children asleep on the shakedown were clean, while the little fellow four years of age, who was apparently prepared for bed as he was entirely naked, but sat as yet upon one of the three chairs, had no speck of dirt upon his fair white skin. A painter should have seen him as he gazed wonderingly upon us, and my respect deepened for the woman who could, spite the hard lines of her rugged life, bring forth and preserve so much of childish symmetry and beauty.

Having absorbed these general facts, I turned to the master of this household. He was a man of small stature but rugged frame, and his left shirt sleeve dangled empty at his side. That adroit Finn, noticing my inquiring look, blurted out: "That arm went in a street accident, I suppose?"

"No, sir; it wint at the battle of Spottsylvania."

Here was a hero! The narrow limits of his humble home expanded to embrace the brown and kneaded Virginian glades, as I saw them just seven years ago, pictured with the lurid pageantry of that stubborn fight when Sedgwick fell. This man, crammed with his family into twelve feet square at the top of Sweeney's Shambles, was once part of that glorious scene. In answer to my test questions he said he belonged to the Thirty-ninth New York, which was attached to the Second Corps, and that he received a pension of $15 per month from the grateful country he had served as payment in full for an arm. It was enough to keep body and soul together, and he could not complain. Nor could I; but I could and did signify to my guide by a nod that I had seen and heard enough, and we went down again into the slimy, reeking court.

Looking upward, I saw the vast tenement house, which contained two hundred such suites of apartments as the one I had just left, rising five stories above the narrow court, and I tried to imagine the vast total of human misery it embraced. The reflective official at my side guessed my thoughts, for he assured me that, coming as I had on a pleasant night of the early summer, I had seen the place at its best. In August, when these two hundred homes had been blistered for two months, the odors would be unendurable by a stranger; and although the atmosphere would be purer in winter, the place was then made as ghastly in a different way by the sight of these thousands of human beings suffering for want of fuel and clothing. For I knew, without being told, that only the wretchedly poor would harbor in these holes. In many of the rooms were widows struggling to maintain children by their scanty earnings as charwomen. Where there was a male head to the family, he was usually either physically disabled by sickness or injury, as in the case of the Pensioner, or was one of the wretched army of unskilled labor. There were however among the tenants some craftsmen, such as printers, carpenters, and in fact representatives of all trades, who had lost their cunning through the bottle; and knowing this fact, "Sweeney's Shambles" loomed into the misty night an irrefutable temperance argument. But whatever the failings of these wretched people, or whatever the reason of their poverty, there could not be any excuse for the barbarity which crams one hundred families into one building having a front of fifty feet, a depth of one hundred and fifty feet, and five floors, when that building is "Sweeney's Shambles," devoid of every appliance for health, privacy, or decency, and with those terrible vaults under the two courts upon which the east and west sides of the edifice open.

Picking our way by the lantern light through such kitchen refuse as remnants of fish and vegetables, mixed with more offensive offal, with which the court was covered, we slowly made our way to Cherry street again. Passing along I glanced through a score of first-floor windows, and saw in every room the same evidences of poverty and overcrowding. Every apartment was a "living-room" choked with adults and children, with such articles of furniture as I had seen in the Pensioner's room, and, worse than all, with foul odors evolved from the room itself and the vaults beneath. It was plain there could be no cleanliness, no privacy, no chance for decency, no godliness among these hundreds of people; and I had the chief moral and sanitary problem of the great city thrust thus forcibly upon me as I made my way through the court, which is the common thoroughfare of all these hundreds, but which the landlord does not light and which nobody cleans.

It was a relief to get out of Gotham Court into the fetid atmosphere of Cherry street, and we passed hurriedly up the court on the other side of the building, for the odors were coming up through the grating from the vault beneath like steam; and I was glad when, at the upper end of the court, we passed into Roosevelt street by a narrow entrance.

I had started out to see the worst human habitation in New York, and was convinced that my object had been fully accomplished. I knew that the law classes all domiciles containing three or more families as tenement houses, and that there are in the city of New York 20,000 such houses, in which 160,000 families and more than a half million of persons are packed. I knew of the cramming and foulness of the barracks Nos. 7 and 9 Mulberry street, where a stray spark from somebody's pipe will some night breed a conflagration which will destroy scores of the wretched inmates. I knew of those vast houses of the better sort in the German portions of the city, which are furnished with gas, have tolerable ventilation, and water as high as it can be forced, but which have narrow halls and steep stairs, to make them in moments of alarm perfected machines for the killing or maiming of a large per cent. of the hundreds who inhabit each of them; in short, I had a general idea of the high state of perfection to which the art of crowding the largest possible number of people into the smallest possible space had been brought in this Christian city, but I had not imagined the possibility of such things as the kennels for humanity which overhang Gotham Court.

The glimpse I have given of one of the 20,000 tenement houses affords a view in detail of the chief evil of the metropolis, but a proper sense of the overcrowding with which New York is afflicted can perhaps be better obtained from some general facts. London has had some centuries of experience in packing away the poor, but that New York, after scarcely a generation of trial, has surpassed her, can be seen by the following comparative statement of the population of the more densely peopled quarters of each city:

NEW YORK.				LONDON.			
Districts.	*No. of Acres.*	*Population.*	*Rate to Acre.*	*Districts.*	*No. of Acres.*	*Population.*	*Rate to Acre.*
Fourth Ward	83	17,352	209	Whitechapel	383	78,970	206
Sixth Ward	86	19,754	230	St. Giles	245	54,076	221
Seventh Ward	110	36,962	187	St. James West	164	35,326	215
Tenth Ward.	198	31,537	287	East London	153	40,687	266
Eleventh Ward	196	38,953	301	Strand	140	42,979	307
Thirteenth Ward	107	26,388	247	St. Luke's	220	57,073	259
Fourteenth Ward	96	23,382	244	Holborn	196	44,862	229
Seventeenth Ward . . .	331	79,563	241	West London	126	27,145	215
Totals and averages .	1,207	293,891	243	Totals and averages .	1,627	381,118	234

This carefully prepared statement, which appeared in the report of the Board of Health for 1869, was based upon the census of 1865, so that now the comparison must be much more unfavorable to us, as the population of the city has increased in an undue ratio in these densely peopled wards. But while this exhibit gives a general view of a gigantic evil, it affords no adequate idea of the exceptional exaggerations by which some portions of these wards become ulcers upon the body politic. There are many blocks where the population exceeds one thousand to the acre, and localities where the living have but little more of the earth's surface than the minimum allotted to the dead. It is not strange then that the tenements become nurseries of social degradation, and only escape being intolerable pests by causing a mortality of seven per cent. per annum of the inmates, as the average of all the houses, while in such dens as 35 Baxter street, where fifty beggars and prostitutes are stowed in indescribable filth, the mortality reaches seventeen per cent.

It has been truly said that the home is the last analysis of the state, and it is not strange that the civic virtues decay in a community where one-half the people have no home in the true meaning of the word. The profligacy of New York, after allowance has been made for the gross exaggerations due to ignorance and partisan rancor, is considerable and shameful; but resting as the city does upon this tenement system, it is wonderful that it retains so much of physical and moral vitality. Family privacy, which is the foundation of public morality and intelligence, is within the reach of but a small fraction of the population. It requires at least $5,000 per annum for a man with even a small family to live in the metropolis with the domesticity necessary to the successful propagation of the home virtues; and as very few possess an income of that amount, the strictly private houses in the city are proportionately scarce. Thousands escape the horrors of the tenements by subletting portions of their houses either to a family or in furnished rooms, and in either case only succeed in mitigating an evil that every year presses more sorely upon the city. But these semi-private families feel only the distant glow of the flame that is consuming the moral stamina of the tenement population. It is not necessary to face the horrors of Sweeney's Shambles and see the Pensioner with his wife and three children, his female lodger and her two children, supplemented by the Buster, enveloped in the foul odors of the vault, and stowed away in a space barely sufficient for the healthful and decent accommodation of at most two human beings, in order to fully realize the individual suffering and public peril which these tenements produce. A stroll at random through any portions of the Tenth, Eleventh, or Seventeenth Wards will force it upon the most careless of observers.

A walk during any hot evening of summer through Avenue A, or any of the streets crossing it at right angles below Fourteenth street, will be sufficient to convince the most skeptical that I have adhered literally to fact. Almost every house in these streets will be found to be a tenement five or six stories high, with two or more human beings gasping for air at each one of the numerous windows, while foot room can scarcely be found on the sidewalks or roadway because of the multitude of children incumbering them. It is only by entering these houses that it can be seen how it is possible for them to shelter so many thousands; and in examining them it must be remembered they are nearly all tenements of the better class, provided with all the appliances for health required by the tenement-house law. Each family will be found to have the inevitable "living-room" and "bedroom," and the improvement in the latter consists in its having a small window near the ceiling opening into the narrow hall, which in its turn has a window at each end opening to the outer air. But at the rear this hall window is of small service, as it looks out upon another tenement twenty-five feet distant which is built upon the rear of the lot; and in this fact the observer has the key to the mystery of housing the thousands he sees at the windows of the front houses, and the other thousands he sees in the streets. Upon each lot of one hundred feet in depth two distinct edifices are erected, with the space of twenty-five feet left between only because it is imperatively demanded by the law; and knowing this fact, the secret of the density of population in these wards is learned. It is not the least painful of the facts discovered in these quarters, that almost without exception the tens of thousands of inmates of these houses thus subjected to physical discomfort and moral jeopardy belong to the industrial classes. The great metropolis, with its vast enterprise, its restless ingenuity, and its imperial revenues, can furnish its skilled labor, upon which its prosperity so largely depends, with no better homes than these. Its mechanics of every grade and trade, who elsewhere would find their wages amply sufficient for the reputable maintenance of their families, and enough to place them in the second class of the population, which is the bulwark of the State, are here compelled by the enormous rents and the high charges for all the necessaries of life to live in these tenements, where they become negligent as citizens, and their children, owing to the influences which surround them, growing dangers to the commonwealth. In a sanitary sense the tenements are a perplexity and a vexation; but it is in their moral and social aspects that they are perilous. There are hundreds of these immense barracks in which from fifteen to fifty families live under one roof, using halls, stairways, closets, and all the conveniences for the privacy of life in common. In every one of these families there are females of course, and there are very few in which there are not several children. No truth is more universally recognized than that barrack life is demoralizing even in the army; and remembering this fact, some idea of its destructive influences when it is inflicted upon a half million of men, women, and children can be formed. With half its population camped in its heart, the city has a disheartening future to the reflective publicist who traces effects to the first cause. The first generation of tenement life has destroyed in a great measure the safeguards which a genuine home erects around a people, and it is inevitable that in the second or third generation it must brutalize its victims, and leave vice and ignorance as the foundation stones of the municipality.

But while the tenements suggest politically these grave apprehensions for the future, to the sanitarian they are a present peril. Since the enforcement of the present admirable law regulating their construction and occupancy, they have been so greatly improved that they are far less of a menace than before to the public health, but they are yet nurseries of disease and death. Dr. Elisha Harris, the late effective Sanitary Superintendent of the city, with the assistance of his learned and careful chief clerk Mr. Norris R. Norton, who is now deceased, did this community an incalculable service by making tenement-house mortality a special study and the subject of full and exact statistical compilation. The last report published by these gentlemen shows a total mortality in the city during the year of 25,167. Of this army of the dead 4,065 had been recruited from the public institutions, 7,817 from private houses, hotels, or boarding-houses, and 13,285 from the tenement houses. In the first class the percentage of the whole mortality was 16.15, in the second 31.06, while the deadly tenements yielded a per cent. of 52.79, or more than half the mortality of the year when we consider only the deaths actually occurring in them. But the tenements are the reservoirs from which the public hospitals are fed, and charging the mortality of the latter to the former, where it rightfully belongs, these dens of death produced 68.94 per centum of the whole mortality of the year. The forced community of families, which is the great social and sanitary evil of the city, can have no more startling commentary than this brief statement of general facts; but some details of these nests where only moral and physical death is hatched will be both interesting and valuable.

These human hives are the natural nurses of epidemics. Smallpox, malignant fevers, and all contagious diseases revel in them. There is hardly a day throughout the entire year when some one of these dreaded foes of human life is not present in these choked centres of population, to occasion public alarm and tax the skill of the health authorities to keep it within bounds. During the past two years the viler of the dens, and especially the cellar lodging-houses, have propagated a new pest in the relapsing fever—that sorrowfully suggestive disease of privation which slays comparatively few, but destroys the physical vigor of thousands, and thereby has become the most efficient recruiting officer pauperism has ever had. Dr. Harris says in one of his invaluable reports that "the inevitable and the preventable among the causes of mortality become strangely blended and combined in the unventilated and unscavenged houses of the overcrowded poor. Consumption and all the inflammatory diseases of the lungs vie with the infectious and other zymotic disorders, in wasting the health and destroying the life of the tenement population." It is not singular, therefore, that the tenement mortality has occasioned the gravest alarm, for these perpetual fever nests not only infect special localities but also the whole city, and render the death rate of the metropolis excessive. It could not be otherwise when a single house in Sheriff street, having fifty-eight persons, had four deaths in nine months, thus giving a death rate of 84 in 1,000. The same grave facts are almost as forcibly illustrated in the block bounded by Madison, Grand, Corlears, Monroe, and Jackson streets. In this area, where the population is so excessive as to give but 9.15 square yards to each inhabitant, there are eighteen tenements containing 153 families, which gave 25 deaths in nine months. One house with a population of 36 had 4, three others with a population of 110 had a mortality of 6 in the same period, and the case was no better in the other. Nor was this block the most serious in its suggestions, for I have been careful to select from a large mass of statistics facts which would present a fair average of the deaths in these overcrowded dens.

The humanitarian might almost refuse to regret that these tenements constitute the modern Herod, for the children who grow up in them are inevitably doomed to a life of infamy or suffering. Breeders of contentions, brawls, domestic murders, these houses subject children from earliest infancy to incidents which must bestialize them. Aside from the intermingling of families so that there can be no such thing as home privacy, these houses are frequently the scene of brutal murder. Almost without exception the domestic murders occur in them, and as these homicides are invariably the results of drunken quarrels, the details of the crime are always sickening to the reader, and must have been terribly demoralizing to the inmates of the house who, as is sometimes the case, stand idly by and see the butchery done. Intoxication is responsible for another horror of these houses. It was but yesterday that one of them was discovered in a Mulberry street tenement. A woman occupying a squalid room not having been seen for some hours, another woman living on the same floor went to the room and found her lying dead upon her "shakedown," with her three children playing innocently about her. Such incidents are constantly occurring, and I have seen more of them than I care to experience again by narrating them.

As briefly as the disagreeable task could be performed, I have endeavored to present the tenements of the metropolis in such matters of detail and generalization that their present and probable future effect upon the community which tolerates them can be fairly estimated. There is nothing in the criminal statistics of the city so alarming as this overcrowding of the population in houses unfit to be the kennels of dogs; and the Nether side of New York has nothing more distressful than these huge contrivances for the production of moral and physical death. Take a common case. An artisan in middle life has growing sons and daughters around him. The mother has gone to her rest, and he, being a man of strong will, struggles with some success to preserve his children from the demoralizing influences of the den in which he is forced to shelter them. Suddenly,

Of all the fevers that infest
His temporary fever nest,
He takes a deadly one. The rest
Is easily conjectured. *

* Some weeks after this article was written, the Board of Health peremptorily closed Sweeny's Shambles as a place of human habitation and compelled the owner to entirely renovate it, so that it is now no longer as I saw it; but it is a type of so many kennels for the poor in New York that I have chosen to let the description remain. If the reader is curious in such matters, the police in any of the lower precincts can show him something distressingly like the den of death in Gotham Court. I may add that the den in Mulberry street did take fire at last, but the accident occurring at midday instead of midnight, only one person—a woman—was burned to death.

OUTCAST CHILDREN.

TEN thousand human beings under the age of fourteen years are adrift in the streets of New York. Four-fifths of them are confirmed vagrants, and the majority are growing up in ignorance of everything but the depravity which is gleaned from the city slums, and all of them are being pushed by the relentless force of untoward circumstances into the criminal practices in which many have become adepts in the dawn of their blighted lives. The major portion are boys rapidly preparing for the almshouses, prisons, and gallows; but hundreds are girls, who have before them the darker horror of prostitution as well as those appliances of civilization for the care or repression of the pauperism and lawlessness which it creates. It is this juvenile army of vagabondage and crime hanging upon the flanks of society, and occasionally startling it from its propriety by manifestations of an immeasurable capacity for mischief, which is a prominent peril and the most sorrowful of the nether aspects of the city.

"Foxes have holes and birds of the air have nests; but the Son of Man hath not where to lay his head," is the most woful declaration of friendless homelessness ever uttered on earth. To-day in the Western metropolis ten thousand defaced images of the Creator are as friendless, as homeless, as abandoned to the wrath of man. However hardened he may have become, no one can encounter this phase of metropolitan life without a fervent hope that the experience may not be repeated. Policemen who, it might be supposed, are indurated to callousness by long attrition with human suffering and degradation, are frequently unmanned by casual meetings with little castaways wailing in the agony of hunger or homelessness, or in the anguish of detected crime; and the mere amateur in such scenes cannot be blamed if he avoids rather than seeks them. For the reason that the facts are so repulsive, they have been collated with extreme difficulty, and no task which I have undertaken has been more onerous than that of presenting the juvenile wretchedness of the city in trustworthy and intelligible shape.

At the beginning of the undertaking I discovered that notwithstanding the many earnest agencies at work among these outcasts to ameliorate their condition, very few precise facts concerning them were known. The intelligent and sympathetic agents of the Children's Aid Society, the Howard Mission, the Catholic Protectory, and other organized charities, were constantly among them; yet no one of them could give any exact data as to the number, haunts, or habits of the outcast children of New York, nor did the reports of any of these institutions contain such information in manageable shape. The moral and physical destitution of these child-vagrants, and the causes which produced them, are the topics chiefly discussed by these societies; but the statements of facts are almost entirely confined to the means of reclamation which they so constantly and unselfishly exert. But by combining information obtained from widely differing sources with personal observations, I have avoided conjecture, although it is of course impossible to give exact statistics where none ever have been or can be collated. The only positive statement I have seen is that "the vagrant and neglected children of the city, if placed in double file three feet apart, would make a procession eight miles long." In this estimate are included the neglected children as well as the true nomads of the streets, and it is under rather than above the truth.

In this army of sorrow there are gradations in misery, but only few resources for its alleviation. The child who is naked has the odds against him who is both hungry and naked, but neither has the advantage of the other in means for the relief of either the one or the other. The first and most natural recourse of the outcast who has just passed from a neglected babyhood into a vagrant childhood, is beggary. It is these forlorn creatures whose naked feet smear the gutter ice with blood, whose hands eagerly search the garbage barrels for morsels of refuse food which the homeless dogs will not touch, but which they devour; it is they whose eyes have the frightful glare only privation can give, and whose voices are often so weakened by want that they cannot audibly articulate their needs at area doors; it is they who are found at night under stoops, in wagons, in lumber yards, or timidly asking for lodging at the police stations. I am fully aware that all this means that there are homeless children who are actually starving in the streets of New York, and I am also conscious that I have not exaggerated nor set down aught in malice. There are such children, and hundreds of them. Despite the constant and systematic efforts made by organized charities, there are constantly in the streets fifteen hundred fragile boys and girls under the age of ten years, who have no conception of the meaning of the word home, and who are dying by inches for the want of sufficient nutriment. These are grave statements, but those noble laborers of every Christian creed, who are working with such unwearying and unselfish zeal to rescue the human drift annually cast up in increasing quantities, know that they are rather below than above the truth.

But these hapless waifs that, living or dead, are rebukes of civilization, do not constitute all of the infantile street beggars. There are half as many more who are less than they pretend to be, but still having a perfect right to be classed as outcast children. They, in common with other classes to be noted, are the victims of debauched and brutal parentage. Born of misery, nurtured by penury, cradled in the filth and degradation of such tenements as that I have described at Gotham Court, having blasphemy and drunkenness as constant companions, there is nothing on earth more pitiful or more painfully suggestive of social ulceration than the child-vagrants of New York.

Crowding all the narrow streets and courts of the lower portion of the city, swarming about the markets and piers, haggard, filthy, the foul blasphemy of experienced depravity constantly on their lips, they at once declare their appalling numbers and their unutterable degradation. They are the *enfants terrible* of civilization, and many of those now specially considered are forced to add hypocrisy to their vices. They are the children of parents who, sunken by liquor below the beasts of the fields, strip their progeny of nearly all their scanty clothing and drive them forth from the kennels which are their homes, to beg for them the means of further indulgence. It is this class which infests the doors of theatres, concert-saloons, and other places of public resort, and which is found in the streets at the latest hours of the night and is most importunate in demanding charity. One special case which happened to come under my personal observation will perhaps fully illustrate this class. A boy was dragged into a police station for the heinous offence of begging at the doors of Wallack's Theatre. It appeared that with two brothers younger than himself —and he was only twelve years of age—he was driven out by his drunken mother every night to beg, and that she compelled them, before beginning their task, to remove their shoes under the stoop of a house near by. Not only were they thus exposed to the bitter cold of an extreme winter, but the beastly mother hovered near to urge them to increased importunity by significant gestures, and regularly rewarded them with brutal beatings if their gains were not commensurate with her desires. It was ascertained that this was the practice of a large number of bestial parents colonized upon the east side of the city, whose children escaped from them when they could to become veritable vagrants and beggars upon their own account. There are others of these child beggars who are still less entitled to sympathy, for their homes are abodes of comparative comfort and they readily obey their parents—who themselves are beggars—and sturdily demand the charity to which they are not rightfully entitled. But the phases of street beggary are as manifold as the shapes taken by human depravity stimulated by greed, and I cannot pretend to do more than make mention of general facts.

Juvenile delinquents are infantile mendicants ripened by time and circumstances. Foremost among them are the boy-burglars and thieves who have become at least a grave annoyance of metropolitan life. There is nothing too trivial to escape the attention of these young marauders, and their physical insignificance is to their advantage in their work of depredation. They go with nonchalant ease where bolder spirits would fear to tread and larger bodies fail to penetrate. Having none of the caution of experience, and able to crawl into the crevices of buildings, all the vagaries of theft are laid to their charge. I could not have an apter illustration than a case which occurred on the day I reached this page in my writing. Three boys, each twelve years of age, having glided in unnoticed during business hours, easily secreted themselves in the premises at the corner of West Broadway and Franklin street until the house was closed; that being done they began operations while it was still daylight, by ransacking the office, where they were in plain view from the neighboring houses. Of course they were discovered, but so small were they that Capt. Petty searched an hour before he found them stowed away in a coal-hole under the sidewalk. Boy-burglars always commit some such blunder as this in their operations, but in spite of blundering are often so favored by circumstances that their enterprises are successful. Their particular depredation is to enter unoccupied houses and strip them of whatever they can conveniently carry away. The summer months, when large numbers of families go into the country for weeks, leaving their homes entirely unprotected, offer an opportunity to burglars which is never neglected, and very few of these houses escape pillage. Sometimes a clean sweep of everything portable is made, which is satisfactory evidence that adults have been at work; and sometimes only a few trifling articles are missing, but much wanton damage is done to what is left, which is sure proof that boys have been about. But the especial field of juvenile burglars is found in houses which are to let, and are therefore left to care for themselves by the police. The boys easily gain entrance, and once in are secure in the intrusion, however protracted it may be. There is nothing to operate upon apparently but the bare floors and walls, but the boys find portable plunder in the gas and water fixtures. Not only do they wrench off fauçets and burners, but they pull the pipes out of the walls, and frequently do a damage of hundreds of dollars in obtaining plunder for which they get only a few cents from the junkmen. The water is very rarely cut off at the street from vacant houses; and where it is not, this breakage of the pipes causes the flooding of the houses, which is often the first intimation obtained of the robbery. While this spoliation of such houses is always done by boys, and cases of it are occurring every day, it by no means absorbs the attention of all juvenile delinquents. There are others who are engaged in breaking show-cases incautiously left on the sidewalks at night and robbing them of their contents.

There are some who loiter about the doors of the smaller shops watching an opportunity to slip behind the counter and rob the till. This also is an every-day occurrence and the small size of the thieves peculiarly adapts them to the crime and renders them remarkably successful in it; where a man or half-grown boy would be sure to be seen or heard, the urchin of eight or ten years glides noiseless and invisible. These same advantages are apparent in his depredations upon the property exposed at the doors of shops where he lingers unsuspected to snatch up a pair of shoes, a jacket, or something of like nature which he can easily carry off.

The principal methods of thievery employed by boys have been stated, but no pretence is made that the list is complete. Every case of crime develops some distinctive features which tend to remove it from the class to which it seems to belong, and the means of robbery are therefore almost as varied as the peculiarities of cases. This is especially true of the depredations of vagrant girls, and I have not therefore attempted to do more than generalize concerning them. They never commit burglary and rarely street robberies or from stores, and they principally confine themselves to what is called "the domestic lay." Gaining access to dwellings by pretence of begging or selling matches carried in a large basket, they snatch up and secrete whatever is presented by opportunity, if it is nothing better than a handkerchief or a pewter spoon. But almost the only method of robbery which is peculiar to vicious street girls is that practised by the flower girls, who are about twelve years of age, rather handsome in features and modest in demeanor. Sufficiently attractive to make the story probable, and having enough adroitness to give it the further probability of an opportunity having been had, they boldly demand hush money of gentlemen for alleged improper liberties taken with them. There are scores of these girl blackmailers, and they are the most dangerous and profligate of all juvenile offenders. It is to the credit of the city that, although yet in existence, they are much less numerous than they were a couple of years ago, when Police Captain Thorne discovered a regularly organized band of them. Such incredible youthful depravity was so clearly shown on that occasion that the story is worthy of brief recital. A gentleman of irreproachable character and extensively engaged in business called upon Captain Thorne and frankly stated that he was the victim of one of these flower girls, who had already despoiled him of large sums of money, and whose persecutions were actually killing him. It appeared that she always came to his counting-house on particular days and, watching until he was alone, went boldly into his private office. In police parlance, they "put up a job on her." Captain Thorne was secreted in a closet in the office the next time she called, and the gentleman talked to her as previously arranged. He began by asking her why she persisted in her demands upon him, for, said he, "you know I never had anything to do with you, never said an improper word to you." The young analyst of human nature answered unabashed, "I know that; but who'll believe you if I say you did?" Captain Thorne, dressed in full police uniform, stepped from the closet with, "I will for one, Mary!" The girl, young as she was, had enough experience in devious ways to see that her game had escaped, and readily, although sullenly, promised to cease exacting tribute in that particular quarter. The gentleman would go no further, and to the earnest entreaties of Captain Thorne to prosecute the girl, both for her own good and that of society, returned an absolute refusal. Captain Thorne was therefore obliged to let her go with a warning not to attempt her operations again anywhere. He also remonstrated with her upon her way of living, and asked her why she did such things. The hardened girl morosely answered that all the other girls did them, and thus gave a clue which was followed until it developed the gang of feminine blackmailers of tender years, working in concert, which has been referred to. Although the band was then dispersed, the method of robbery it employed survived, and is yet extensively used by scores of girls under the cover of selling not only flowers, but apples and other fruits.

It is impossible to give the exact numbers of the juvenile thieves of all classes to be found at all times in New York. All outcast children are so liable at any moment to pass the line between vagrancy and crime, that the two classes are practically only one. But there are two phases of infantile misfortune presented in the streets which are distinguishable from all others, and from each other. One is the children temporarily lost, who are outcasts for a few hours, and crowd into that brief time unnecessary but unutterable misery. In the past ten years 66,809 children have come into the hands of the police as lost, which is an average of 6,680 per year, and of nearly 19 per day. Most of the cases, however, occur in the summer months, when the children, getting into the street to play, wander off a few rods, are unable to find their way home, and soon attract attention by their lusty lamentations at the discovery. They are then handed over to the first patrolman who is met, who takes them to his precinct station. They are retained until nightfall, when they are sent from all portions of the city to Police Headquarters, No. 300 Mulberry street, where a large dormitory has been prepared for their reception on the top floor of the building. They are kept there in charge of a judicious matron until claimed by the parents; but if this does not occur within three days, an accurate description of the children is taken and they are sent to the Commissioners of Charities. But this rarely happens, and if the children are not claimed at the stations, as many are, they are so generally sought by the parents at Police Headquarters, that very few remain even through one night.

The foundlings have a far different fate. During the past ten years 939 of the waifs on the sea of sin, who are outcasts from the moment of their birth, have been picked up in the streets; and it is a notable fact, upon which I do not care to moralize, that 161 of these foundlings were picked up by the police in 1870, and 178 in 1869, although the Foundling Asylum was in full operation during 1870, and for that reason a large diminution in the police cases had been expected. Formerly, when these castaway babes were found in the streets, it was the custom to transfer them as soon as possible to the care of the Commissioners of Charities, by whom they were placed in one of the public asylums, where most of them speedily, and as a matter of course, died. Being now committed to the more careful charge of the new Foundling Asylum, a larger proportion of them survive to become public burdens during the years of infancy, and to be in after life whatever chance may determine for a child who never had a home. It does not come within the scope of the present article to deal with the causes of infant abandonment nor with its effects either upon its subjects or the community. I give now only the bare record of the number of these castaways as sufficient for my purpose.

There are other juvenile outcasts who are self-helpful, and therefore less painful to the observer than the classes which have been mentioned. These are the thousands of boys and girls who are in great part friendless and homeless, but scour the streets for a livelihood to such good purpose that few of them actually suffer for the necessaries of life. Chiefly newsboys and bootblacks, they are the gamins of an advanced civilization, and could exist only where the undue aggregation of humanity has produced the poverty which inevitably attends such herding. Generally ragged, often hatless or shoeless, or both, unclean in person and language, the newsboys are a class by themselves. Nowhere else, and among no other human beings, is there so much energy, independence, effrontery, cunning, shiftlessness, and contentedness with the lot fortune sends. Out at four o'clock in the morning to crowd the folding-rooms of the morning newspapers, they can be seen from then until late at night, when they are vending the evening journals, scouring every part of the city and heard everywhere shouting their wares into the general ear. Each sale they make yields only a cent or a fraction of a cent profit, and it can be readily seen that they must make many sales, involving hours of time and a terrible strain upon youthful muscles, for them to gain even a scanty subsistence. If a boy sells one hundred papers per day, he is doing more than an average business, but his profits amount only to about fifty cents; so that three dollars per week is more than the general reward of an occupation that consumes fourteen hours per day and requires a daily capital almost equal to the weekly profits. Out of these scanty earnings, got at such a great cost, the newsboy can, if he will, live cleanly and comfortably. Although as a class improvident in the last degree, hundreds of the newsboys take the benefits of the practical philanthropy of the Children's Aid Society, which has established the Newsboys' Lodging House at No. 49 Park Place, where a boy can obtain wholesome meals and a clean bed at a cost of six cents each. Less than half his petty profits therefore suffices for his sustenance and shelter, leaving him twenty-six cents per day to provide him clothing and other necessaries. Human thrift has never had a more extreme example than that out of such gains as these a fund of $2,433 60 has accumulated in the savings bank attached to the lodging house, from deposits made by 1,104 boys of their surplus pennies. But cheering as this fact is, when others are considered, the improvidence of the mass and the vast total of homeless boys remain uncontradicted. During the year 1870, 8,655 different boys were inmates for differing periods of the lodging-house, and of this number 3,122 were orphans, 3,651 were half-orphans. Of the whole number 33 per cent. were received at the lodging house gratuitously, because they were destitute; and we are thus brought face to face with the appalling fact that during 1870 2.500 boys under the age of fourteen years sought in vain in the streets of New York for the subsistence that costs only twenty-four cents per day. That this is a misery that is forced upon and not sought by its victims, is shown by the fact that during the year only 713 of those admitted to the lodging house were found to be truants who had fled from comfortable homes from an uncontrollable spirit of adventure. All the others were actually homeless, nor did they constitute the total of the infantile privation of the year. All those admitted to the lodging house do not sell newspapers, nor do all who do seek its comforts. There are hundreds, many of whom are girls, who are suffering the martyrdom of profligate parentage. Less fortunate than their orphaned comrades who can find refuge in the sanctuaries provided by a wise beneficence, these outcasts must go at night to brutal parents in foul tenement dens, to be kicked, cursed, and despoiled of every penny of their earnings for the benefit of the rumseller. Taken altogether, the newsboys are subjected to great privations and terrible temptations. Among them are many who, surviving the one and proving superior to the other, are to emerge from this shrouded infancy into an honorable manhood. But among them are many others who are to escape all evil in a pauper grave before childhood is passed, or failing this beatitude are to become confirmed vagrants and thieves.

Akin to the newsboys in many respects are the bootblacks, who are, however, a much smaller class, as their calling has of late years greatly decreased as a street pursuit. It has now become a common thing for a boy to have a number of customers whom he serves every morning at their places of business, at a fixed rate per week; and some of them make more money than unskilled adults, as their gains amount to $12 or $15 per week. But these are not common cases, and the average is about $8 per week for those having regular customers. The nomads who roam the streets or lounge in the public parks, depending upon chance patrons, do not average more than $5, and many of them glean much less from the many hours of the day and night which they devote to their calling. Nor is the meagreness of its rewards the only hardship of their avocation. Of all street children seeking an honest livelihood, the bootblacks are most liable to temptation. Necessarily having much time unemployed by their trade, they use it in penny-pitching or other methods of petty gambling. They learn to chew tobacco and to smoke by picking up the ends of cigars which have been cast into the gutters. They become more proficient in profanity than the Water street roughs, and rival the most degraded in obscenity. The rivalry of an overdone trade makes them adepts in lying. Brought in contact with all classes of men, they are reached by the burglars, who so often need a "kid" in their nefarious enterprises, and thus lead these hapless boys to deadly familiarity with crime. Keeping in mind these general facts, I have not been surprised to find so many of the bootblacks passing so readily into criminal practices. In their homes these Arabs of the street are no better and no worse off than their comrades of all classes of outcast children. When their hours of seeking for labor are brought to a close by the thoroughfares becoming solitudes, they must kennel like dogs in some area, must go to the foulness of some tenement, or must seek some one of the lodging houses which the charity of New York has provided for the little wanderers in its streets.

The army of juvenile vagabondage has been briefly reviewed in its leading divisions, and the sources of its recruitment can be briefly and distinctly stated. Liquor is at the bottom of all of it. If not the immediate cause, the traffic in alcoholic liquors is remotely responsible for the casting adrift from the anchorage of home of every juvenile outcast found in the streets. Years ago I read in an English periodical the short, sad story of Elsie, a St. Giles child. The father died, and

'Twas hard upon his death, I think,
That Elsie's mother took to drink,
And harder still on Elsie.

That told the whole story. The St. Giles unfortunate became an outcast and worse. In New York and in London the same causes produce the same effects. Only the rum traffic could make the tenements of Greenwich and Cherry streets possible, and only the profligate debauchery produced by it could cast ten thousand children out of a million of people, in such a country as this, homeless upon the world. Every agent of every organized charity engaged in the labor of saving these children will bear witness that he has found the parents, if living, drunken wrecks, or if dead, the victims of intemperance. Ordinary prudence and industry will enable any adult in the United States to earn sufficient to keep those dependent upon him from want, and I dare affirm the same of a place so exceptional to the country at large as New York. But there is not ordinary industry and prudence in the mass of the population of a city which has 7,500 grog-shops, or one to every one hundred and twenty-six of its people. At least $15,000,000 are swallowed up every year by these grog shops, and three dollars in every ten come out of the pockets of the tenement classes. The $5,000,000 thus wasted, if legitimately used, would more than provide a comfortable home for every vagabond child in New York.

Talking upon this subject with Mr. Charles L. Brace, the accomplished Secretary of the Children's Aid Society, he held that orphanage was a leading cause of juvenile vagrancy; but when I came to inquire as to the orphanage, it was found to be caused in almost every case, directly or indirectly, by intemperance. Of course people would continue to die if there were not a drop of alcoholic liquor in the world, and would die at all ages; but fewer of them would die in middle life, and still fewer leaving their families totally unprovided for. Alcohol, therefore, as found in intoxicating liquors, if not immediately, is remotely chargeable with the mass of misery which I have presented. Of the immediate causes the figures of the Newsboys' Lodging House show that orphanage is a principal one, and conversation with the outcasts proves that parental profligacy is another. "They beat me so I couldn't stay," or "Father and mother fought so much I run away," are common excuses of the children who are found wandering destitute in the streets; but in every one of these cases which has been fully probed, whiskey has been found to be at the bottom of it.

There are some of these outcasts, however, who cast themselves upon the world from a spirit of adventure. Every year many boys and a few girls are picked up in the streets who have drifted into the city from the surrounding country. There is a delusion that New York is an El Dorado to every one who can reach it, and the delusion drags thither hundreds of children as well as thousands of adults. The former come in during the summer months by the canals, as helpers, or on foot, begging or filching their food *en route*, and reach the city, where they expect to find money as easily as thistles on their native heaths. Hundreds of such cases are picked up in the streets every year, and in the majority of them it is found that the boys left good homes, impelled by an uncontrollable desire to make their fortunes in the metropolis or see its wonders, foremost among which the theatres are always found. Nor do the theatres lure country boys alone, for the sensational drama as found in the Bowery has enticed shoals of city boys from their homes and into criminal practices. That I may show that this is no mere assertion, it is proper to state that a leading laborer for juvenile reformation recently conversed with fifty young convicts picked at random from the penitentiary on Blackwell's Island, and found that all of them, with very few exceptions, had become criminals when small boys, by the theft from their parents, or wherever else they could find them, of the few cents required to secure admission to the pit of the theatre. One of the exceptions had done this also, but he rather prided himself upon being a natural thief, for he boasted that when only four years of age he had stolen two cents from his mother, and the cunning and delight with which he hid it seemed to be still one of his chief pleasures.

Vast as it is, the evil would be much greater but for the constant and intelligent efforts which are made for its amelioration. The saving and reformatory agencies which have been at work for many years in the gutters of the city, have left behind them, as we have seen, a terrible total of juvenile misery and depravity; but without the work they have done the criminal and pauper classes would be twentyfold what they are. It is almost painful to contemplate what would be the condition of the city if these classes had been dealt with by the law alone. It requires considerable patience to look upon the law dealing with any class of offenders, but Job himself would have been unequal to the task of viewing its proceedings with children.

If any one desires illustrations of the stupid carelessness of the law in dealing with juvenile delinquents, they can be found any day in the procedings of the police courts. Taking a most common case, I will however cite that of the two boy-burglars caught coming from a store in Greenwich street, to which they had made burglarious entrance through the skylight, which they had reached from the roof of the adjoining tenement. These facts being stated in the fewest possible words to the magistrate, without the slightest inquiry as to their past history, they were sent to a cell in the Tombs. But they had been attendants for a short time of one of the industrial schools of the Children's Aid Society, were searched for by its agents, rescued from prison, and although many months have since elapsed, neither has again transgressed, and there is a chance of saving both of them. I must also tell of the experience of Dr. Elisha Harris, Secretary of the New York Prison Association, with a boy of fifteen years whom he found in jail, and who had spent three years of his brief life in penal confinement for petty thefts. Anxious to know what effort had ever been made to reclaim the boy, Dr. Harris asked him what the Judge had said to him when he was arraigned. It appeared that it had been his misfortune to encounter the same magistrate on the occasion of each transgression. The first time he was asked if he were not ashamed of himself, the second time was told that he was an incorrigible young rascal, and the third time was informed that he was sure to be hanged. The boy, who had been more thoughtless than criminal, speedily became a believer in his own total depravity; but the words of kindly advice addressed him by Dr. Harris had such effect, that he was anxious to know if he could have a chance to learn a trade when he got out, and do something besides steal. There is at least a chance that, despite the strenuous efforts of the law to make him a confirmed criminal, the boy will find more remunerative employment than petty thievery. These cases might be multiplied endlessly, but the mass would only be cumulative evidence that the law as administered in New York, and (so far as I have seen or read) everywhere else, is either criminally careless in dealing with juvenile delinquencies, or is a devout believer in original sin and compelled to meet children in the spirit of the theology that dooms babes to perdition.

Nor has the institutionizing—if I may be allowed to coin a needed word—of outcast children done much better than the law. Space will not permit the citation of facts, much less an argument against the huddling of children in public reformatories, and I must be content with stating that Dr. Wichern's paradox, "The strongest wall is no wall," has been signally illustrated in the Indiana House of Refuge and the Ohio Reform Farm, where the "family plan" of dealing with juvenile delinquents has been found a vast improvement upon the old semi-penal system yet in use in New York. The city has, however, many private charities working on the same plan with the most beneficent results. The Children's Aid Society and the Howard Mission herd children as little as possible, and do the work of salvation by transplanting them to homes which are found for them in the Western States. During the year 1870 the former took to the West, where they were scattered among the thrifty farmers, 2,757 persons, nearly all of whom were children; and since 1854 it has in like manner rescued and transplanted 21,829. This is God's work. No agency is to-day doing a higher service to mankind; none is doing half so much for the city of New York, where to-day but for it all these thousands would be paupers or criminals

PAUPERISM.

THIS is a city of princes and paupers. Great wealth and extreme poverty are found elbow to elbow almost everywhere from the Battery to Spuyten Duyvel. Here is the stately mansion, there the tumbling tenement. In the one are all the appliances of luxurious ease which money can procure, and in the other only the scantiest necessaries in their rudest forms. In the one is every opportunity to cultivate all the refinements of life; in the other no chance to save even its decencies. In the one, existence is a feather weight scarcely felt; in the other, it is a burden that bends and racks the burdened. Nowhere on the Western continent are there such contrasts as here. No other city can equal our splendor, none exceeds our squalor. Nowhere else does the carriage of the millionaire spatter the gaunt beggar at every hour on every crosswalk. No other human hive can show the counterparts of Fifth avenue and Baxter street. No other city is so deceptive in its physical aspects. The raggedness of our water fronts implies that we are poor indeed, and the massive grandeur of our central plateaus declares that we are rich beyond computation. Both are exaggerations of the actual facts. I believe there are agencies at work in New York which, left unhampered, will sooner or later make one or the other true. I do not pretend to guess which it will be, for I hope the social conditions which render either possible will be exterminated. To that end all facts are wanted. I have shown hitherto how more than half the population of the city is crammed into the deadly tenements. I now deal with a smaller but more helpless and useless class.

In its lowest and most repulsive form our pauperism appears as the station-house "bummer." A creature more degraded, more utterly worthless in human economy, it is impossible to find anywhere on earth. I have been so often in contact with these lazzaroni, learning how irreclaimable they are, how helpless the law is in handling them, that I have ceased to have charity for them. I defy any one to share a night-watch with the sergeants at any police station in the city without having his heart sealed against these bummers. I would wager he would even be mentally inquiring, long before his vigil ended, whether it would not be a kindness to them and the community to pitch them off a pier with stones tied to their necks, as is done with worthless curs. It would be murder doubtless, but you almost feel certain that you would not only have the approval of your conscience, but that any jury knowing merely the surface facts would bring it in justifiable homicide. It is these surface facts which are so distressingly aggravating. On any one of the muggy, chilly nights so common during the fall and winter, the inquirer can see them all by merely standing for an hour or two in the office of any one of the police stations below Fifty-ninth street. There are twenty-four such houses, but perhaps those which can show the most and the worst of the evil are those in Oak and Mercer streets. But at all the houses the bummers are sure to appear with nightfall. While daylight yet lingers you will see them huddling in adjacent doorways. They are ragged, greasy, their faces foul, their hair matted. They look rotten, and have the odor of a damp cellar from which the air has long been excluded. But they have another aspect, and the more sickening stench of the vile liquor of the bucket-shop, which the slums, always felicitous in nomenclature, have called benzine. These creatures are so plainly full of it that no insurance surveyor would even consider a risk on a house which harbors them; they are so full of it that you wonder every minute why they do not explode, and you would not dare light a match near them lest you might be involved in the sudden and general conflagration that would be certain. And you keep your distance for another reason. You see even from a distance that they are infested with all manner of vermin.

If any one believes I have exaggerated, let him go and look for himself. The trouble will not be much, for wherever he may be he will have a police station within ten minutes' walk, and any patrolman will direct him. But when he goes let him do the inspection thoroughly. Wait in the office and see these beasts troop in one after another, demanding "A night's lodging, sur," as if claiming a vested right. After thirty or forty males and a quarter as many females have been told to go back, let him ask the same privilege. It will be readily accorded, and in rear of the main building he will find a smaller one two stories high. The first floor has the cells for prisoners, the second the lodging-rooms for tramps. These are two in number, one being for males, the other for females. Put your nose in the former, and you will be amazed at the suddenness with which you will cast up accounts with your last meal. But do not desist for any such trivial incident as this; look again and see for yourself the degradation and squalor which a Christian city can harbor. The air in the room is thick with foulness; but look steadily and you can drag the horrors from these mists. The room is not more than eighteen feet each way, and at least thirty, sometimes as many as seventy, filthy men are crowded into it for the night. The first comers carefully close every avenue for ventilation, and lie down on the planks, which are the rewards of priority in arrival. Their successors stretch upon the stone floor, or on each other, and, steaming in the foul exhalations from their bodies, sleep till daylight, when they are turned out to tramp the streets till nightfall again. But before they sleep a third of the tramps spend an hour in picking the vermin from themselves and depositing them on their neighbors. A few are even more radical, and having washed their clothes in the water-trough which fills one corner of the room, hang them around the red-hot stove and lay themselves naked on the floor.

In the female room are the same scenes and stenches, mitigated only by the smaller number of occupants. Men and women are alike in these holes in their filthiness, laziness, drunkenness. Both go out at daylight to wander the streets, begging food at basement windows, draining the dregs from the beer kegs set outside the saloons, earning a dollar occasionally by some short job of light work, and invariably spending it in liquor. Both get their ragged raiment by brazen beggary, and both are incapable of the persistent labor necessary to raise them out of their degradation. Neither will work except for an hour when driven to it to obtain a dose of alcoholic stimulant. I have seen it tested so often that I am quite sure of the fact. Philanthropists, who were strangers to the characteristics of the bummers, have often been shocked by their condition, and have made exertions to procure them remunerative employment. Sometimes the bummers have pretended to be eager for the chance, and have promised to appear at an appointed place, but they never kept their promises. More often they have not made even a pretence of desiring employment, but have flatly refused it or made impossible demands as to wages. Time and again I have seen them offered the opportunity of getting out of the vilest of the city slums to become laborers in the rural districts, and I never saw one of them accept the chance. Yet many of them are apparently robust men and women, capable of any amount of physical exertion. Why they do not fall to pieces from mere rottenness it is impossible to conjecture, but they do not. Year after year they appear at the station-house seemingly none the worse. Any old police captain or sergeant can point out several of these bummers whom they knew as such years ago, and who have slept every night in the noxious air of the lodging-rooms, but are to all appearances yet in vigorous health. I never knew of any pestilence seizing them except the relapsing fever, and that killed only a few of them. They are satires upon the hygienic laws which declare foul air to be fatal to life, and personal filthiness to be a repulsive but swift method of suicide. They are evidence in rebuttal of the general belief that vile liquor is poisonous and tends to shorten life. Soaked in filth and rum, they live on year after year, and seem to keep robust on an experience that ought to kill them in a month.

Such creatures as these make up the bulk of the station-house lodgers. The Police Commissioners report 140,000 lodgings granted during the year at the several stations of the city, which is an average of about 5,000 to each station. Some of these, however, such as the Twelfth, Thirtieth, Thirty-first, and Thirty-second, being remote from populous portions of the city, have very few; and some other houses, such as the First, Second, Third, Ninth, Eleventh, Fourteenth, Sixteenth, and Twenty-eighth, have limited accommodations. The 140,000 lodgings were therefore mostly granted in the Fourth, Fifth, Sixth, Seventh, Eighth, Tenth, Thirteenth, Fifteenth, Seventeenth, Eighteenth, Nineteenth, Twentieth, and Twenty-second, some of which during the winter have had as many as 100 per night, and the daily average of several during the entire year has been 35. Of all the lodgers in all the houses a large portion are bummers who sleep always in these places, and are repeated in the records almost every night in the year. Refused admittance in one house because of the frequency of their applications, they go to another, where they have been partially forgotten, and continue going until the officers there also refuse to shelter them any longer. They thus make the rounds of all the houses, but every night can be found in some one of them. Knowledge of this fact robs the figures of the Commissioners of much of their significance, and shows the station-house lodgers to be a much smaller class than these statistics would indicate. The bummers are about 300 in number, and represent 110,000 of the 140,000 lodgings granted. Of the remaining 30,000, four-fifths are represented by a class known as repeaters, from the fact that they repeat their visits several times each, but still do not become such permanent residents as to be classed as bummers. The remaining 6,000 represent the actual casuals, for whom these refuges were designed. None of them are repeaters, and the 6,000 lodgings therefore are equivalent to 6,000 different persons who during a single year found themselves upon some one night utterly homeless and forced to escape the inclemency of the weather by huddling with the bummers and repeaters. It is these unfortunates who are the real sufferers in the station-house lodging-rooms, and the most painful of all its aspects. The detection of the casual in one of these rooms by a visitor is easy and unerring. He will always be found in one of the corners as remote as possible from the mass of filth about him, and an expression of unutterable loathing for his surroundings upon his face. But he can rarely be found at all in the overcrowded rooms of the central stations. In one of these I have seen hundreds of cases where a man decently dressed, and whose extremity was plainly but temporary, has furtively entered the office and asked the sergeant for lodging. He has been shown the way to a horror of which he before had not the slightest conception, but has returned with his guide, and, saying that he cannot stand that, has gone out to walk the cheerless streets during the whole of a bitter night.

Liquor leads the bummer to his degradation, and sometimes reconciles the repeater to his fate, but it has nothing to do with forcing the casual to become a station-house lodger. Almost invariably the casual is entirely sober when he makes his application, and shows no signs of dissipation. He is always decently dressed, and of such cleanly appearance that he is never mistaken for other than he is, although he seldom volunteers any reason for seeking the shelter of the station, and it is never asked in any case. Some, however, drop a word explanatory of their condition, and from these, heard occasionally during some years, it is not difficult to ascertain the sources of this temporary distress. Very many, probably the majority, of the casuals are strangers who come to the city for a day or two, with just money enough to get them home again, but happening to fall among thieves are plucked of every dollar. A sharper or a man of nerve under such circumstances would play a daring game of bluff with the landlord of a first-class hotel; but the casual, being honest and timid, descends to trick and device only to obtain the stamp necessary to carry a letter to his home explaining his condition. Then he wanders the streets until exhausted, and having not even an acquaintance in this vast hive of humanity, which to him is a solitude, he is finally driven to ask a patrolman for advice and is directed to the station-house. Thus he becomes a casual; and if he endures the horrors of a midwinter night in one of the central stations, he is likely to obtain a loathing of the metropolis which lasts his lifetime. But these strangers do not constitute all of the casuals. There is a remorseless freebooter in New York who calls his plunder "rent" and his victims tenants. He has a delusion that he has given an equivalent for his exactions in the occupancy of his house; but as he demands and gets his money in advance of any such occupancy, it is easy to see how very weak is the delusion. If he does not get it, he pounces upon his tenant with a "dispossess warrant," and pitches him with his family and household goods into the street. These victims furnish another considerable portion of the casuals; and wherever you see a whole family of cleanly aspect entering a station to seek lodging, it is not necessary to ask the reason. Another class of casuals are the young men who are suddenly turned out of their boarding-houses for non-payment; and there is no lack, in such a city as this, of such sudden reverses of fortune that a man lodges one night in splendor and the next in a station. Even the repeater may have lately been a man of substance, and such is the elasticity of metropolitan life that he becomes such again. I have known of many cases where a man who has been knocked by a rude blow of fortune into a station lodging has tarried there a few nights, but finally managed to give Fortune as good as she sent, and in a short time was forehanded again. This recuperative power is possessed only by men not broken down by age or disease, and it is abnormally great in the plucky youths who are plentiful in this city. One such two years ago was flat on his back, but by explaining his needs and prospects to a stranger who met him in the station-house managed to borrow $5; with that he started in business again, and in a few days was on his feet, and ever since has staid there. I might multiply such cases indefinitely, not only among men, but women also, for a part of the lodgers of all classes are females. They become such from the same causes as males, but in much smaller numbers, as they did not receive more than a fifth of the lodgings granted last year, and nearly all of these were granted to female bummers, without whom lodgers of their sex would be very few.

There is no one thing in the nether aspect of New York more calculated to excite contempt for the administration of affairs than the fact of these comparatively few male and female bummers gorging the public lodging-rooms year after year, monopolizing the scanty shelter the city has provided and intended for the casual poor. It seems incredible that an enlightened city should foster vagabondage, yet this is precisely what New York is doing and has been doing for years. There would seem to be no great difficulty in weeding out a class that is so small as this, but the policy which has been adopted has both perpetuated and increased it. In other cities which in many ways are less enlightened than New York, these confirmed vagrants, who are found to some extent everywhere, are made more than self-sustaining. In some cities they are set to work cleaning or repairing streets, but the more sensible method of disposing of them is their commitment to farms owned by the corporation, where these incorrigible idlers are compelled to labor to such purpose that they yield a profit to the public treasury. The plan has the further effect that the bummers acquire habits of industry, and when their terms of service expire a large porportion of them wander off into the country and earn their way as farm laborers. In New York nothing of the sort is even attempted. The bummers are allowed to lounge about the streets by day and sleep regularly in the station-houses every night, until some police captain becomes disgusted with the nuisance they create, and, making a sudden foray upon those who happen to be at hand, arrests them as vagrants. They are then arraigned before a police magistrate, who has a peculiar method of disposing of them which he calls committing them to the "care of the Commissioners of Public Charities and Correction." This ought to mean a protracted term in the workhouse, but it really means detention for a few hours either in the prison of the court or in one of the penal establishments in the charge of the Commissioners, after which the bummers are turned out to resume their filthy vagrancy. If New York had a reform farm where these idlers could be compelled to labor, they could be entirely extirpated within six months. Year after year the Police Commissioners, and latterly the Charity Commissioners, have called attention to the inadequacy of the public lodging-rooms at the station-houses, but have not asked for the little legislation which would render them more than sufficient for the demand. On the contrary, there is evidence that the bummers are to be perpetuated in the fact that a large building has just been secured which is to be used exclusively as a lodging-house.

After the station-houses, the cellar lodgings furnish the most repulsive aspect of our pauperism. There is no means of knowing exactly how many persons lodge every night in these holes, where a bed can be had for a few cents. They are the men, women, and children who are met in the streets by day ragged and filthy, and generally endeavoring to gain the means of living by petty traffic, although some of them are professional beggars. The crowding in these dens is somewhat less than in the station-house lodging-rooms, but the atmosphere is equally foul. In some cases actual cellars many feet under ground, and invariably below the surface of the streets, these lodgings have long been one of the greatest dangers to the public health to be found in the city, and have been actively warred upon by the Board of Health. Formerly they were much more numerous and many degrees more filthy than they are at present, when the worst have been closed altogether, and those which remain have been much improved by the rigid enforcement of sanitary regulations. In the old days, prior to the establishment of the Metropolitan Board of Health, when no sanitary control was exercised over these slums, the cellar lodgings were even more of an affront to health and decency than the station-house rooms can ever become. A tour among them now will show how great must have been an evil which it is claimed has been vastly mitigated. Decrepit men and women, whose gray hairs and bent forms tell of years of suffering, are stretched on attenuated bunches of straw stuffed in ragged ticks, and beside them gaunt children who have known no childhood and whose fleshless limbs prove the privations they have endured. Mixed with these are men and women in middle life, wrecked by rum or shiftlessness, stranded at maturity and sure to be public burdens for the remainder of their lives. In the dens thus occupied, and in which the occupants are constantly changing, are engendered the infectious diseases which are constantly threatening the city, and which are prevented from becoming epidemics only by the constant exertions of the Board of Health.

Only a step above these wretched lodgers are the poor who have not yet utterly lost foothold in the world, but manage, by the various devices to which poverty is so accustomed, to pay the pittance necessary to secure them in the possession of some squalid room which they can call home. They are found in the leaking lofts of rear tenements, where pure air cannot come and water can be brought only in driblets. Exposed in these wretched eyries to all the privations of extreme poverty and the moral degradations of tenement life, they comprise nearly all of that army of pauperism known in the administration of the public charities as the "outdoor poor," as they receive relief from the public purse without becoming inmates of an eleemosynary institution. This army during 1870 comprised 5,541 families, in which were 1,986 adult males, 5,354 adult females, and 15,442 children, making a total of 22,782 human beings. Upon these wretched creatures $123,836.85 was expended during the year, and every penny was for the relief of actual suffering. To New York belongs the high credit of being not only a prodigal but a judicious and honest almoner. While the administration of all other departments of municipal affairs has been charged with corruption, the depth of degradation which robs the poor of the money set apart for their relief has not been even approached. And while every dollar has been appropriated to its legitimate use, the most careful research is always had to make sure that every penny is properly expended. In the relief of the outdoor poor this research is exhaustive in every individual case, and there is a positive certainty that every cent has been used for the relief of absolute want. By means of a Board of Visitors, a member of which makes a personal investigation of the condition of every applicant, the whole is learned. No one except a few impostors apply for this relief until extremity has been reached, and no one receives it until it has been passed. These 22,782 persons therefore are not merely the poor wanting some of the comforts of life, they are paupers needing all of its necessities.

It is impossible to portray the terrible scenes of human suffering which the visitors of the Commissioners of Charities are forced to encounter in the discharge of their duties. As the figures show, a male head is found in only about one-third of the families, and where he is found is a bed-ridden man, reduced to a skeleton by disease and want, and only adds to the horrors of the scene; for around him, as he lies stretched on a bundle of straw, are his gaunt wife and children, who in many cases are too weak from want of food to move. Where the father has been carried to a pauper's grave before relief is sought, the scene is scarcely less terrible. There are hundreds of cases where a widow has been found, on days when the mercury was shrinking near zero, huddling with her children around the embers of a few chips which emitted less heat than the flame of a candle. Emaciated by starvation and clothed only in a few thin rags, the utmost exertion and most careful application of restoratives has often been needed to rescue these sufferers from death by freezing. But even without the horrors attendant upon a low temperature, these scenes are sufficiently suggestive of extreme destitution. In the fervent heats of summer these wretched women and children have been found so enfeebled by lack of nourishment that they were helpless in the fetid atmosphere that must soon have brought them the sure relief of death. Both in winter and summer, when there is a male head and when there is none, the surroundings of these families are those of the most abject poverty. They have yet a roof over them, as they have managed by the sale of one after another of their articles of clothing and household goods to pay the rent of one squalid room thus far; but when the visitor reaches them they are sure to be turned out on next rent day, for they have nothing left to sell. After there is absolutely nothing left, families have been found in rooms which did not contain a single article of furniture, and some of the members of which were entirely naked. In other cases there have been a few broken dishes, a skillet, one or two broken chairs, and perhaps a table; but in almost every instance the simplest conveniences of the rudest life were lacking.

This is extreme wretchedness, but extreme as it is and vast as it is the Visitors of the Commissioners do not find all of it, nor hardly the worst of it. In previous articles I have shown that we have half a million of people crammed into the deadly tenements, and that ten thousand children are constantly adrift in the streets. A city of which these startling things can be said must have a vast pauper population. But while its pauperism is its shame, the charity of New York is its glory, and covers a multitude of its sins. The city has one hundred and five private charities fully organized, and constantly engaged in succoring the distressed. Such institutions as the Five Points Mission, the Children's Aid Society, the several orphan asylums, homes for the indigent, and hospitals for the sick, which are mainly supported by private funds, are aggressive charities. They seek suffering instead of waiting for it to seek them, as almoners of public funds must always do, and they find a vast deal more of it. While they do not wait for the last extremity of distress before extending relief, they discover cases of poverty as urgent as any which have been stated, and many only a little less abject, which never come to the knowledge of the public functionaries. In the relief of such destitution as they find, these private charities expend more money annually than is required by the Commissioners of Charities and Correction for all the sick, destitute, and criminals coming into their charge. It is therefore apparent that hardly half the pauperism of the city is a matter of official knowledge, and the gaunt legion of 22,782 starving people is but a fraction of the army of misery which the city can muster. At least 50,000 more must be added to the rolls, and then the exhibit will not contain all the human creatures who during the last year have in this great commercial city been dependent to a greater or less degree upon charity for food, clothing, or shelter. Many of these, it is true, are temporary recruits, and need but little relief to enable them to become again self-sustaining. But the permanent pauper population is much greater than should be found in a community so young and so rich as this. There are scores of buildings scattered through the city, in addition to the receptacles provided by the municipality, which are constantly filled with decrepit or disabled men and women, or with helpless orphans. But for these private charities, which are constantly engaged in clothing the naked, feeding the hungry, and housing the homeless, it is difficult to imagine the condition to which the city would speedily be reduced. Public benevolence is always stinted, never seeks for its objects, and aims only to prevent the reproach of a death from starvation or exposure coming upon the community in whose behalf it is exercised. The public charities of New York are liberal, and as wisely administered as it is possible for a public trust to be managed; but if the city had nothing else to depend upon for the relief of its pauperism, it would speedily be disgraced by a bread riot.

These statements may be considered reckless exaggerations by those who have paid but little attention to this subject. It is possible for an observant man to walk the streets of the city for weeks together and see nothing of this extremity of wretchedness or of the constant and extended efforts made for its relief. Where he meets one genuine mendicant he will encounter five charlatans of pauperism; and nothing is more natural than that, classing all seekers of alms as impostors, he should conclude there is little real distress. The man, however, who being a householder spends his mornings at home, and who is called by his vocation into the streets at late hours of the night, reaches a very different conclusion. During the last summer pauper observations were thus forced upon me, and I estimated probabilities that were appalling even to one who knew something of the real truth. There has been an average of five demands for relief per day at my house since May; and although some of the applicants have called more than once, taken altogether the five applications represent at least half as many different persons. No one of all these claimants was an impostor; no one ever asked for money, and none wanted clothing. In every case it was food that was wanted, and there was no occasion when the broken scraps from the table were not eagerly accepted. Making inquiries among my friends, I found that mine was only the common lot, and I was forced to conclude that, vast as are the charities of New York, they are not equal to the need of them. And so the evidence obtained at my area door has been strengthened by the experience of every night when I have been at late hours in the poorer quarters of the town. Nor do I call as witnesses a single one of the hundreds of importunate beggars who, moth-like, flutter about the flame that consumes them, and, hovering about the doors of bar-rooms, cannot conceal the purpose for which they want the money, which they demand with more of the earnestness of footpads than the shrinking sensitiveness of mendicants. But I do call scores of witnesses from darkened doorways, where they crouch to escape the rigor of the weather and the police. They are sometimes men or women, but oftener children. Coax them out into the glare of a street lamp, and you will see upon them the marks of want in shrunken limbs and gaunt faces, which so competent a judge as Mr. Job Trotter declared could not be got up, like his piety, for an occasion. Take any one of these into the nearest bake-shop, and the reality of the distress you have encountered is painfully evident. In the later summer and early autumn nights there is nothing more sadly suggestive of the bitter poverty prevalent than those of these outcasts who strive to keep the wolf from the door by selling hot corn. Wearied with the fruitless toil of the night, they can be found after midnight sitting on the steps of houses, or, utterly exhausted, stretched out upon the stone steps fast asleep. They are mostly Italians, are all old women or young girls, and among the latter are many of those faces of delicate beauty characteristic of their race. I have not the space to give in detail all the sights and sounds of sorrow in the streets at night; but whoever believes that I have exaggerated the pauperism of the city should see and hear them. I have aimed to give merely a hint of what the observer will find forced upon him almost everywhere in his rambles through the city, as a justification for statements that are sufficiently startling to require evidence to support them.

Another and perhaps more sorrowful phase of human helplessness is found in the public hospitals; and it is equally convincing proof of the fact that New York in her youth is afflicted with the disease of pauperism to an extent normal only to a city in its decrepitude. Bellevue Hospital at the foot of East Twenty-sixth street, and Charity Hospital on Blackwell's Island, which are the two great receptacles for the sick and injured thrown upon the public authorities, last year received 17,190 patients. Of this army of the helpless, many when in health were self-sustaining, but all, with a few exceptions among the victims of street accidents, belonged to the class that is constantly doing uncertain battle with the wolf at the door, so that if disabled even for a day they must receive charity. In this sense they are paupers and to be added to the public burdens. Besides these, the hospitals for contagious diseases received during the year 6,165, and the Bureau for the Relief of Outdoor Sick prescribed for 16,850 persons, who become paupers for the hour by some simple sickness for which they could not provide the means of relief. Grouping now all the poor for a general view of this metropolitan misery, I must add to the list the 4,315 permanent inmates of the public almshouses, which brings the startling total of 66,286 persons dependent during the year upon the public charities. To these must be added at least 50,000 succored by the private agencies, making a grand total of 116,286 human beings who, in the year 1870, in this city of New York, were the recipients of eleemosynary aid. This shows the poverty of the city complete; but to see its poverty, its improvidence, and its crime at a glance, add to the figures given the 40,205 who during the year applied for work at the Labor Bureau of the Commissioners of Charities, and the 71,849 who became inmates of the various prisons and reformatories of the city. Here we are face to face with the fact that 228,330 out of a population of 942,292, or only a small fraction less than one-quarter of the whole population of the city, were dependent during the year, in whole or in part, upon the other three-quarters. It does not detract from the gravity of this exhibit that the greater portion of these figures represent only transient burdens, and that a smaller part of them stand only for idlers, asking the public charity to find them work. Making more than due allowance for all these facts, it is yet undeniable that a fourth of the population, as criminals, paupers, or idlers, were public burdens long enough to become part of these suggestive statistics. Nor is it more encouraging to admit that there has been no material increase in the pauperism of the city during the past six years. There has been no decrease, on the other hand, and the statistics of successive years show only that we are to have the poor always with us.

There is little space left to state the causes of this overgrown pauperism, and it needs little. To my mind two undeniable facts of our social condition are sufficient to account for the whole of it: the existence of one rum shop to every one hundred and twenty-six of the population, and the superabundance of unskilled labor. These are the recruiting-sergeants of poverty and crime, whose success is so marked that it should receive more general attention than has been accorded it. A community that herds half of its population in tenements, that has occasion to thrust almost a ninth into jail each year, that must relieve the distress of an eighth, that has tens of thousands of idlers in its midst, and that harbors such social degradation as is typified by the bummers, has problems before it which cannot be too soon or too carefully considered

PROSTITUTION.

TAKE the lowest type first, and find it in the middle of any night by merely sauntering through Broadway from Grand to Fourteenth street, or again from Twenty-third to Thirtieth street, or in some of the side streets. The type is the night-walker, and gradations of the class are almost as numerous as its representatives. To meet the worst, Greene, Wooster, Houston, Bleecker, or Amity streets must be traversed. There was a time, and it is not long past, when only the Fourth Ward could show the prowling prostitute in her most abject degradation, but it is not necessary now to get lost in the tortuous mazes of the old town, to find the most repulsive phases of female frailty. The Eighth Ward has taken the place of the Fourth, and the stranger need only turn three hundred feet out of Broadway anywhere between Grand and Amity streets, to encounter the most startling evidence of the possibility of total depravity.

To see the worst, stand for the hour before midnight on the corner of Houston and Greene streets. In that time a hundred women apparently will pass, but the close observer will notice that each woman passes the spot on an average of about twice, so that in fact there are not more than fifty of them. This frequency of appearance leads to the supposition that they do not go far, which is the fact. Each set of prostitutes has its metes and bounds laid down by an unwritten code of its own enactment, which is rarely violated. The set now under consideration travels Houston, Bleecker, Wooster, and Greene streets, with occasional forays upon Broadway, which is the common property of all. But these poor fallen creatures rarely go there to put themselves in fruitless competition with more attractive sin. They are poorly dressed, have nothing of beauty in form or face, and are always uncouth or brazenly vulgar in manner. They are miserably poor, herding in garrets or cellars, and are driven by their necessities to accost every stranger they meet with what the silly law of New York calls "Soliciting for the purpose of prostitution." When a woman offers to sell her body to a man she never saw before, for fifty cents, she has fallen low indeed, and this offer will be made at least a dozen times within the hour to any observer at the spot mentioned, whose appearance does not absolutely forbid advances.

Next stand for the same period at Amity and Greene streets. As many women will pass, and in about the same ratio as to reappearances. They are a shade better in appearance as to dress, and some of them have the faint remnants of former personal beauty. They are vulgar yet, but are a vast improvement on the set first seen. All of them will so look at you as to invite advances, but only about one in five will speak first. When they do, it is merely to say "Good evening" or "How are you, my dear," instead of a direct invitation to go home with them, which is the first greeting of the other set. These Amity street women are, as a rule, better housed and fed than the first set, as they live in the houses bordering their tramping-ground, which are all well built and finished. Some of the women have attained to, or more correctly speaking, have not fallen below the prosperity of occupying a room in one of these houses alone, and none of them have more than one female room-mate. Instead of the rough pine furniture of Houston street, the rooms here are given an almost decent appearance by imitation oak, or else are filled up with those strainings for respectable adornments known as "cottage furniture." Another decided proof of better condition is the absence of the cooking stove, for these girls either board with the "Madam" or obtain their food at restaurants. This class, which is thus better housed, better dressed, better behaved, has the middle rank, and contains the majority of all women plying their vocation in the public streets. Although I have mentioned only Amity and Greene streets as a post of observation, it can be seen at many other points, and notably so at Twelfth street and University Place, which latter stately thoroughfare has lately become a chief tramping-ground for abandoned females.

There is yet another grade of these night-walkers, and it can be best seen at Broadway and Washington Place, or Broadway and Twenty-fourth street. But whoever wishes to observe this class must go earlier, as these women have nearly all retired from the tramp by ten o'clock, and can be seen in greatest numbers only between eight and nine in winter or nine and ten in summer. Almost without exception, they seem in the faint light of the streets to be dressed with elegance and taste, to be handsome in feature and form, and to have left in them something of womanly reserve and modesty. True, they are out in the streets at unseemly hours without male escort, but walking quickly as they do, without looking to the right or the left, the unpractised observer doubts that they belong to the *demi-monde*, and charitably supposes that they have been compelled to leave the shelter of their homes by sudden sickness in the family or by some equally urgent necessity. If the stranger is bold enough to accost one of them, he is even less sure than before of her character. She does not exactly repel his advances, but she does not invite them, and is sufficiently adroit to assume a maidenly reserve that perplexes while it allures him. She will not stop to talk with him, but if he walks beside her she will converse on ordinary topics and use language to which no exceptions can be taken. There is nothing essentially vulgar, much less indelicate, about her words, demeanor, or appearance, and by the time a novice has walked a block in her company he is in a tremor of apprehension that he has committed the grave indiscretion of speaking to a lady who happened to be unprotected, and who is luring him on to be cowhided by her brother or husband. If she succeeds in getting him to her home he finds it a house of respectable exterior and furnished within with some pretensions to elegance. As there was nothing indecent about the woman herself, so there is nothing bawdyish about her home. The pictures which adorn the walls are not, as in houses of a lower grade, suggestive of the vile lives of the inmates; the furniture is handsome and of a kind to give an impression of a quiet, reputable life. Under such circumstances as these the chances are that the stranger has been lured to the lair of a "badger" and is about to undergo the operation known as the panel game.

As this species of robbery must be described somewhere in this volume, I may as well pause here and have done with the disagreeable task. No kind of theft is so commonly practised, none yields such large returns, nor is any so safe to the spoilers as this. Formerly it was achieved by a contrivance by which it gained its name, but latterly it has been much more simple in its operation, as a consequence of its more general use. When thieving by prostitutes first became a distinct branch of criminal art, it was done only by mechanism specially prepared for the purpose. A whole house, or at least a floor of a house was hired, and one room was prepared with a secret door called a "panel," which could not be seen by even the closest scrutiny of the walls, and which, opening into another room, gave easy access to the "badger," as the male confederate of the prostitute is called. When the woman had lured a stranger to this room she always created a sense of safety in his mind by an ostentatious locking of all doors. She was always troubled with a modest reserve, and would proceed no further until the lights had been extinguished, and the victim rarely objected to a proceeding so manifestly proper. When the proper time arrived, of which he could easily judge, the "badger" stole into the room through the secret door, which opened without making the slightest noise, and having rifled the clothes of the stranger, which had been placed upon a chair, of all they contained, crept back to his hiding-place and closed the panel behind him, without having betrayed his presence by the faintest sound. Having succeeded in effecting the robbery, it was a matter of entire indifference to both the badger and his confederate when it was discovered. If the victim found his pockets empty before leaving the room, he might make as much outcry as he chose, as it would avail nothing; he had seen all the doors locked, he was sure no one but the woman and himself had been in the room, and she, while indignantly denying that he been robbed there, was extremely anxious that her innocence should be thoroughly established by a strict search of the room, where, as she well knew, none of the valuables would be found. Sometimes this was done, but more frequently the victim said nothing whatever about his loss, either before or after he had parted with his frail companion. His mouth was closed by the disreputable circumstances attending the robbery, as he was usually a married man, and always one who would submit to any loss rather than compromise his character by admitting that he had been in such company.

This was the original panel game, but it has long been utterly obsolete, and in its place devices have been adopted which are equally effective and have the added advantage that they can be used in rooms which have not been specially prepared for the purpose. The most common of these devices is transparent enough, but it is none the less successful for that reason. As has been hinted, the first-class panel women are the most elegant in appearance and coy in demeanor of all who are found on the street, and they are, moreover, capable of selecting the proper kind of victim. They are rarely deceived in their choice, so that the men who are picked up by them in the streets are almost invariably married, of good repute, and with money about them. A man of this kind falling in with one of these women, and accompanying her to her home, will sacrifice anything to keep all knowledge of the fact from his family and friends. Hence he is nervous, and an easy prey of the thieves from the beginning of the adventure. When a knock is heard at the door the moment it has been locked behind him and his companion, he is startled; when the woman simulates the greatest terror and declares the knocker to be her husband or lover, as she may happen to select, he is really terror-stricken, and so rushes about looking for a way to escape as to give her an excuse to put her arms about him to keep him still, while she begs him for his life's sake not to make any noise. At this moment the robbery is committed by the woman herself, and such is the condition of the victim that she is rarely detected in the operation, although she generally relieves him not only of his wallet, but of his watch, and any other valuables he may have about him. All this time the knocking has been getting more peremptory, and at last she thrusts the visitor under the bed or into a closet, and opens the door. Explanations ensue between her and the knocker, which tend to convince the victim of his narrow escape from death at the hands of a jealous rival, after which the two go off together, leaving the door open and their victim to go away when his fancy may dictate. With some variations in its details this is the way in which the panel game is now worked, and it is made to yield a princely revenue to the operators.

But the wretched girls by whom it is done get only a small fraction of its products. The "badger" always takes the valuables from her the moment the robbery is accomplished and only returns her so much as may happen to seem just to him; and there is one noted scoundrel in the city known as the "King Badger," of whom it is known that he pays several girls a regular salary to "work the panel" in his interest, but makes no division whatever of their spoils with them. He furnishes them, however, with their rooms and clothing, which his own interests require to be of the best quality, so that none of the unfortunates of the streets are so well housed or so elegantly dressed as those who are in his pay, and none are so little coarse in language and demeanor. But all the thievery brings no addition to their fortune, as all these female panel thieves, whether in the pay of the King Badger or not, are in their turn remorselessly robbed by their male confederates. The chief excuse put forward by the latter for taking all the spoils, is that they must give a large proportion of it to the police captains to purchase immunity. However false this may be, I know that the women really believe it, and talking among themselves, freely mention the amount which each panel-house pays the police, which is never, according to their belief, less than fifty dollars per week, but in some cases is treble that sum. I have no proof except the assertions of thieves that these are facts, nor can any other be obtained; and I do not therefore assert them to be facts, and it is urged in behalf of the police that if they were to try their utmost they could not extirpate a system of robbery which exists chiefly because not one in a hundred of its victims can be induced to make a complaint against the thieves, much less to prosecute them. The excuse is plausible, for I can remember only one case where a man prized his money so much above his reputation as to press the charge against his despoilers to a conviction, and he was ruined by it. The revelations of the trial caused him to be deserted by his family, expelled from his church, and compelled him to leave the town where he had established a prosperous business. His experience is not likely to produce imitators, and where such results await complainants I am loath to believe that the badgers are such fools as to surrender any considerable amount of their spoils to police captains, who are impotent to do more than annoy them. But it is also true that the captains can so harass them as to make it a good investment to give them a very small interest in the robberies, which the sums mentioned represent. While the proof necessary to a conviction can very rarely be obtained against any panel house, there is always enough of suspicion against all of them to excuse their seizure; nor can the "badgers," who are everywhere held to be outlaws, ever appeal to the law or to public sentiment to protect them from these arrests. It may therefore be that they purchase toleration rather than be subjected to the annoyance and loss of constant moving from house to house, or of having a policeman constantly in front of their premises to warn all strangers about to enter, of its character. While I more than suspect that this has been done in many cases, I can assert nothing positive as to the division of the products of the panel game, except that the outcast women, who are its chief operators, find only a beggarly fraction falls to their share. In the aggregate these products must be very large, as the comparatively few cases which are heard of amount to tens of thousands of dollars per annum. And all of this property is irrevocably lost, for it consists of money and jewels which can never be identified, even if recovered from the thieves, which barely happens.

This phase of New York prostitution is sufficiently important to justify the space which has been devoted to it, but it is not that which is most prominent to the philanthropist or to casual observers in the public streets. In all the great cities of the United States, so far as my personal observation extends—and I have been in all of them—the walking of the streets after nightfall by prostitutes has become an alarming evil; but New York is entitled, I am afraid, to preëminence in this respect. Not only is the city first in the number of its street-walkers, but nowhere else has the class become so degraded. I have hinted something of the profanity and obscenity of the women who can be found after midnight in any of the side streets, but it is not possible to describe in detail the scenes which will be forced upon the observer any night in Houston, Bleecker, Amity, and Fourth streets, as well as in the lower Bowery, Chatham street, and some other east-side thoroughfares. Singly, in couples, or groups, these girls, many of whom are mere children and very few of whom have scarcely passed maturity, plunge along the sidewalks, accosting every man they meet, or, stopping at the street corners, annoy all passers until they are driven away by the police. Many of them are under the influence of liquor, and not a night passes but some of these degraded creatures are carried into the station-houses helplessly or furiously drunk. Until within the past two years I never saw any of these women drinking in public bar-rooms, but now it has become so common that it has ceased to be remarked; it is true there are few of the saloons which will serve them, but there is always one on each route of the tramps which will sell to any one, and here these poor painted wrecks of womanhood can be seen standing at the bar, drinking vile liquors until they have won the beatitude of stupefaction, or until they reel out into the streets indecently drunk. If the unconsciousnes of inebriety is ever a blessing, it is such in the case of these lost women, as it permits them for the time to forget what they are and must be always. Often suffering for the necessaries of life, burdened almost without exception with "lovers" who despoil them of the pittance they receive for moral and physical death, harassed by the police, shunned by their more prosperous sisters in sin, corroded morally and physically with the leprosy of their vice, no class needs so much of pity, none has less of it, and none is so little aware that it needs commiseration. Calloused by crime which is unnatural and bestializing, the street-walkers have forgotten that they were ever undefiled and lost all desire to be other than they are. Numbering about two thousand, constantly infesting the public thoroughfares, inoculated and inoculating with loathsome diseases, they are the great danger and shame of civilization found in all cities, but here more numerous more dangerous and more shameful than anywhere else on the continent.

It has not been from any wish to pander to a morbid desire for the repulsive that I have set this type of prostitution in the foreground, Palpable facts cannot be ignored, and a vice that is thus obtruded upon every passer through the public streets cannot be too soon or too fully described; but having presented the facts in such plain terms that they cannot be misunderstood, I gladly take leave of this lowest type of metropolitan prostitution. It is hardly more agreeable to speak of the next grade, which is found in the lowest of what are known as "parlor houses." The chief difference between the inmates and the street-walkers is that the former do not cruise the streets to entice strangers to their dens. If this is a comparative virtue it is the only one these women can boast, as they are fully as bestial in every other respect as their sisters of the pave. The houses in which they live and ply their infamous vocation are always unmistakable even to the novice. In Greene and Wooster streets several blocks are almost wholly taken up by such houses, but others but little less open and degraded can be found in many other quarters of the city. In many of these houses there is a public bar; in all of them the orgies are indecent to such a degree that they cannot be described. Next above these dens are houses a shade more sufferable, which attempt to hide their infamy behind cigar stores or some other kind of shop, and are filled with women who do not shock at the first glance. Above these again are houses which really have parlors, and in which the women make a pretence to decency in their demeanor while in public. After these come the grand saloons where the evil is painted in the most alluring colors. The houses are of the largest and stateliest, the furniture the most elegant, the inmates beautiful, accomplished, captivating in dress and manner, who, with woman's only priceless jewel, would adorn any circle. It is difficult to persuade one who has no personal knowledge of the matter, that, taken into the parlors of one of these houses and meeting the inmates without a previous intimation of the character of the place, he would believe himself in a pure, refined home. Yet such is the fact. Such houses as these can be found in every desirable neighborhood, and no man can be sure that he has not one of the sepulchres next door.

But the vice has taken in New York a more insidious if less alluring form than this. For some years past a most deplorable change has been going on which has had the effect of greatly decreasing the number of parlor houses, while houses of assignation have multiplied in the same ratio. The effect has been to intrude prostitution into circles and places where its presence is never suspected. Hundreds of houses are thus defiled, and the corroding vice creeps into families of every social grade. Women of high position and culture, no less than the unlettered shop girls, resort to the houses of assignation, which are of every grade, from the palaces in the most aristocratic quarters of the city to the frowsy rooms in the slums. Many of the frequenters of these houses are married women, who are driven by an insane desire for display to thus add to a scanty income; others are young girls led astray by faulty education, and yet others are driven by starvation to sell their virtue to any casual buyer. Many of these cases have come to the knowledge of the police, and there is nothing which pleads so strongly against the flagrant injustice which has closed the doors of productive industry against women, as the fact that when forced to fall back upon their own resources, so many of them have been compelled to choose between prostitution and destitution. But for this fact the chief evil of the age could not have become so prevalent as it is. Woman is naturally chaste, and if those who have fallen can be induced to tell the cause, it will be found that at least six in every ten are forced by sheer necessity to become confirmed prostitutes. I do not mean to say that they will plead this as the cause of the first lapse from virtue, as nine cases out of ten of them will charge that to their betrayal by men whom they loved. But after that first lapse, and after their desertion by these men, they claim they had no choice between their way of life and death from starvation. The story is told by types of every class of prostitutes, from the adroit adventuress who lays her snares in the great hotels, to the poor drunken creature who tramps the streets, and there is so little variation that one will answer for all; that one was told a few nights ago at a station-house desk by a young girl of rare beauty, who had been taken from a house which had been seized by the police. Having given her name, age, and birth-place, she was asked the usual question as to her occupation, and answered, "I am what men have made me." Then she went on speaking rapidly, as if to have her revenge upon society before her resolution failed her:

"Sir, only a year ago I was a happy innocent girl in my father's house in a town near this city. I had a lover everybody thought an honorable man, and we were engaged to be married. I adored him, father trusted him, all my friends envied me because of him. Well, I was weak, he was mean, and he betrayed me. After that he deserted me; the consequences of my sin after a time could not be hidden. Then my father cast me off, and all who had ever known me shunned me. In that town, sir, there was no human being who would shelter me or give me a crust; but *he*, mind you, was received among them all just as before, except father. Of course I had to starve or come here. I hadn't nerve enough to kill myself, so I went to the house where you found me to-night. That's a "disorderly house" you say—perhaps it is—I know it's vile enough, but ain't the men you found in it as bad as the women? You don't seem to think so, for you've let the men go and we women are to be locked up. I'm young yet, sir, but I'm old enough to have found out that all the sin and shame of this thing falls on us; the men get none of it, yet they cause the whole of it."

With some variations in immaterial details, I have heard this story so often, and from women of every type, that I am convinced that they believe it to be the cause of all the prostitution with which we are cursed. There is the corroborative fact that the majority of all the public prostitutes in the city are from the country, and drift hither from the towns and villages within two hundred miles, when they enter upon their career of open shame. Many are from the New England States, as many from New York State, a few from the other Middle and the Western States, and the others are produced by the city itself, and, as they claim, by like causes. From all I have seen of the vice I am constrained to believe that the perfidy of men is chargeable with the greater part of it, and of nearly all of that which is most open and bestial. There is enough in the mental and moral characteristics of these weak, thoughtless, hapless women to sustain the indictments which they present against their betrayers. All prostitution cannot of course be thus explained, for there are women who have deliberately chosen it, as there are others who have been led astray by love of dress and other equally unworthy motives. For the first there should only be boundless pity, for the others only measureless scorn.

From the commencement of this chapter I have written under manifold difficulties. I have striven to present only general facts and to present them so that the full measure of the shame of the metropolis in this respect can be seen, without rudely shocking the false modesty which is so prevalent. Of the dangers which threaten us from this cause it is hardly necessary to speak in a work of this character, as they are the same here as in other cities and not much greater here than elsewhere in proportion to numbers, unless it is in the corrupting influence of vice upon the domestic life. It may be that here the evil in its covert form is more general in its ramifications through all circles of society, and is thus corroding where its presence is not suspected. I believe such to be the case, and if it is, the moral stamina of the community is being undermined, and it is impossible to imagine what will be the debasement it will entail upon the next generation. It is a terrible state of affairs when the chastity of men is hooted at as an absurdity, and the virtue of women seeming to be virtuous is suspected; yet such is the condition of New York. That such things can be asserted and believed is in itself a proof of a profligacy that has become ominous; that houses of assignation into which women can steal from reputable homes have gradually replaced the houses of prostitution, is a startling evidence that there is too much foundation for these assertions and this belief. As I look upon it in the light of many facts which are of such character that they cannot be hinted at, much less mentioned, the chief danger that threatens the city from the social evil does not come from the street-walkers, nor the inmates of public houses of prostitution. These are women known to be unchaste, who are without home ties and without influence except to a very limited extent. On the contrary, those women who are unsuspected prostitutes occupy and defile the holiest positions of domestic life, and there is no limit to the evil which their crime produces. And this form of the plague is more deplorable because it is one which no law can cure, although it might be mitigated to some extent by statutory remedies.

But as yet there has been no attempt to apply any remedy to any form of this vice. Chiefly because of a senseless delicacy the subject has not been sufficiently agitated to compel the Legislature to attend to it, and the consequence has been that prostitution has gone on unchecked until it threatens to ulcerate the whole body politic. What little demand has been made for putting it under legal restraints, has been for such expedients as have been adopted in some European cities with a view to ameliorate the physical consequences of debauchery, and has been met by the Pecksniffian objection that such laws are viler than the vice they regulate. These cavillers declare that every man should be compelled to take the possible consequences of his sin, and that to lessen the chances of these consequences occurring is to increase rather than diminish the evil. It is useless to tell them that prostitution has always existed and always will in every segregation of mankind, and there is little sense in attempting to ignore a thing that every one knows to exist. Yet it has been ignored by the law-makers of New York, with the exception that they have declared that it shall be "unlawful to solicit men on the public streets for the purposes of prostitution." No Legislature has, however, ever been induced to enact that all houses of prostitution or assignation shall be licensed and a register kept of the inmates and frequenters, although it is evident such a law would materially decrease both the number of houses and of prostitutes. There is nothing so certain as that New York must do something to check this evil, if it does not desire to be known the world over as a marvel of lechery within the next twenty years, and it is as sure that while statutory restrictions may assist to that end they cannot alone accomplish it. The moral character of this people needs to be rebuilt from the foundation. Public writers and speakers must make unceasing warfare upon this form of iniquity until unchastity in males as well as females is once more an outrage upon the social code. The truth as to the facts must be plainly told, and no prudish delicacy must be allowed to prevent the adoption, much less the suggestion of the needed remedies. I may be all wrong, but I have always had a fancy that when profligate men are socially outlawed, a great deal will have been done to exterminate profligate women. It would not, as nothing else will, exterminate prostitution, but it will do more to mitigate it than anything else.

The full measure of our danger from prostitution cannot be seen from the meagre statistics on the subject which are attainable. A census of all public prostitutes is taken each year by the police, and the last enumeration shows 351 houses of prostitution with 1,223 inmates, and 113 houses of assignation. Two years before there were over 600 of these houses, and when some one complained to Mr. John A. Kennedy during the last of the ten years that he worthily filled the office of Superintendent of Police, that this was too small an exhibit to be a true one, he answered that if all these houses were together they would line both sides of Broadway from the Battery to Houston street, and he thought New York ought not to have more than three miles of houses of ill-fame. That is true, but there is vastly more of prostitution than these figures show, for the reason that they do not give any of that covert class to which I have alluded. This class to a large extent are domiciled in tenement houses where two women live together occupying a suite of rooms; but there are others who belong to a higher social grade and living unsuspected as members of respectable families are frequent visitors to houses of assignation. It is evident that none of these get into the police statistics. The full measure of our shame exceeds this showing as to the number of women who sell their virtue in the open market, at least three times, and to a far larger extent as to those who go astray from less sordid but equally unworthy motives. What we must acknowledge we have of the vice is enough to move us as a community from our apathy regarding it; what we have good reason to dread that we have is enough to startle a people more debauched and debased than we have yet become.

ABORTIONISTS.

ON that night in August, 1871, when the "trunk mystery" was fully solved through the exertions of Inspector Walling by the arrest of Rosenzweig, alias "Dr. Ascher," a party was assembled in front of Police Headquarters discussing the matter of abortions, which was then uppermost in all minds. The intense stupidity of Rosenzweig in packing the body of his victim as he did, so that discovery was inevitable, being mentioned, one of those present who had long been suspected of being an abortionist blurted out:

"Why didn't the cursed fool pack it in charcoal, I always do!" Seeing in an instant, however, how his remark could be construed, he added:

"You know, of course, I mean when I ship subjects."

But his auditors smiled; and one was bold enough to hint, under cover of playful railery, that perhaps the "doctor" had told the truth, unwittingly, not only of himself but of his fraternity.

There was something horrible in this suggestion of human bodies packed like carrion in trunks or barrels and shipped on railroads, yet the revelations of the Bowlsby case had shown that it could be done, and the thoughtless remark of the quack raised the presumption that it was of frequent occurrence. While there are many phases of nether life more sensational because more open to the public view, there is none more sickening than the work of the abortionists, who ply their infamous trade to a far greater extent than is believed by those who have not studied the matter.

These wretches seem to never lack patrons, and secure them chiefly from three classes of females. The one which is smallest in numbers, and perhaps the worst morally, is composed of married women, who commit a crime to avoid the first duty of marriage. This crime is daily becoming of more frequent occurrence, and the desire to commit it is so intense and wide-spread that reputable physicians are often importuned to abet it, and when refusing, as they invariably do, they are often beseeched to direct the inquirers to some one more pliable. The causes of the steady increase of this offence among married women are found chiefly in the hollowness of their lives. They are too intent upon frivolities of social life to spare the time necessary for the bearing and rearing of children, and are eager to sacrifice a newly-quickened life to avoid any interruption of their giddy pleasures. There are a few of these women, however, who seek the aid of these monsters, who are actuated by less unholy motives. With some of them it is a hard choice between their own life and that of the babes, as they are unable for physical reasons to bear the pangs of maternity, and others are conscientious in the belief that they have no right to bring human beings into the world whom they cannot support properly; and therefore when such number of children have been born as they think they can provide for, they crush all future germs of life as a matter of duty. The lax morality of the day has greatly increased this class, and any observer can see for himself how frequent must be this or some similar outrage upon nature, by merely noting how few of the couples of his acquaintance married during the last ten years have more than three children, and how many of them have only one. I am supposing these observations to be made among the middle or upper classes and I feel certain that the result will be that, taking couples married five years, six out of ten will have only one child. There is a villanous notion abroad that few children is a mark of aristocracy, and nothing which cannot be proved is so certain as that the innocents are slaughtered by the thousands every year, that parents may seem to have the impotency of long established wealth. I am speaking of a thing which any reader can put to proof by merely looking about and drawing inferences which are unavoidable. Take a husband and wife who are each one of a brood of eight or a dozen, and both of whom are young and in vigorous health; if after a half dozen years of married life they have but one child, what must you think? As there are thousands of such cases, is it necessary to wonder that the trade of the abortionists has increased so alarmingly of late years?

But the prevailing profligacy of the age is perhaps best shown by the fact that the majority of the patrons of these rascals are unmarried women who move in respectable society. This is a fact of which I am sure if the abortionists themselves can be believed, and there are occasionally cases which so drag the terrible business out into public view, as to convince the most skeptical that these vile practitioners do speak the truth. The most startling of all these instances was that of Alice A. Bowlsby, which became the celebrated crime of 1871, as the Nathan murder had been that of the previous year. This young girl had always moved in the most reputable circles, and had never been suspected, even by her most intimate friends, of any impropriety. Yet she was forced, in order to be rid of the consequences of her transgressions, to resort to the man in whose hands she died. Up to the moment when the identity of the corpse found in the trunk at the Hudson River Railroad dépôt was established, there was no young woman of fairer reputation; but the revelations following her death rolled away the closing stone from a whited sepulchre, so that all the world looked in upon a mass of corruption. Close upon this case came another, less startling in its tragical features, but showing the same profligacy, and the two unloosed tongues that could tell horrible tales. The consequence was that more was learned in a week of the secrets of the abortionists than had ever been known before. It was found that unmarried women of every social rank went in such numbers to these medical adventurers, that all who advertised their business had new patients constantly making applications for relief, making a frightful total per annum, the majority of whom were unmarried. The whole of this immorality could not be charged to the metropolis, as the abortionists declare one half of their patrons to be unmistakably residents of the country or of rural towns, and of those coming from the city many were girls working in shops or factories, but many were also young women from what are called the first circles of society. All of these women in their homes and among their associates were of good repute, and it was plain that women no less than men live lies. The poison of this immorality has entered every grade of life, and the same abortionist who chuckled over the huge fee he had received from a young woman of fashion, laughed immoderately at the fact that a wretched creature whom he called a "nigger wench," had applied to him for professional attendance. And while it is true that nearly all the patrons of these quacks come from the ranks of reputable society, many prostitutes also ask their aid. These women consider it no offence whatever, and resort to these unnatural means to avoid child-bearing without the least hesitation or compunction. Some of them have done it so often that they have learned the art themselves, and swindle the abortionists by practising it upon themselves. It is difficult to blame them, even upon moral grounds, when it is remembered what sort of parentage and tutelage their children must have; there is no sight in all of metropolitan shame and crime so sad as that of young children inmates of brothels, and one is almost forced to feel thankful for the crime that makes it of such rare occurrence.

There is extreme difficulty in telling how all these women fare after they get into the dens of the abortionists, as the subject is one of which the whole truth cannot be told without again shocking that mock modesty to which I referred in the last chapter. Several of these pretended abortionists, however, are nothing worse than unconscionable swindlers, who profess to commit a crime that they have neither the intention nor ability to perpetrate. The worst of these is a fellow to whom large numbers of women resort, from whom he takes fees, but no one of whom has he ever relieved or even attempted to relieve. If you call this fellow an abortionist he is down upon you with great vigor as a liar, and proceeds to vindicate himself by proofs that he is only an exceedingly mean thief. When a woman comes to him to arrest the course of nature, he demands his fee, receives it, professes to be ready and willing to do all that is required of him, and proceeds to beguile her with bread pills or some other equally innocuous deception; when she returns after a time to demonstrate the inefficacy of his remedy, he declares the case one of unusual difficulty, demands another fee, which he gets, and then sends her away with something equally harmless. She comes, of course, a third time, when he boldly asks her if she takes him for a murderer, frankly avows the cheat he has practised, and sneeringly asks her what she is going to do about it. She can do nothing. She does nothing, and he knew perfectly well in the outset that her mouth never could be opened to accuse him of the fraud. This confidence game he has played over and over again during the past few years, and is yet engaged in it, to his own great profit and the unutterable anguish of hundreds of women. I have spoken of this one man only because he is the breeziest rascal of the gang, but he is not without imitators, for there are ten or twelve of the professed abortionists who are only swindlers. In fact there are only three who are really what they claim to be, and will unhesitatingly perform an operation on which two human lives depend, without the least hesitation and with as little qualification for the task. One of them is an ex-cobbler, another kept a lager-bier saloon, and one was for a few days porter for a physician, but neither of them has the slightest knowledge of surgery or anatomy, and all of them are ignorant in fact of everything but the vile arts of knavery. To them the other abortionists who advertise to "relieve ladies without danger or chance of publicity," send their patients to be operated upon, and divide with them the spoils. Of these last there are less than a dozen, making the total of professed abortionists in the city less than twenty, and in making this statement I am fully aware that two hundred has been mentioned in the public prints not only as the probable number, but once with such positiveness as to seem that it was the result of an actual count.

While my number seems small in comparison with the mischief done, I yet have enough of these vultures to do all the preying upon human life and morality which I have charged to their account. Each has hundreds of patients, and it is fortunate for life that so many of them lack the nerve to execute as they promise. If this were not so the community would soon cease to be startled with such affairs as the Bowlsby case, because of their frequency. As it is, women are wasted away by noxious drugs into premature graves, but their exit from the world is commonplace, and does not attract attention to them or to their slayers. Much has been said of the low standard of physical health among American women in cities, and it has been charged to faults of dress and habits of life, to which it is mostly due, but of late years the advertisements of these abortionists of "Portuguese Female Pills," "Infallible French Pills," and other nostrums which "will remove any obstruction with perfect safety and certainty," have had a vast deal to do with undermining the health of women. Many of these "remedies" are in the highest degree hurtful to the human organism, and all of them are certain sooner or later to make a physical wreck of those who use them. Yet thousands who would shrink in horror from a personal visit to an abortionist, send for these "remedies," and use them, and it is because of this fact that these professed abortionists are so dangerous although so few in number. Picking up the last number of a journal which they patronize, I casually light upon the advertisements of Madam Restell, Fifty-second street and Fifth avenue; H. D. Grindle, 120 West Twentieth street; Dr. Bott, 60 Bond street; Dr. Franklin (late of Prussia), 161 Bleecker street; and a rural rascal who calls himself C. H. Chester, M. D,, Lock Box 4, Reading, Pa., who advertises "an entirely harmless preparation, which may be applied by any female, and will remove any disorder in four hours." He is no worse, however, although more verbose than the others, none of whom are so vague in the declarations that their purposes can be mistaken. Those mentioned, although all who happened to make announcements of their hideous trade in the number of the journal I consulted, are by no means all who advertise. There appears to be more of them than there really is, because of the fact that some of them advertise under several different names, no one of which is the real one. Take as examples "Dr." Franklin, whose real name is Jacoby, the man Rosenzweig, who now, happily for mankind, is in Auburn prison, whose professional title was "Dr." Ascher, and Thomas Lookup who is keeping Rosenzweig company, and who was most known in his trade—I cannot call it profession—as "Dr." Evans.

In order that I may show how few in fact are the abortionists who profess to be such, while many of them are not, I mention in addition to those named all who advertise. Foremost among them is Dr. Mauriceau, now or lately of 129 Liberty street, who is the proprietor of the infamous Portuguese Female Pills, and whose real name is said to be Loman; Dr. Selden, 241 Bleecker street, who proclaims himself the best physician for ladies in trouble, and adds "that thousands are relieved without accident;" Mme. Van Buskirk, whose real name is Gifford, noted as one of the boldest and worst of her tribe, and whose den in St. Mark's Place, has long been known as one of the most infamous places in the metropolis; Mme. Maxwell, a pupil of Van Buskirk, publicly declares that she does not humbug ladies with medicine, and Mme. Worcester, another of these pupils, has or had a den in Charles street for the reception of the victims of all the operators. All of these people have become reckless by long immunity, and notwithstanding the fact that during the year 1871 Wolf, Lookup, Rosenzweig, and Mme. Burns, were convicted of the crime of abortion and sent to State Prison, they yet continue to advertise their business, and what is worse, to do it. There is little circumspection needed in making the first advances to any of them. If a woman enters and inquires as to their ability and willingness to remove a physical difficulty, they are instantly assured of both with great volubility and distinctness. In nearly all cases the offices of these practitioners are easily accessible to the public and are well appointed. Their incomes are sufficiently large to justify them in surrounding themselves with some of the luxuries of life. The house of Mme. Restell, which is in the midst of the most aristocratic quarter of the city, is one of the most imposing of that quarter, and is furnished with great splendor.

The house of Rosenzweig when he was seized by the police was comfortably appointed; and when Mrs. Burns was sought by the officers of the law she was found in her costly country mansion on Long Island, entertaining a company of friends who had no suspicion of her real character. On the other hand, the den of Lookup in Chatham street when it was taken possession of by the police, was found to be one of the foulest in the city; but it was soon discovered that its condition was a matter of choice rather than necessity. He had a splendid farm worth $100,000 on Long Island, and his receipts had been so large that he had expended $1,000 per week in advertising under his several aliases of "Old Dr. Ward," "Dr. Elliott," "Dr. Thompson," "Dr. Powers," and "Dr. Evans."

Generally those of these people who really do what they profess, have two places, as Rosenzweig, who lived in Second Avenue had his office in Amity Place, as the upper block of Laurens streets, now dignified as South Fifth Avenue, was called. In the office the operation is performed, and the victim is then sent to another place to await the consummation, which is generally some house that several use in common for that purpose; but Rosenzweig appears to have used his private residence as his hospital, for he sent Alice Bowlsby there to die, and by her death to rouse the community momentarily to a sense of the horrors in its midst. But, by better luck or because of greater skill in making away with the bodies, such cases rarely happen. I have often wondered what the abortionists do with their adult dead, for these butchers must have many every year, and being unable to obtain burial permits they must get rid of them clandestinely in some way. Some of them may be shipped to confederates in other cities as freight, some may be taken beyond the city limits in boxes or barrels and buried at night in the fields, and other may be put under ground in tho cellars or yards of the houses where they die. Certainly the large number of young women who every year are "missing" and of whom no trace is ever afterward found, combined with the proved practices of the abortionists, is enough to suggest the most frightful possibilities. What these monsters do with their infant victims is not matter of conjecture, for it is perfectly well known that the slaughtered innocents are buried in the yards or cellars, or, carried out wrapped in an old piece of cloth, are cast into the rivers or dropped in the streets; there is not a day that the finding of the bodies of still-born children is not reported to Police Headquarters, and they are always found under such circumstances as to make the detection of their murderers impossible. Many bodies of course are never found at all, and those which are picked up are useless to fully unveil the horrors which they prove must exist in the midst of this great centre of modern civilization which nurtures a worse than Herod.

Another, and in comparison with those which have been treated, a pleasanter phase of the abortion business, is presented in such advertisements as that of Madam Grindle, who has openly notified the world that she has "pleasant rooms for nursing," by which she means that she has an asylum for outlawed motherhood and for children who come unhallowed into life. A visit to the establishment of Madam Grindle showed it to be of large capacity and elegant appointments, in which women about to become mothers under such circumstances that they dared not for their reputation's sake let the fact become known, could be treated during the crisis, and that over, after paying a large bill, could go their ways and leave their offspring behind them to be "adopted out" by the Madam, or to take such other pot-luck with the world as might befall them. It is something to the credit of us all that the women who resort to such places as this, of which there are several in the city, do not seek to have their children murdered outright—not much certainly, but still it is something to be put to the credit of poor, frail human nature, and counted for what it is worth. This Madam Grindle is reported to have lately said to a reporter who pretended to seek her services: "We have had hundreds of them. Poor unfortunate women! How little the world knows how to appreciate their trials! We think it our mission to take them and save them—a noble work it is, too. But for some friendly hand like ours, how many, many blasted homes, scandalized churches, and disorganized social circles there would be. Why, my dear friends, you have no idea of the class of people that come to us. We have had all sorts of politicians bring some of the first women in the land here. Many, very many aristocratic married women come here, or we attend them in private houses." "What are your charges, Madam?" "Three hundred dollars cover all expenses, and we see the patient through—unless it occupies more than a week. Then we charge an extra medical fee and board money." "What about the child?" "Well, we adopt it out in good hands. One hundred dollars extra is our fee for that."

Whether this be a correct version of the interview or not is immaterial, as this woman, or some one else engaged in like business, has often enough said something substantially the same. And there can be no doubt that very much of what all these traffickers in life and virtue promise, is never performed. In some cases, doubtless, the infants are adopted out, but even in such cases no care whatever is taken to procure them proper homes. The great anxiety is to get rid of them, and latterly it has become the custom to throw them into the receiving basket of the Foundling Asylum as the quickest and easiest method of attaining that end. Before the establishment of that charity the unfortunate innocents were dropped in the streets, to be picked up by the police and handed over to the Commissioners of Charities, to die in the hospital on Blackwell's Island, as ninety per cent. of them speedily did. I have mentioned the number of these castaways found by the police and received by the Foundling Hospital, in the chapter on outcast children, and it is not necessary to repeat the statistics. Suggestive as they are, they but faintly tell the dreadful story of the terrible waste, in this city, of life and morality by means of its abortionists.

In this chapter and the previous one I have hastily dealt with incidents of our social life which are so foul that they cannot be handled effectively. I have endeavored to speak as plainly as possible, in order that there may be no mistake as to the facts. New York has nothing like the number of public prostitutes accredited to it, but it has more than enough for its safety; the city has less than a tenth of the professional abortionists assigned it, but it has enough to bestialize all the women in the world. I have shown how weak the law has always been, and is yet, in handling the vice of prostitution, and it is as silly in regard to abortionists. Clothed in such vague terms that it is almost impossible to secure a conviction for the offence, it permits a maximum punishment of only seven years in State prison, when the offence is proven. As an illustration of the absurdity of the law, I must again cite the case of Alice Bowlsby. The details of the case, as they were published in the newspapers, were such as to horrify and scandalize the public; the affair in all its incidents was one of the most atrocious crimes ever developed, yet Rosenzweig could only be awarded seven years in State prison. To accomplish even this the law was terribly strained, and Rosenzweig was convicted more by prejudice than proof. There was no doubt in any reasonable mind of his guilt, but the unreasonable law had very grave doubts. The proof was clear that the young girl had died from the effects of an abortion, and it was equally clear that the trunk containing her dead body was removed from the house of Rosenzweig. This was enough to remove any moral doubt, but the legal doubts yet wanted to be shown when, where, and how the accused ever met the deceased during her life; and under the ordinary rules of evidence these doubts were entitled to be satisfied. Legally, I am convinced that gross injustice was done Rosenzweig by his conviction on the evidence in his case, which, however, was much more direct and positive than in the case of any other abortionist convicted during the past year, except in the case of Mrs. Burns, in which the jury had the *ante-mortem* statement of the deceased that the prisoner had operated upon her. The lameness of the law has been felt and acknowledged of late by the authorities, and at the last session of the Legislature of New York, an amendment to the law was passed by which the judges are given a discretionary power in the infliction of punishment, even to confinement for life. The definition of the offence has also been so altered as to make it more easy of proof, and the new law is in every way a vast improvement upon the clumsy statute formerly in force. But even this amendment does not go far enough and make an outlaw of every man and woman who advertises his or her willingness and ability to violate nature.

But while statutory enactments of the right kind would do much to lessen this evil, it can be eradicated only by moral agencies, if at all. In the chapter on prostitution I have stated what I believe to be the only remedy for that evil, and the same remedy will deprive the abortionists of the majority of their victims. Both these evils are based on the licentiousness of the people, and whatever decreases that will lessen both. When, in plain language, the social code dishonors a man for seducing a woman as it dishonors a woman for being seduced, there will be much grief among the abortionists and the proprietors of such places as lying-in asylums. They would lose at once nine-tenths of all their customers among unmarried females, and in time lose them all. Then society must change its code as to married life. Children must be made the brightest jewels in woman's crown. The high premiums which society gives for violations of the law of nature must be withdrawn, and the place of honor given her who fulfils her functions, and not to her who avoids them by the aid of the abortionists. How this is to be done may be more difficult of statement. The evil has become so widely and deeply seated that only protracted and persistent efforts will uproot it. The press and pulpit must make common cause in its extirpation, but especially the latter. As a first step it is necessary to reform what are known as "fashionable" churches, where preachers who are outrageous burlesques of Him who preached the Sermon on the Mount, mince into their pulpits to smooth the primrose path to heaven, for hearers who are satires on the Christian faith. No church at all is better than a church false to itself; no religion better than a religion that condones offences against its code by its devotees. Travellers have told us of savages who have as little enlightenment as monkeys, but yet, guided by uncorrupted instincts, and nothing else, are pure in their domestic lives. We had better be such savages than the victims of a civilization that is eating out our vitals. The time has fully come when we must do something if we would be saved, and that something must be to restore purity to the homes of the people, and, above all, to the marriage tie. That can never be done so long as fashionable congregations, led by pastors false to their duty, fall down and worship gold, and that magnified, instead of "Christ and Him crucified."

HAUNTS OF VICE.

PROTRACTED investigation is not necessary to learn the outlines of a city. If a casual observer should occupy only a few days in acquiring a general knowledge of the physical aspect of New York, he would have a large store of facts, which, however superficial, would nevertheless have both interest and value. If he should begin his observations at the point where Broadway debouches into the Battery, he would first encounter those old, high-gabled houses which show in their rigid fronts the stately and stable craftsmanship of the seventeenth century. But the quaint old houses bear new signboards, which proclaim that they have become the abodes of that modern enterprise which has conquered time and space, even to the spanning of the great deep. Here the casual runs upon the two truths, that in business, as in social life, "birds of a feather flock together," and that the ocean common carriers have congregated at the foot of Broadway.

The first fact is thrust upon him everywhere. In New street, Broad street, and part of Wall street is the fast and feverish life of the money centre of the continent; Beekman street and Maiden Lane remind us of the ills that flesh is heir to, by the great drug houses that occupy them; Ferry and Spruce streets are given up to leather, while stoves predominate in Water. Hardware manufactories, with the great Hoe press foundry in the van, topple over Gold and Cliff, and nothing of consequence can be bought in William except blank books and stationery. The silent and grim customs warehouses frown upon Stone, Marketfield, and Bridge; Beaver and a part of Pearl have the fibry appearance proper to localities doing the greater portion of the cotton business of the western world. Flour and ship chandlery monopolize South street; clocks give Cortlandt its distinctive character; while Front, West, Washington, and Greenwich have the stench and stickiness inseparable from wet groceries. Getting at last out of the labyrinths of the lower town, the observer finds that dry goods and kindred fabrics occupy Broadway and Church street, and all the intervening cross streets from Chambers to Canal. Noting only these most obtrusive facts, and ignoring many specialties he sees wedged in here and there, he has gained a very correct idea of the city in its present outward and commercial aspect.

But having learned all this, he knows the city thus generally only as it is to-day; and wandering among the huge homes of a world-wide commerce, the observer listens with incredulity to some modified Wouter Von Twiller who tells strange stories of these localities. No city, with perhaps the single exception of Chicago, ever experienced in the same period of time such vast and violent changes as has New York in the past twenty years. The trade that had abundance of accommodation in the few blocks around South Ferry has absorbed the whole island up to Canal street, and has naturally driven all other forms of human action before it, so that the prim dwellings of the last decade have been swept away in company with the haunts of its poverty and vice. The merchant of the last generation, coming suddenly upon the city as it is to-day, would be perplexed; and the pauper, *roué*, or ruffian who should now seek his old resorts, would find not even a reminder of former familiars. Time works no such wonders anywhere as in this changeful metropolis, and in many cases it has been as sudden and complete as though it were a work of necromancy. Only a dozen years ago such streets in the Fifth Ward as Leonard and Franklin, now fronted with stately warehouses, were wholly filled with dwellings which were once occupied by respectable families, but many of which in the end were the abode of gilded sin so notorious that the House of Mirrors, which was one of them, became known the country over for its unique splendor. Even less than a dozen years have elapsed since the Eighth Ward, which was the chosen home of middle-class good repute, was seized by shame and squalor. The wave of change has rolled even further, and in Bleecker and Amity streets converted the abodes of aristocratic respectability into dens of the lowest vice; but while this has been doing, Mercer street, which lately had an infamous notoriety, has been nearly reclaimed by legitimate traffic. There seems to have always been in the city, between where reputable people live and where they do business, a region where only crime and poverty find refuge. This territory has shifted with the changes of the city, and it is my present purpose to give its present location and appearance, supplemented with facts picked up in the colonies it has planted in other portions of the city.

There was a time, which has hardly yet passed, when the vilest region of the metropolis was known the world over as the Five Points. Located in the most depressed spot of the Sixth Ward, and getting its name from the fact that five tortuous streets there converged together, it once deserved its reputation. Only the vilest quarters of London could match it, and we fell to describing it over and over again, as though it was rather creditable to us to have crowded so much of vice and squalor into so small a space. Presently it became a generally accepted fact that all of outcast life which the city contained was to be found in the Five Points, and the delusion has continued to the present day. Once the worst locality in the city, it years ago became almost reputable. A sturdy, practical Christianity, getting hold of the spot, robbed it of its distinctive features, and now the Five Points Mission House, with other structures of similar character, occupy the site of the old rookeries that harbored the harlotry, thievery, and poverty by which the spot was made infamous. But the fact of this reclamation, which is of such great good cheer and excellent promise for the future of the city, does not appear to have even yet become known, and the Five Points is yet constantly and exclusively cited as illustrating the worst aspect of the nether side of New York; while the Arch Block, which is fast becoming entitled to that bad eminence, is never mentioned.

Life is a most undesirable condition as seen in the region bounded by Thompson, Sullivan, Broome, and Grand streets, with the ragged fringes of the adjacent territory. Like the Five Points the ground is low. Unless it is because the dregs must settle to the bottom, I do not know why it is that the vilest population of great cities is usually found in their most depressed areas. Certainly there appears to be something inimical to skulking crime and slothful poverty in the high, breezy table-lands of towns, and successful search is rarely made for either on the hill-tops. Whatever the explanation may be, the fact is beyond dispute, and has never been more plainly proven than in the Arch Block, a name which is due to an open archway under the houses from Thompson to Sullivan street, midway between Broome and Grand, which has often served thieves and brawlers a good turn in enabling them to escape the pursuing police. The Arch Block has always been subject to miasmatic odors from natural causes, but these have been multiplied and intensified by artificial means. The population is dense, and as little addicted to cleanliness as godliness. The streets, which until a short time ago were rudely paved with cobblestones, are generally matted with the foulest garbage, thrown from the houses in defiance of law and decency. The sidewalks are strewn with the decaying refuse of green-grocers, and the arm of authority is so weak that even in the fetid days of midsummer the attempts to remove this death-producing filth or to prevent its accumulation are few and feeble. In winter huge heaps of ashes are added to the piles of kitchen and grocer garbage, both intermingled with fouler filth, so that the roadways are passable only to horses and vehicles specially adapted to scaling an infinite variety of short ascents; and I can compare their floundering, when the task is undertaken, to nothing but a ship tossing in a chopped sea. In summer these heaps disappear only because the heat spreads them more evenly and thickly over the roadways, while at the same time it liberates the noxious vapors the cold had imprisoned, adding them to the natural miasmas of the place; so that the atmosphere during the close sultriness of later summer would enliven the undertakers but for the fact that the inhabitants who breathe their last of it are as undesirable customers in death as in life.

The houses enveloped in these rank odors, and crowded with a population as wretched and debased as New York or any other metropolis can show, have seen much better days. Built many years ago, when the city had but little crime or poverty, and originally designed for respectable middle-class people, by whom they were first occupied, they were once as much a credit as they are now a disgrace to civilization. The majority of them being on the same plan, they are forcible examples of the simplicity of structure which answered all the needs of two generations ago. Few of them have more than three floors, and many of them not more than two with an attic. All of them have the first floor, which is raised only one or two steps above the pavement, divided into a hallway and two rooms; and the upper floors are on the same plan, except that half the hallway, front and rear, is partitioned off to make those last abominations of builders known as hall rooms. These houses will not average more than ten rooms each, but in many of them the ground floor has been taken for the petty trade of the quarter, leaving the average of living rooms not more than eight to each house. These may seem to be trivial facts, but they become important when the population which these houses harbor is considered. So also do the other details that these domiciles, almost without exception, are destitute of water or gas; that they are dirty and dingy beyond description; that many of them have so lurched to the southward, owing to the settling of the ground on which they were built, that articles of furniture slide from one side of a room to the other; that the stairways have fallen into decay, and the floors are so worn that they are in many places thin and insecure. Painters and glaziers know of no such locality as the Arch Block, because of the long lapse of time since any of them were called there to exercise their arts; and house carpenters are aware of these crumbling structures only by traditions transmitted from their ancestors who helped to build them. Illuminated at night by kerosene, frowsy and repulsive in the glaring light of day, crowded day and night with people to be described, the Arch Block presents the most striking view which can now be obtained of the vice and squalor of the great city.

How vile a spot can be found in the heart of a metropolis, and how bestial humanity can become, can be best seen during the early hours of any hot summer night, when Arch Block life is at its windows, in the streets, or lounging at the doors of the groggeries and groceries. Among all the thousands of human beings, of whom nearly half are negroes and the majority of the remainder Italians, there will be hardly one cleanly, pleasant, humanized face. The men, with few exceptions, are idlers, brawlers, thieves, or something worse than either, and the women harlots or something still less reputable.

Adhering as I have throughout this series to facts, without attempting to philosophize upon them, I do not try to explain why negro prostitution is viler than that of any other race; but that such is the fact no rambler through the streets bordering the Arch Block can doubt for a moment. At every step he will encounter hideous women of every shade of color, from bleached yellow to the deepest black, who leer at him with an attempted wantonness that would be ludicrous if not so disgusting, and who, if encouraged by even so much as a half glance, brazenly make the most unnatural propositions. If the rambler hurries on without response, he is wiser than if he dallies even for a moment with this extremity of sin; for his refusal at the last to accept the hideous proposals is sure to be followed in his retreat by a torrent of foul profanity that will make him shudder, however accustomed he may be to indecent language. It is only in their fastness, where the police have ceased from troubling them, that these negro prostitutes are thus obtrusive; and one who sees them only in Broadway or adjacent streets, which they nightly hunt for prey, would be certain that I have done them gross injustice.

It is not only the women in the streets who seek to entice the stranger. There are others standing in the doorways or leaning out of the windows who begin their acquaintance with you by calling out, "Say, fellar, ain't you gwine to come in?" and being answered with a contemptuous refusal, pour out obscene objurgations which startle even hardened sinners, and which a patrolman new to the post once said "made his hair curl." I do not wish to be understood as saying that these flagrant exhibitions of indecency are habitual in the locality, for I have so often seen its evils in a mitigated form that I am forced to believe that the population is only equal to them when crazed with the frightful whiskey of the place, which they call "benzine," or made savage by a long-continued and extraordinary run of bad luck at the game of policy, which is their chief pursuit and sole amusement. But I do say that any day and every day more of total depravity can be seen in and around the Arch Block than anywhere else in the city. It is not alone that the women are viler than the vilest, but the men are vicious, cruel, and cowardly. A majority of them being petty thieves or gamblers, or worse than either, dependents upon the earnings of female prostitution for subsistence, they are a burden and a danger not only to the immediate vicinity but to the whole community. Standing about the corners or infesting the groggeries of the block during the day and early evening, drinking and brawling, it is not possible to say with certainty where or how the later hours of the night are spent. They are of a nomadic race, and prowl for prey in distant streets. They have little respect for law, and less for its guardians the police, who have paced around the block for years without doing anything to curb the constantly increasing wickedness. Whenever, as frequently happens, an affray occurs, the assailant is arrested if he can be found, but the wars of words nightly waged between conflicting gangs pass unnoticed. It would be such an innovation for a policeman to order one of these gangs to move on or to desist from insulting passers by, that the occurrence would occasion universal astonishment, to be followed by general derision. The outcast men and women who predominate in the Arch Block, making it the moral cesspool of the metropolis, might possibly be coerced into the appearance of decency if the most energetic means were used, but they cannot be cajoled into it. There seems to have been a tacit understanding among the police for some years past that the ills of the spot were incurable, and there has consequently been but little decided effort to apply any serious remedy. Therefore the outcasts have gone on almost without hindrance, quarrelling, fighting, stealing, plying prostitution without disguise, and only when they occasionally broke out into the more serious offences have they been molested. Every great city must have in it somewhere such an ulcer as the Arch Block, and the authorities have perhaps concluded that it does no more harm where it is than it would anywhere else.

Wishing to obtain a closer view than I had ever had of all this shameless sin, I lately made a night tour through the segregated infamies of the region, in company with a detective. By pretending to be in search of an imaginary thief the officer went where he chose; and I following as the victim to identify the rascal if found, which of course he never was, we penetrated with safety dens we should not have dared to enter if provided with no better excuse than curiosity. First of all we scrambled down eight steps and reached the "dive," in Grand street, of a mammoth African known as Big Sue. The place was a cellar rather than a basement, so far was it below the street; and opening the door, we were halted for a moment at the threshold by an odor compounded from an adjacent sewer, the bodies of the negroes in the room, and several kerosene lamps. The room was scant six feet from floor to ceiling, the walls were mildewed, the wood-work unpainted and crumbling. The furniture was in character with its surroundings. On the floor was a patchwork made up of old remnants of ingrain and rag carpets, the chairs were of rough wood, the stove made for cooking purposes; and faded calico hung from the ceiling divided this repulsive apartment, which was evidently the reception and living room combined in one, from the dormitories at the rear. I had seen all this indistinctly in the semi-darkness, and it was not until my eyes had become more accustomed to the feeble light emitted by the kerosene lamps, that sputtered so viciously as to suggest the danger of an immediate explosion, that I could plainly see the persons in the "dive" besides "Big Sue," whose huge proportions blocked the doorway; but at last I saw clearly enough that there were three women who were full-blooded negroes, one who was unmistakably Caucasian, and three men, all of the latter race. The white woman was seated alone in a corner of the room, abandoned to her own reflections, if she was capable of any, while the three white men were deeply engaged in "chinning" with the black women, as such creatures call the conversation of which they are capable. Shutting out all other views of the white race but the one obtained in that room at that moment, its superiority over the negro seemed a philosophic crotchet without a leg to stand on. I must, however, do these men the justice to say that they were thoroughly ashamed, not of their position, but of being discovered in it; and as we stood near the door talking to "Big Sue," whom I could not help imagining to be a huge turtle which was somehow standing on its hind legs, they moved off from the inky women with kinky hair, and sought to hide themselves in the distant corners where the dim light was dimmest. We were in no hurry to relieve them from their embarrassment, but conferred leisurely with the turtle concerning one apocryphal Smith who had stolen a wholly imaginary diamond pin, and of whom the turtle declared: "Fore de Lord, I nebber knowed him; I 'clares to goodness I nebber did." Being informed of his personal appearance, she was "suah I nebber seed him," and was heartily glad he was "nuffin but poor white trash anyhow; niggahs don't go totin' off things in dat way."

Satisfied that I had seen the every-night aspect of the "dive," and not caring to probe its shameless mysteries further, I ended this talk by giving a preconcerted signal to my companion, and we ascended to the street. As we walked away he boasted with professional satisfaction of the one virtue of "Big Sue." She was very fat, horribly ugly, outrageously profane and obscene, but she wouldn't steal. He was sure of that, for he had never had a complaint from any of her customers, and, as more satisfactory proof, mentioned that he had known her to scour the neighborhood at one o'clock in the morning to get change for a hundred-dollar bill given her by a patron too drunk to have ever recollected the incident, and, not getting it, turning the patron and his money over to a patrolman that both might be safe. He could not say so much for the women Sue harbored, for he had sometimes had "squeals" on their account from men whom they had lured into the dive; but he insisted that "Big Sue" prevented thievery in her den to the extent of her power.

Sauntering on through the slums, made doubly repulsive by the mugginess of the night, we reached Laurens street, which some foolish Aldermen thought to make more reputable by changing its name to South Fifth avenue, in which undertaking they failed miserably. Pausing at the lower end of this street, my guide, pointing to a row of nine dilapidated three-story brick houses on the rear of the lots which the widening of the street had exposed to view from the sidewalk, said, "There's one of the worst 'dives' in New York." And here let me explain that in detective parlance every foul place is a "dive," whether it be a cellar or garret, or neither. Inquiring for details as to this particular dive, I was told the tenements contained a dense population of white and black, mixed together in filth and wickedness; that thievery and harlotry were the chief pursuits of nearly all the inmates, among whom wrangles and fights were frequent. But he could not give me any special case which would fitly illustrate this outcast life, and declining the proposal to enter one of these houses and see for myself how indescribable was the condition of these people, we turned away and sought the Arch, only a block distant. There is nothing startling or peculiar in this open roadway under the houses, although it has not its counterpart anywhere in New York. At night, however, it seems a perilous way, for it is unlighted from end to end; and on this night, as we stumbled through it, I mentally rejoiced that the garroting method of robbery had been extirpated by the energy and severity of the authorities. But we met no one except a pair of skulking negroes, and half way between the streets there was a sort of open court dimly lighted from the lamps in the overhanging houses, and here some children were playing in the mud, who were half naked, and in the scanty light seemed half starved. This open court and these houses distinct from those facing the public streets were new to me, and I inquired as to the inmates. "Rag-pickers, beggars, and the like, miserably poor, but most of them honest, and nearly all Germans," was the answer. But aside from this knowledge of reputable poverty, walled in from the world by vice and crime, the journey through the Arch was unprofitable. We had entered from Thompson street, and as we emerged into Sullivan street the detective paused and summed up the region: "All around here is about the worst slum in New York. Quarrelling, fighting, thieving, and cutting are going on all the time; but we get few prisoners here, as we don't have any 'squeals.' If a man is robbed by one of these women, he isn't very likely to tell about it; and these people won't make complaints against each other on account of affrays, because none of them can afford to have daylight let in on them. Negroes always use a razor in their fights, and it's a savage, silent, but not often a deadly weapon, the way they handle it. We don't have murders here yet very often, but it's coming to that fast enough, and there's plenty of dives about here where a man isn't sure of his life for five minutes together. The fact is, this is getting to be what the Five Points was. The old-clothes dealers know it, and see how they are turning all these little six-by-nine cellars into shops."

He was right; and the proof of it was thrust upon us at every step as we walked around the block and saw those things which I have before mentioned, and which are too repulsive to be repeated in more detail. As we walked away toward the light and purer life of Broadway, we saw the vileness from the nest we had left behind overflowing into the street up to Greene. Parting with my companion, I made a détour to the corner of Prince and Wooster streets, to look in upon the accomplished thieves who resort to the hotel there. In the shameful days when the might of the Tammany Ring was unshaken, this St. Bernard Hotel used to be a pivot of political power. The outlaws who frequent it were adepts in the sort of cumulative voting known as repeating, which was the basis of Ring supremacy, and they were courted accordingly. But this disgraceful time being past, the thieves have nothing to do but pick pockets, and have devoted themselves to their vocation with redoubled energy. When I looked in upon them, they were engaged as usual in smoking cigars and drinking whiskey or playing billiards. There were about a dozen of them, who are well-known as among the most skilful pickpockets in New York. Without exception they were well dressed; all had delicate hands with long slender fingers, and none were repulsive in features or manners. Next to a confidence operator, the successful pickpocket is always pleasing in appearance and address when in public, and I found them no less so when in the retirement of their home. Their talk here certainly was flashy, but at the same time they were, as they always are, wary in their words, and no hint of their accomplished or contemplated crimes could be obtained from their conversation. They are jovially sociable among themselves, and spend their money with as little compunction as they get it. Merely noting as I pass that this house is the best known resort in the city of the better class of thieves, I do not stop to describe it in detail. If any one is curious to know more of the place, it is entirely safe to see for himself, as these gentlemanly marauders never "take a trick" at home; so far, I am informed, no robbery has ever been committed in the house.

It is very different in the den of a lower class of thieves, who are mostly ruffianly burglars, in a cellar at the corner of the Bowery and Hester street. This is a veritable "dive," for it is many steps below the street surface, and nobody but an idiot would expect to enter it and not get robbed. It is always filled with fellows who do business in a rude way with crowbars and slungshots, and who are experts in nothing but slangy talk. Many of them are convicts, and all of them would have that distinction if the interests of society were conserved. Uncouth in appearance, demeanor, and language, these ruffians could never be mistaken for other than what they are.

These two resorts of thieves are fair samples of all to be found in the city, of which there are not more than a dozen altogether; and taken singly or collectively, they are by no means the most dangerous dens to be found in the metropolis. There is a sporting house in Houston street, one block east of Broadway, which has long appeared to me to be the most demoralizing place to be found in the city. The resort of a low class of prostitutes, and of the ruffians and idlers who support the prize ring, there is nothing in the country to compare with it in its malign influences. I have not stated this fact without proper investigation, for I have gone there often enough to be sure of its character, and I do not doubt that the most general description of it will enable the public to reach the same conclusion. Known the world over in sporting circles as Harry Hill's, the house itself, which has lately been enlarged to accommodate the increasing debauchery, is of brick, two stories high, and painted white. Over the entrance in Houston street is a huge ornamental lamp, and beside the door, where every passer must see them, are a dozen lines of doggerel lettered on a signboard, which invite to deep potations, and two of which declare that within are

Punches and juleps, cobblers and smashes,
To make the tongue waggle with wit's merry flashes.

The bar-room, with this enticing but false announcement—for the liquor there has nothing but headaches and fights in it—is even with the street, and is too much like scores of other houses frequented by a low class of topers and idlers to need particular description. The wickedness of the place is reached by paying twenty cents at the bar, and ascending some narrow stairs at the rear of the groggery. Gaining the floor above, the visitor finds himself in a large room with a very low ceiling, which is furnished with numerous chairs and tables, a bar, and a raised platform with some rude scenery, which is used as an excuse for covering the orgies of the den with a theatre license. There are many placards on the walls which instantly remove any doubt a stranger may have as to the character of the place. One is a repetition, with the phraseology slightly altered, of the doggerel at the door; another is a blasphemous justification of deep drinking by perverted quotations from the Bible; and others request "gentlemen not to smoke when dancing with the ladies," and to refrain from certain other acts equally impossible for any gentleman to commit.

There is never a midnight when this mill of vice and demoralization, which grinds not only surely, but fast and furiously, is not in full operation. Scores of abandoned women are seated at the tables drinking deeply of the vile liquors of the place, or smoking strong cigars, to which only long experience is equal. There are as many men who are doing the same things, and who, paying for all this dissipation, have and expect no better recompense than talking with these painted women in the slang language in which they are alone versed. These women are in keeping with the place, for being public prostitutes, they are social outcasts; but some of the men seem startling incongruities. While the majority of the males plainly belong to the vicious class, there is never a midnight when there are not many actively engaged in the debaucheries who claim to be and are generally accepted as members of reputable society. I do not now refer to the curious who visit the place but once or twice to get a view of its iniquity, but to those who are seen so often as to be classed as customers, and who receive the familiar greeting of established acquaintance from the bar-maids. Among them are men of every calling, who in their business and domestic life are surrounded by reputable influences, but who, sneaking from these with nightfall, can be found in Houston street wallowing in corruption, and eagerly filling the coffers of vice in exchange for moral and physical death. Every night men can be seen there who were lately of great promise, and who have been wrecked by its debauchery? but the sight of them rarely awakens pity. When men and women voluntarily congregate night after night, in this public manner, for the indulgence of bestial passions, the women are already lost and the men scarcely worth saving.

Outbreaks of brutal violence are as frequent in this place as in others which are frequently pounced upon by the police as dangerous to the public peace. Latterly, I admit, these exhibitions have not been so frequent nor flagrant as they were, but I can recall several such occasions during the past few months without trouble. Only the night before I write this page, a woman crazed with the liquor of the den suddenly made an indiscriminate attack upon its occupants; but being pushed, pulled, and parried into the street, she there had a protracted fight with a policeman, all the time screeching out obscene profanity in a voice that mingled it with the roar of Broadway. At last, finding that she was being conquered, she threw herself upon the sidewalk, where she kicked and screamed until, other policemen coming up, she was picked up bodily and carried off to a station-house cell. All this had been witnessed by hundreds of men, women, and children, and it is hardly necessary to say to any enlightened reader that no one was improved by the incident. Not long ago there was a general fight in the dance-house, in which men were gashed and women had their teeth knocked out; and fights of a milder type are of frequent occurrence. Nobody has ever been killed outright in any of the orgies of the place, and it may be the police are waiting for a startling homicide to occur before interfering with this murder machine, erected under the shadow of their headquarters, which has heretofore worked so awkwardly that it has never fulfilled the purpose to which it is naturally adapted.

A dance-house for prostitutes, a resort for prize-fighters and the idling ruffians who hang upon the edge of the roped ring, a rendezvous for the vicious of all classes, and a place where the potations are interspersed with suggestive dancing and the performances of the lowest type of a "variety show," this Houston street den is more of a public peril than any of those Broadway waiter-girl saloons which are again becoming numerous and dangerous, and which were lately vivified by a descent upon them by the police, when there was a greater straining at gnats and more readiness in swallowing camels than the city ever saw before. The raid ending as usual, the saloons, after being closed one night, reopened with their women in scantier costumes than ever; and there are now, from Prince to Fourth street, a distance of about a fifth of a mile, seven of these alluring doorways to moral death, so obtrusively conspicuous that the stranger needs no guide to find them. One occupies the whole second floor of a large building near Bleecker street, and has its front illuminated at night by hundreds of gas jets; while the others are in basements equally large, and, having their lights even with the sidewalks, are even more conspicuous. In all of them is the fevered life of gilded vice that leads unto perdition. There is everything in the embellishments to please the eye and stir the prurient imagination. There are young girls with enough womanhood left in their appearance to lure men whose manhood has not been utterly destroyed. There is liquor not so bad as to disgust a cultivated taste, and there is music execrable enough in the main, but relieved sometimes by a pure soprano voice almost artistically managed, or by some more than passable pianoforte execution, which is well worth hearing. The place, the wine, the women, the music, entice thousands, and hold hundreds in the corroding cords of vice gayly caparisoned, long enough to pass them on fully fitted for the pastimes of the Houston street hell or the Arch Block. Suppressed for a time by the rigid execution of the metropolitan excise law, which prohibited the sale of liquor after midnight, these saloons have again become aggressive. Without the wine the women palled even upon debauchees, and the saloons closed their doors for want of patrons, leaving the metropolis with one terrible temptation the less. Now the glare and glitter of sin, in the most alluring shape it ever took in public, have come again, and with more power for evil than ever before.

While the danger to public morals from these saloons, which, seated in the artery of the city, are poisoning the whole body, is rapidly increasing, what little risk there ever was from the Water street slums is fast diminishing. The dance-houses and other places of vile resort in the Fourth Ward were never so enticing nor so numerous as they have been painted, and, bad as they might be, were frequented by and debauched but a comparatively small portion of the population. Strangers, and sometimes citizens, went to them as one of the sensations of the metropolis, but always under police protection, and therefore escaped pollution. Their patrons were sailors on a carouse, or thieves and ruffians who would have been just as bad without them. These resorts were undoubtedly deadly in their effects, but they swept off what was past or not worth the saving, and never scattered the seeds of death broadcast to undermine the moral stamina of a whole people as do the Broadway saloons or the Houston street hell. I have spoken of the Fourth Ward slums in the past tense, and in so doing have but slightly anticipated events. I made the tour of the dance-houses a few nights ago, and was highly delighted at finding them in a comatose condition. The women were few in number, and apparently in most rotund condition, but my more experienced companion pricked the bubble by the remark, "Bloated, that's all; come and see them in the morning if you don't believe me." But I was willing to take his word, and decidedly averse to visiting the dives a second time. They were, without exception, perfectly ghastly in their loneliness. Half a dozen large coarse women, soggy with rum, and dressed so as to expose the largest permissible portions of their repulsive persons, moving lazily over the sanded floor of a room which had no other occupants except three or four ruffians stretched half asleep on the rude benches, and the two fellows who scraped untuned violins in the corner, was the most depressing depravity I ever witnessed. When my detective guide told me that this has come to be the usual aspect of the Water street dives, I was convinced he was telling the truth, and that this particular wickedness is happily in the last stages of a rapid decline. The dens in Greenwich and other water-side streets are almost in the same condition.

In the briefest terms I have endeavored to sketch the plague spots of the city as they are in the present. Some of them, as the Arch Block, are beyond the surgery of the law. Every vast city must have a vile population, and it will herd together. But other of these evils could and should be eradicated. The law as it is, and executed as it could be, is amply able to root out such things as the house in Houston street and the Broadway saloons. I do not claim that the proprietors could be convicted of any specific offence, but I do assert that things are constantly occurring in them to excuse police descents, and that they could thus be harassed out of existence. There is little sense in the city making exertions for a purity which it is impossible to attain, but it is suicidal folly to permit the growth of ulcers which are destroying the moral life of a million of people.

WILL MURDER OUT?

AT seven o'clock on the morning of the last day of 1868, Charles M. Rogers, an elderly gentleman of primitive habits, living at No. 42 East Twelfth street, in the City of New York, stepped out upon the sidewalk in front of his house. At the moment two outlaws happened to be passing. Taking off his light drab overcoat, the smaller one handed it to his taller companion, who crossed the street, whence he remonstrated "Jim, don't do it." But Jim, made of more reckless stuff, snatched the old gentleman's watch, and simultaneously jerking his wallet from his pocket, transferred these articles to the pocket of his blue flannel sack-coat. The robbery accomplished, Jim would have gone his way rejoicing, had not Rogers seized him by the collar of his coat, with the hope of compelling a return of his property. The struggle that ensued was brief but terrible. At the same instant of time Rogers tore from his assailant exactly one-half of his coat, and the thief, in his eagerness to escape, became an assassin, by plunging a huge knife into the abdomen of the man he had despoiled. Public as was the street, and clear as was the light of day, the affair had not been witnessed by any human eye, and the murderer and his passive accomplice fled untracked. A moment later Rogers was found dying on his own threshold. He was able to give the outlines of this last instance of New York lawlessness, but expired after two days of semi-consciousness.

The murderer had left behind him his hat, the sheath of his knife, and the fragment of his coat. In the pocket of the latter was the watch and wallet he had risked his neck to get, and also an envelope, from which the letter had been taken, and which was superscribed, "Jams Logan, N. Y. Cytty—this will be handed yu by Tom." The police, taking up the clue thus offered, began a vigorous, but somewhat disjointed search for a certain James Logan who had been shortly before discharged from State Prison. Within a week this theory was exploded, by the self-surrender of Logan, as that act was accepted as sufficient proof of his innocence. Forced to begin the search anew, it was next discovered that the letter had been written by a Sing Sing convict named Tom McGivney, alias Jim Rice, who, in prison and out of it, had been an intimate associate of Logan's. This convict, desiring to communicate with his comrade, who had been discharged, sneaked down to the river, with the intention of sending his missive by one of the hands of a sloop lying at the wharf at Sing Sing. Finding the sloop for the moment deserted, he took advantage of the opportunity thus given him, to escape, and, secreting himself in the vessel, got to New York, carrying his own letter. He could then, of course, communicate in person with Logan; and, having destroyed his letter, in a careless moment left the envelope in his pocket, to be the most important link in a strong chain of circumstantial evidence seeming to bind him to a terrible crime.

The murder of Rogers was an event so startling in itself, and the subsequent developments were so singular, that the affair became the sensation of the dawning year, and was for many days the chief topic of journalism and conversation. Among the police, especially, it was the absorbing theme, and it dragged up many long-buried crimes for the purpose of comparison. Generally, the case was conceded to be without a prototype; and Inspector James Leonard, who had been a prominent and valuable police officer of New York from 1845, admitted that it had no exact parallel in his experience. But when the case occasioned the assertion that "murder will out," and that no lapse of time or combination of circumstances can ever shield the assassin from ultimate detection, he cited many cases in rebuttal of the adage, and among them those which are appended.

THE BUCKSON CASE.

In the year 1851 Captain John Buckson lived, with his wife Nancy, in a handsome cottage in the village of Seakonk, near Providence, Rhode Island, in the enjoyment of a competence acquired by many years of frugal industry. He was, however, often absent from home, as he still pursued his vocation, and was master of the sloop "Oregon," plying between Providence and Norfolk, Virginia.

He had then reached his fiftieth year, and his hard seafaring life had not made him look younger than he was. He was tall, gaunt and angular, weather-stained and storm-beaten. His short, stiff hair was grizzled, and his long narrow face furrowed by deep lines, but his physical powers appeared to be still untouched, and he seemed assured of a long continuance of active life.

His temperament was favorable to a lusty longevity. He was patient, and apparently so passionless that he stared at the cares and troubles of life, as at strangers with whom he could not possibly have dealings. He avoided quarrels and all unseemliness with scrupulous care, and was known on his vessel and in his village only as a sedate, God-fearing man, kind-hearted and even-tempered.

But he had positive points in his character, and the requisite friction would produce the natural glow. As in all equable men, his anger burned with dim light but intense heat, and hence, with him, a knitting of the brows or twitching of the hands, meant more than the wildest signs of passion in other men, and his word of wrath was weightier than the brawler's blow. But he so loved peace, and so sedulously courted it, that his most intimate associates remembered as memorable epochs the rare occasions when his temper had given way.

The only trouble of his life brooded upon his own hearth-stone. Mrs. Nancy Buckson was many years his junior in age, and in important respects his opposite in character. To her youth she added comeliness of person. Though a thoroughly good woman at heart, she yet embittered her life and his by constant efforts to do more than her duty. Nervous and irritable, she became fretfully voluble in her assertions of her own merits and his short-comings. So in the summer of 1851, the neighbors began to pity poor Captain John as a henpecked husband, and the inroads of the wife upon the domestic quietude were noticed as of constantly increasing frequency and bitterness. Captain John, however, bore the infliction with his accustomed patience.

But the end was at hand. One evening in the last week in July, a neighbor, James Pauls, in passing the house, heard Nancy's tongue going at an unusual rate, and glancing through the window saw Buckson standing before her. He seemed roused at last, and although Pauls could not hear his words, he saw the knitted brows and twitching hands, in one of which a stout whipcord was convulsively grasped. The scene was indelibly stamped by after-events upon the memory of the accidental witness, and he could always see, even to the most minute details, the enraged woman, confronted by that quiet, concentrated man, struggling with his passion, and fidgetting with a whipcord. At the time, however, Pauls gave no especial weight to the circumstance, and stopping at the village inn on his way home, only casually remarked to the inevitable loungers, that he "reckoned Nancy would keep on a naggin' of Captain John until she riled him."

The next morning the cottage was closed and deserted, but the circumstance did not excite, remark. Buckson, it was presumed, had gone to Providence to prepare his sloop for sea, and Nancy had a habit of making sudden pilgrimages to the neighboring towns. The event, then, was so far from being suspicious that it was not even unusual.

In those days a magnificent forest stretched to the northward from the little town, interspersed with patches of open land where the blackberry grew in great abundance. This wonder and delight of the American glades had fully ripened under the hot July sun, and the children of the village were busily employed in gathering the fruit. That afternoon the patches were unusually crowded. One group of children started home just before sundown, taking their way direct through the wood without regard to beaten paths. They had gone but a short distance when the little dog that was with them stopped, and began to sniff eagerly at a spot of ground which appeared to have been recently disturbed. Giving a long mournful howl the dog scratched furiously with his paws in the sand, and in a moment had uncovered a human hand. Howling more mournfully than before, he bounded off a couple of feet, and tore at the ground with redoubled energy. He soon completed his task, and the children saw a woman's face, pale and rigid, imbedded in the moist clayey earth. With but one glance at the horror, they dropped their pails and fled to the village. The dog detective remained yelping over the crime he had unearthed.

Every village, probably, has its sensation at some time, and that of Seakonk came with the story of the children. As the tidings spread from house to house the people gathered at the inn, and eagerly discussed what should be done and who should do it. At last, all the male inhabitants, headed by the Squire, bearing a lantern, and piloted by the children, started out to investigate the matter. But the pilots were not needed, as the dog still maintained his watch; and with his mournful howlings echoing through the dim woods, the party could not go astray. Reaching the spot, they gathered around it, and the Squire advanced and, kneeling down, wiped the dirt from the face of the dead woman with the skirt of his coat. Then he held the lantern over it.

"It's Nancy Buckson!"

He fell back a few paces with the exclamation, and his companions turned to imitate the conduct of the children shortly before. They rallied, however, at his summons, and fell vigorously to work to exhume the body. A few shovelsful of earth, and the body of a woman, without shroud or coffin, but fully dressed in the ordinary garments of life, was exposed. About the body a white substance was plentifully sprinkled, and was found to be chloride of lime, doubtless placed there to insure speedy decomposition.

Every one recognized poor Nancy Buckson, and saw the ridged and livid mark upon the neck, pointed out by the Squire. It was plain that she had been murdered by strangulation, and tossed, dressed as she was at the moment of her violent death, into the rude grave where the dog had found her.

The neighbor, Pauls, now recalled the quarrel of the preceding day, and told how Captain John had stood before the angry woman, playing with the whipcord. The cottage was searched, and a cord was found lying on the floor of the room, which, when tried upon the woman's neck, fitted exactly the ridged and livid circle. In the cellar was a quantity of a white substance precisely similar to that found in the grave, and those articles belonging to Mrs. Buckson found upon the corpse were missing from the house. There could be no more doubt as to the criminal than the crime.

Captain John Buckson was not found in the village or in Providence; but it was ascertained that he had sailed with his sloop, and the presumption was raised that he intended to touch at New York, and there, leaving the vessel, seek to elude the officers of the law in the labyrinths of the great city. A messenger was, therefore, dispatched in great haste to reach the city before him, with a requisition for his arrest.

His authority was placed in the hands of Police Captain Leonard—the officer referred to in my preamble—who searched diligently among the shipping, until he found the sloop "Oregon," moored at an East River pier. Going on board, Captain Leonard greeted Buckson, who was seated on the deck.

"Good-day, sir."

The sailor scarcely looked up, as he mechanically returned the salutation.

"I'm sorry to trouble you, but I've a warrant for your arrest."

"Arrest! For what?"

The exclamation and succeeding question were those of a phlegmatic man slightly astonished.

"For the murder of your wife."

"Murder of my wife! Squire, that can't be. Nancy isn't dead."

"Yes, she is—strangled with a cord."

Buckson rose to his feet and, looking the officer steadily in the face, said slowly and solemnly:

"Squire, if Nancy's dead I don't know it. I had a quarrel with her the night I left, and gave her a piece of my mind, but God is my witness that I didn't put a hand upon her!"

The officer looked with some interest upon a man who could thus deny a crime with which he was so clearly linked by circumstantial evidence, but without further parley took him from the sloop and placed him in a cell of the station-house. He made no resistance, and did not trouble himself to again volunteer any protestation of his innocence. While in the station-house, and during the journey to Providence, whenever the question was directly put to him, he always denied his guilt in the same emphatic terms, but he was never the first to broach the subject, and it was especially noticed that he never made any inquiry for the details of the murder.

When the officer and his charge arrived at Seakonk, the latter seemed amazed to find himself the object of universal execration. When he reached the village and while he walked beside his captor through the street to the jail, he was surrounded by a hooting mob, that pelted him with opprobrious epithets, and with difficulty was restrained from doing violence to his person. He bore himself bravely and undismayed through it all. But his conduct was noted only to his discredit, and the citizens could not remember any hardened wretch who had ever so flaunted his crime in the face of an outraged people.

In due time the grand jury was convened and his case considered. There was no more doubt of his guilt in that official body than in the community at large; and he was formally indicted for the murder of Nancy Buckson.

When the news was taken to him in his cell he only said: "God's will be done!"

His perfect resignation had, by this time, won slightly on the jailer's heart, and he inquired if he did not wish to engage counsel to defend him at the approaching trial. Buckson's face brightened with this first faint sign of sympathy, but he answered:

"I thank you, friend, but I don't need a lawyer. God knows I am innocent of this crime and He will prove it in His own good time."

The day appointed for the trial of the prisoner was close at hand when the quiet village was startled by a new terror. One pleasant September morning a ghost descended from the eastern coach and walked leisurely, and with every semblance of life, up the street toward the long-deserted cottage. It was a horrible ghost, for it nodded familiar greetings to several persons it met upon the way, and once tried to pat a shrinking child. It almost seemed endowed with human passions for many were ready to make oath that they saw its cheek flush with anger when it found the entire town avoiding it in unconcealed terror. But it was a persistent ghost, for it walked steadily on until it reached the gate of the cottage-garden, which it found nailed up; and it became a talkative ghost when it discovered the pigs running riot in the garden. In the very voice of the dead Nancy Buckson, it said in a peevish tone:

"That John Buckson 'll be the death of me yet! Just see how he lets these pesky hogs root up things!"

It was, indeed, Nancy Buckson herself.

It is needless to prolong the story. On the night of the quarrel Captain John had left, as usual, to take out his sloop, and Nancy, smarting under the severe censure he had, for the first time, expressed, had gone off on foot, during the night, to a neighboring town, where she was unknown, and had there taken a coach to begin a journey to Maine to visit a sister. Her absence from the cottage was not known until after the finding of the body, and its identification was so absolute that of course no search was made for a woman known to be dead. On the other hand she had heard nothing, in a retired spot of a distant State, of her supposed death and the subsequent events; and her return, timely as it was, had been purely accidental. She was horrified when confronted with the results of her thoughtless freak, and, although she made no noisy demonstrations of regret, and was not profuse in promises of amendment in the future, it is pleasant to know that this terrible experience was not without fruit. Buckson was, of course, immediately released from prison, the legal proceedings against him at once dismissed, and thereafter he found in his home a haven of rest that was a recompense for the suffering by which it had been purchased.

But a mystery has always brooded over the cottage, and the murder always remained an insoluble enigma. Eighteen years have elapsed without any second identification of the body unearthed by the little dog, and, as a consequence, without any detection of the murderer. The clothes in which the body was dressed and the ear-rings and articles of jewelry upon it, were undoubtedly the property of Mrs. Buckson, for, upon her return, she found these articles missing from the house. A close scrutiny of the cottage showed that the woman had not only been there, but had probably been murdered there during the night, after Buckson and his wife had left. The cord found in the room had fitted the neck, and the chloride of lime in the cellar had evidently been disturbed. Many articles of value, too, were gone, and the house generally disarranged. Upon these circumstances a theory was founded that the woman was one of a party of burglars that had entered the cottage, and finding it deserted, had leisurely ransacked it. The woman had arrayed herself in the property of the absent mistress, and afterward some quarrel had arisen and she had been murdered by the other members of the party. Subsequently this theory was, in part, thoroughly established, when a complete female outfit, of coarse material, was accidentally fished out of an old and unused well in the cottage-garden.

Detectives are apt to attach the names of noted criminals to extraordinary crimes, and, many years after the events narrated, a rumor was prevalent among the police of Providence that the murdered woman had been the wife of an English burglar named Collins, then living in Providence, and celebrated all over the Union for his success and recklessness. The rumor had no better foundation than that Collins and his wife disappeared at about the time of the murder, and it only lived because theories always thrive when facts are impossible to obtain.

The case yet remains among unfinished police business. No human effort has ever learned more than was discovered by the brute instincts of the dog when he pawed the secret of the murder from the shallow grave in the dark forest.

THE RICARD CASE.

One spring morning, during the first year of the war, a barrel of pitch was found to have disappeared from a Jersey City pier, and the porter in charge, when reporting the fact to his employers, took occasion to speak of the river-thieves in no very complimentary terms.

On the same day, Ada Ricard, a woman of nomadic habits and dubious status, but of marvellous beauty, suddenly left her hotel in New York, without taking the trouble to announce her departure or state her destination. The clerks of the house only remarked that some women had queer ways.

A few days after these simultaneous events, the same porter who had mourned the lost pitch, happening to look down from the end of his pier when the tide was out, saw a small and shapely human foot protruding above the waters of the North River. It was a singular circumstance, for the bodies of the drowned never float in such fashion; but the porter, not stopping to speculate upon it, procured the necessary assistance, and proceeded to land the body. It came up unusually heavy, and when at last brought to the surface, was found to be made fast by a rope around the waist to the missing barrel of pitch. There was a gag securely fastened in the mouth, and these two circumstances were positive evidence that murder had been done.

When the body was landed upon the pier, it was found to be in a tolerable state of preservation, although there were conclusive signs that it had been in the water for some time. It was the body of a female, entirely nude, with the exception of an embroidered linen chemise and one lisle-thread stocking, two sizes larger than the foot, but exactly fitting the full-rounded limb. The face and the contour of the form were, therefore, fully exposed to examination, and proved to be those of a woman who must have been very handsome. There was the cicatrice of an old wound on a lower limb, but otherwise there was no spot or blemish upon the body.

In due time the body was buried; but the head was removed, and preserved in the office of the city physician, with the hope that it might be the means of establishing the identity of the dead, and leading to the detection of the murderer.

The police on both sides of the river were intensely interested in the case; but they found themselves impotent before that head of a woman, who seemed to have never been seen upon earth in life. They could do nothing, therefore, but wait patiently for whatever developments time might bring.

Chance finally led to the desired identification. A gentleman who had known her intimately for two years, happening to see the head, at once declared it to be that of Ada Ricard. The detectives eagerly clutched at this thread, and were soon in possession of the coincidence in time of her disappearance and that of the barrel of pitch to which the body was lashed. They further found that, since that time, she had not been seen in the city, nor could any trace of her be discovered in other sections of the country, through correspondence with the police authorities of distant cities. They had thus a woman lost and a body found, and the case was considered to be in a most promising condition.

The next step was to establish the identity by the testimony of those who had known the missing woman most intimately. The detectives, therefore, instituted a search, which was finally successful, for Charles Ricard, her putative husband. He had not lived with her for some time, and had not even seen or heard of her for months; but his recollection was perfect, and he gave a very minute statement of her distinguishing marks. He remembered that she had persisted in wearing a pair of very heavy earrings, until their weight had slit one of her ears entirely, and the other nearly so, and that, as a consequence, both ears had been pierced a second time, and unusually high up. He regretted that her splendid array of teeth had been marred by the loss of one upon the left side of the mouth, and told how a wound had been received, whose cicatrice appeared upon one of her limbs, stating exactly its location. He dwelt with some pride upon the fact that she had been forced, by the unusual development, to wear stockings too large for her feet, and gave a general description of hair, cast of face, height, and weight that was valuable, because minute.

When he gave this statement he was not aware of the death of his wife, or of the finding of her body, and without being informed of either fact he was taken to Jersey City, and suddenly confronted with the head. The instant he saw it he sank into a chair in horror

His statement having been compared with the head and the record of the body, the similitude was found to be exact, except as to the teeth. The head had one tooth missing on each side of the mouth, and this fact having been called to his attention, Ricard insisted that she had lost but one when he last saw her, but it was highly probable the other had been forced out in the struggle which robbed her of her life, and the physician, for the first time making a minute examination, found that the tooth upon the right side had been forced from its place but was still adhering to the gum. He easily pushed it back to its proper position, and there was the head without a discrepancy between it and the description of Ada Ricard.

The detectives found other witnesses, and among them the hair-dresser who had acted in that capacity for Ada Ricard during many months, who, in common with all the others, fully confirmed the evidence of Charles Ricard. The identity of the murdered woman was therefore established beyond question.

Naturally the next step was to solve the mystery of her death. The detectives went to work with unusual caution, but persisted in the task they had assigned themselves, and were slowly gathering the shreds of her life, to weave from them a thread that would lead to the author of her tragical death, when they were suddenly "floored," to use their own energetic expression. Ada Ricard herself appeared at a down-town New York hotel, in perfect health and unscathed in person.

The explanation was simple. The whim had suddenly seized her to go to New Orleans, and she had gone without leave-taking or warning. It was no unusual incident in her wandering life, and her speedy return was due only to the fact that she found the Southern city only a military camp under the iron rule of General Butler, and therefore an unprofitable field for her.

The ghastly head became more of a mystery than before. The baffled detectives could again only look at it helplessly, and send descriptions of it over the country. At last it was seen by a woman named Callahan, living in Boston, who was in search of a daughter who had gone astray. She instantly pronounced it to be that of her child, and she was corroborated by all the members of her family and several of her neighbors. The identification was no less specific than before, and the perplexed authorities, glad at last to know something certainly, gave Mrs. Callahan an order for the body. Before, however, she had completed her arrangements for its transfer to Boston, a message reached her from the daughter, who was lying sick in Bellevue Hospital, and so the head once more became a mystery. And such it has always remained. The body told that a female who had been delicately reared, who had fared sumptuously, and had been arrayed in costly fabrics, had been foully done to death, just as she was stepping into the dawn of womanhood—and that is all that is known. Her name, her station, her history, her virtues, or it may be, her frailties, all went down with her life, and were irrevocably lost. There is every probability that her case will always be classed as unfinished business.

THE BURKE CASE.

It is not often that a merchant going to his place of business in the morning, finds his stock of rich goods dabbled the whole length of his spacious store with blood, and under his open window looking out upon such a thoroughfare as Broadway, sees the mangled remnants of a faithful servant on whom thirty-six stab-wounds had been inflicted before he would yield up his life. Such a scene as this was encountered in the case now to be narrated, and which remains, after the lapse of sixteen years, unsurpassed among remarkable murders.

When, early on the morning of the 18th of July, 1856, a clerk of Samuel Joyce, tailor, whose shop was on the second floor of No. 378 Broadway, attempted to to enter the establishment, he was much surprised to find the door locked. Bartholomew Burke, the porter, had slept in the store for several years, and had never before been remiss in opening it at the proper hour. The clerk stood, puzzled and wondering, until he caught sight of a faint blood-stain on the handle of the door. The marks of murder make men wonderfully cautious, and he hurried into the street to find a policeman. Jourdan was encountered near by, and going up stairs he looked curiously for an instant at the stain on the handle, and then kicked in the door. Entering the room he encountered a spectacle that his experience had not then, and has never since equalled.

The instant he opened the door Burke had been assailed, and fought long and bravely. The weapons used in the terrible affray both remained in the room as frightful evidences of the horrors of the night. Beside the dead man lay a pair huge shears, plainly witnessing that they had been his weapon, but they were no match for the short keen-edged sword, blood-clotted to the hilt, which the murderer had dropped close by.

The struggle must have occupied at least ten minutes, and could not have been entirely noiseless; and yet no intimation of it reached any human ear. It occurred in a room with a window partly open, which looked upon the great artery of a populous city. A score of persons must have passed the building while the tragedy was going on; but to none of them came any knowledge of it, and the family occupying the floor above slept, unconscious of the bloody work.

The assassin had gone from the building unseen. He had washed his hands and face at the wash-stand, in a front corner of the room, and had probably removed every sign of the murder from his person. But he had received a slight cut in the hand, that had persisted in bleeding, and hence the stain upon the door-knob and a few spots of blood upon the stairs. He had, however, gone from his work without physical exhaustion or mental trepidation. He had walked steadily down stairs, and had not only thoughtfully locked the door and removed the key, to make sure that the murder should not be discovered until after daylight, but, at the bottom of the stairway, had remembered that the trickling from his hand was leaving a red trail for the officers of the law to follow, and he had bound up his wound. He left no more of the tell-tale spots behind him, and, in stepping from the entry-way into the street, all signs of his existence vanished, except that, a hundred feet from the door, a belated citizen met a man walking leisurely, and carelessly whistling a popular air, whose face he did not see, and whose person he did not note, except that he had a bandaged hand.

Murder in that day was a crime in New York, and that of Burke had been so atrocious in its details that it created intense excitement, and George W. Matsell, who was then chief of police, put his best detectives on the track of the murderer. It was naturally inferred, at first, that the porter had been slain in an endeavor to protect the property of his employer from some friend who had determined to turn thief; but, when an examination of the stock was made, it was found that not a dollar's worth of the property of Mr. Joyce had been stolen. The trunk of Burke was found open and in disorder; but there was no evidence that anything of value had been removed, and, as the shop had certainly not been robbed, greed had plainly not been the motive for the crime.

This discovery completely baffled the officers, and placed the affair among the extraordinary murders. Burke had been a man of humble station and retiring habits, with few or no intimate associates, and it was found impossible to gather such details of his life as would be of service in pursuing his assassin. The officers had not only to track an unknown murderer, but to discover a motive for his crime, and this fact added immensely to the difficulties of the task.

There was, indeed, a glimmer of hope in the circumstance that, about half-past nine o'clock on the evening of his death, Burke had been in the saloon in the basement of the building in which he was employed, in company with a man with whom he had drunk. The two men had gone out together, Burke carrying a pot of beer which he had purchased; and, about ten o'clock, a citizen, passing on the opposite side of the street, had seen two men sitting at the front window of Joyce's shop, with two empty beer mugs on the window-sill before them. But this man was a stranger to every one who had seen him, and no one was able to give any satisfactory description of his person. So, in pursuing him, the officers found themselves in chase of a shadow that constantly grew more unsubstantial.

The sword was, at first, eagerly seized as a means of discovering the murderer. It was so peculiar in itself, and so unusual a weapon for an affray, that a search for the owner, as a starting point in the pursuit, was begun, with the greatest confidence in its success. But even this resource failed, and no one could be found who had ever seen it before Jourdan picked it up, blood-clotted and blunted, from the floor where the murderer had dropped it.

The investigation by the coroner extended through three days, and was thorough and exhaustive. The detectives followed diligently such slight clues as they could find, and produced, at the inquest, several persons who had known the murdered man; but, in the end, their testimony proved valueless. They knew him, as had all his acquaintances, as industrious, and generally sober-but none of them knew of any one who bore him ill-will, or who had cause to wish him dead. It was developed that he had saved $900 during his employment with Mr. Joyce; but the money was found untouched in the savings' banks where he had deposited it, and no attempt had ever been made by any unauthorized person to withdraw it. The coroner and his jury were baffled at every turn, and were driven at last to the unsatisfactory verdict of death "at the hands of some person unknown."

No progress beyond this verdict has ever been made. No one has ever been even suspected of having committed the crime; and for thirteen years the assassin has so preserved his dreadful secret that the case still remains as unfinished business.

THE LUTENER CASE.

On Tuesday, the 10th day of January, 1854, Dr. William R. T. Lutener, at an early hour of the morning, left his residence, in One Hundred and Twenty-eighth street, near Fourth avenue, to go to his office, on the second floor of No. 458 Broadway, and arrived there safely at nine o'clock. He went down town that wintry morning, one of the most favored of men, both by fortune and nature. He was thirty-one years of age, and had been six years married to an amiable and beautiful lady. He was of splendid person, remarkably handsome features, and of more than average intellect and culture. He had become celebrated as an aurist, and his practice had become so extensive and lucrative, that he had already amassed a competence, and had surrounded himself, both at home and in his office, with all of the comforts and many of the luxuries of life.

He entered his office in thorough good humor, and, speaking cheerily to his charwoman, sat down near a front window, facing it; and, as a consequence, with his back to the door. He picked up a morning paper, and as he opened it the woman left the room and he remained alone. Having a visit to make to a sister, on the eastern side of the city, the woman left the building at half-past nine o'clock, and was absent an hour.

During that hour, and, as nearly as he could judge, at about ten o'clock, a gentleman hurrying to keep an appointment with a bank president, when passing the building, No. 458, thought he heard the report of a pistol. He paused a moment, and looked anxiously about him, but seeing no apparent cause for the noise he had heard, rushed on and thought no more of the matter, for he was intent on negotiating a loan, and was a little behind time.

At about half-past ten o'clock—people are rarely exact as to time—the charwoman returned and on her way up-stairs paused to look in and see if the doctor wanted anything. She rushed screaming from the room, and in a moment scores were crowding into it to be horrified by the sight that had affrighted her. Dr. Lutener lay dead upon the floor, his face pressing the carpet immediately under the front window, and his hand closed with the rigid clutch of death upon the newspaper he had been reading. It was plain that he had been shot from behind as he sat reading, and had tumbled from his chair, done with the world and its joys forever. There could not be an instant's doubt that it was murder.

Almost the first development at the coroner's inquest was the fact that there had been trouble of some kind between Lutener and William Hays and his wife, who resided in his vicinity. Almost the first act of the coroner was to order the arrest of Hays and his wife, and both were taken during the day.

The inquest was immediately begun, was continued during six successive days, and a large amount of testimony was taken on each day. No one had seen the murder done, and, with the exception stated, no ear had heard the report of the pistol, but several persons passing up and down the stairs, had seen a woman thickly veiled pass into Lutener's office and come out again almost instantly. It was theorized, therefore, that a woman was the assassin, and every effort was made to bring the crime home to Mrs. Hays, and to her husband, as an accessory before the fact; but they were all fruitless. The witnesses could not identify Mrs. Hays as the woman they had seen enter the office, and she on her part proved a complete and positive *alibi*, showing that at the hour when the murder was committed she was transacting some law business in an office in Wall street, and was seen there by several reputable witnesses. The coroner's jury, therefore, were forced to bring in a verdict of death at the hands of a person unknown, and Hays and his wife were discharged.

Where the coroner left the case it still remains. For fifteen years the detectives have been powerless to unearth the assassin. It remains upon the books, classed, as it has been all these years, as unfinished business.

When the Inspector had pulled these stories, with many others of like character, from the shelves of a memory that was overburdened with the details of many horrible crimes that long ago passed out of general remembrance, I had very little respect left for the venerable axiom that "Murder Will Out." Having selected from his tales such as were typical of all, I was desirous of adding to them any homicidal statistics that would determine how often the axiom has been disproved in the late police experiences of New York.

There was but one way of approximating the truth, and I pursued it. Visiting the coroner's office and beginning with the last recorded case of 1868, I worked patiently backward through the mortuary records, until I began to stumble in the scrawling illegibility prior to 1856. As I progressed in my work I encountered facts of such interest, that although not strictly pertinent to the object of my search, I took note of them. I found, for instance, that one person had died of "stricknine," and another by "strycknine;" that one had perished by "poisonous sassage," and another by "gluttony," no particular food being charged with the offence. One man had been "accidentally stabbed while skylarking"—whatever that may be—and another had died of "an overdose of laudanum, but whether taken *internally* or not the jury are unable to say."

Keeping my main object steadily in view, when I had concluded the examination of fifty-two huge volumes, I was able to compile the following startling table:

HOMICIDES OF SIXTEEN YEARS.

Year.	By persons known.	By persons unknown.	Total.
1856	24	11	35
1857	42	13	55
1858	47	12	59
1859	36	15	51
1860	32	5	47
1861	37	15	52
1862	31	15	46
1863	38	11	49
1864	42	8	50
1865	49	12	61
1866	26	9	35
1867	24	10	34
1868	39	9	48
1869	36	5	41
1870	37	4	41
1871	34	8	42
Total	574	172	746

In this table are included as homicides only cases where death was conclusively ascertained to be the result of violence inflicted by human agency. I went over very many cases where the verdict was "from causes unknown," or "supposed drowning," or "injuries received in some manner unknown;" and, giving humanity the benefit of the doubt, classed them all as accidents, although there is every reason to believe that in some of these vague surmises of juries groping helplessly for facts, homicides are hidden. Nor did I seek to swell the list by including among the homicides the nine men who were slain in the Bayard street riot of 1857, nor the ninety-four who were found by the juries to have perished in the great riots of 1863. The table does include, however, seventy-four cases of infanticide, and it is a terrible proof of the ease and safety with which this crime can be perpetrated in a large city, that in only thirteen of these cases were the juries able to discover the criminals.

I must give one more credit to humanity and say that only a very small per cent. of these homicides were murders. Some of the affairs bordered closely upon accidents, others were killings in self-defence, and very few of them ranked legally above manslaughter in the first degree.

Homicidal acts in the metropolis have always been unartistic and hot-blooded, as is conclusively shown by the weapons used. These appear upon the record to have been fire-arms, knives, razors, sword-canes, swords, cords, bludgeons, bayonets, cart-rungs, tumblers, bricks, fire-tongs, smoothing-irons, axes, mallets, hammers, paving-stones, glue-pots, boot-heels, and once the point of an umbrella. It is remarkable that only eight times in these thirteen years has murder been artistically done by poison, and more singular still that in five of these cases the criminals were detected, notwithstanding the popular belief that this meanest and stealthiest mode of feloniously taking life is also the safest. These facts make it apparent that while the average of homicides in New York has been a fraction over one per week for thirteen years, there have been comparatively few wilful and malicious murders. It is true that within the period examined thirty-three wives were slain by their husbands, but even in nearly all of these cases, the "malice prepense," which is the essential ingrediment of murder, and the sign of "the wicked and depraved heart" required by the law, was wanting. The killings by persons unknown were more frequently wilful than in the other class, but even here the testimony taken by the coroners shows that the purpose to take life often was not mentally formed before the deed had been physically accomplished.

Deducting the sixty-one infanticides where the culprits were undiscovered, and it is apparent that nine-two adults have, in thirteen years; met violent deaths, and the assailants have escaped detection.

Lest some devotee of proverbs may yet insist that "Murder will out," I append some facts concerning a case later and more celebrated than any yet mentioned.

A CELEBRATED CRIME.

NOTHING so startles a people as a mysterious homicide, and nothing is more ephemeral in its interest. The cases cited have not more completely passed out of the public mind than have their successors, even including the great case of 1870, known as the Nathan murder, at No. 12 West 23d street, which occurred between the hours of 12:30 and 3 o'clock A. M. of Friday, July 29, and which, from the character of its victim and its startling incidents, became a celebrated crime. Everywhere it was for many days the prevailing topic of conversation, and the columns of the leading journals of the country were almost monopolized with the statement and discussion of its facts. There was nothing in the popular interest to indicate any morbid taste for the horrible, but the universal excitement caused by the event was due to the fact that it appealed with irresistible force to the fears of every individual. It was a foul murder done in the presumed security of the home of the victim, and no man could be sure that he would not next be sacrificed to secure the safety of prowling brutality.

Having briefly given the leading facts of the murder, so that subsequent revelations can be understood, it is my main purpose to relate the thus far unsuccessful groping of the police for the assassin. The narrative will offer cumulative evidence that murder will not "out" at any man's bidding; but on the contrary, that when unwitnessed, if the murderer leaves no positive proof of his identity behind him, ingenuity and energy are frequently powerless to make it out.

Benjamin Nathan was a millionaire of New York, well known and highly esteemed for his personal qualities. Descended from an old Jewish Portuguese family, he was a native of New York, as his father had been before him. Born to opulence and correct principles, he had added to the one, and closely adhered to the other, through his life of fifty-six years. An Israelite in his faith, he was catholic in his sympathies, and gave of his abundance to the needy of all creeds. A man of culture and refined tastes, he moved in intelligent and accomplished society. The peaceful and natural death of such a man would have caused public expression of sorrow; but when his son, who went to his bedroom at 6 o'clock in the morning to call him to a devotional duty of the day, found him lying upon the floor bloody and mangled out of semblance to his kind, with nine gaping wounds upon his head, it is not surprising that there was a general cry of horror, and that the people with one voice demanded the capture and punishment of the murderer.

Superintendent Jourdan and Captain Kelso, who immediately took personal charge of the case, saw all its difficulties at a glance. In some respects the crime told its own story too distinctly for Jourdan, who years ago became known as the keenest detective on the continent, to believe himself mistaken as to the leading facts. It was plain to him that the event had lifted a criminal from ordinary larceny to a murder of rarely paralleled brutality. Intent only upon theft, the intruder rifled the clothes of the sleeping man, which lay on a chair remote from the bed, of a Perregaux watch, No. 5,657, three diamond shirt studs, what money the pocket-book contained, and the key of the small safe which stood in the library beside the door opening into the bedroom. Going to the safe, he knelt down before it, opened it, and began his examination of its contents. Some noise he made awakened Mr. Nathan, who sprang from his bed, and the thief springing up at the same moment, the two men met in the doorway, the face of the thief being brought into bold relief by the gaslight to his left. Not knowing of Mr. Nathan's defective vision, he saw himself identified, and believing his retreat cut off, he struck savagely at Mr. Nathan with a short iron bar turned at the ends, which soon became famous as a ship carpenter's "dog." From this point there is a succession of enigmas until the assassin left the room, after rifling the safe of whatever portable valuables it contained. Carrying the "dog," he went stealthily down stairs, unfastened the front door, which had been carefully secured at 12:20 o'clock A. M., laid the "dog" down on the hall floor, and passed out into the street. From this point there are other enigmas, but not so baffling as those within the house.

The weapon and the unnecessary brutality were the chief difficulties. There were puzzling questions as to how the outlaw had entered the house, as to the manner in which the blows had been given, as to how the stricken man had fallen, as to how the blood smears had got upon the wall and door-casing, with others of less interest; but none of these were vital to the pursuit, and they were considered more as a relaxation from the weightier matters involved than for their intrinsic importance. The weapon was, as Jourdan remarked, the "great puzzler." Had any ordinary burglar's tool been used, or the instrument been one that any thief of high or low degree had ever been known to use, the case would have been clearer, and Jourdan would have known what sink of iniquity to stir in order to start the murderer; but this "dog," whose appearance indicated long use in its legitimate sphere, led only into the mechanical world, and widened the circle of inquiry from tens to tens of thousands. But paralyzed as the detectives were by the "dog," the effect of that mangled corpse in the same way was scarcely less. Rarely had murder been more cruelly done, and never since Bartholomew Burke was found with his body gashed by thirty-six wounds had the police been confronted with a sight so horrible. Jourdan, looking upon such a sight as this, asked what burglar or sneak-thief would have wasted time and courted destruction by work like this, but found no answer in his long experience or intimate knowledge of the habits and impulses of outlaws.

There were other baffling facts encountered at the outset of the investigation, secondary in importance it is true, but of such gravity that in ordinary cases they would be considered insuperable obstacles. Groping his way from the time and place of the murder, Jourdan speedily found that prior to the crime no one had been seen lurking about the house who could be connected in any way with the deed. Again, there were no marks of violence upon the house. There was nowhere the faintest trace of a "jimmy" upon a door or window, nor any sign discernible of a burglarious entrance. Nor had the murderer left any trace of his personality, except that perplexing "dog." Not a scrap of his clothing had been torn from him to tell the tale of his identity, nor had he left anywhere in the house the imprint of either his hand or foot. Attempting to glean something of value from the time intervening between the murder and the moment of its discovery, Jourdan found nothing but a doubt and another perplexity The policeman upon the post persisted resolutely in declaring under oath, that when he passed the house at 4:30 A. M. he tried both front doors, and they were fastened; and when he passed again a little before 6 o'clock, he noticed that the hall door was closed. There was positive and stronger evidence, however, that the door was not only unlocked but partly open at least an hour before the murder was discovered. The testimony on this point also introduced a man in laboring dress, carrying a dinner pail, who at 5 o'clock ascended the steps of the house, and, having picked up a paper from the topmost step, went on his way. That man and that paper at once became and yet are mysteries.

It will be seen that Superintendent Jourdan had only negations to go upon. As a first and obvious step, the house was thoroughly searched, first for signs of the murderer, and, these failing, for the missing property. From cellar to garret it was thoroughly examined, even to the furniture and carpets. But nothing was found. Next the water-tank was emptied, without result; and lastly the waste-pipes of the closets and wash-basins were flushed, and the street sewers carefully examined for a long distance in all directions, but no trace of the articles was found. Absolute proof having thus been obtained that the missing property of the murdered man had been carried from the house on the person of the murderer, Jourdan next caused the flooring of the stable to be taken up and the edges of the boards to be examined by experts to determine whether such an instrument as the "dog" had been used in putting it down. He received a negative reply.

Now, Washington and Frederick Nathan, sons of the deceased, Mrs. Kelly, the housekeeper, and William Kelly, her adult son, were sleeping in the house when the murder was committed, and their sleep was undisturbed throughout the night by any suspicious or unusual sound. All of the search of the house which has been referred to was accomplished without the knowledge of its inmates, who were separately subjected to a rigid examination. As the result of all this labor, Captain Kelso, standing at the side of the murdered man, said to Superintendent Jourdan, "An outsider?" and the Chief answered decisively, "No doubt of it." There was the gratifying fact, however, that the officials, within six hours from the discovery of the crime, were in possession of various facts subsequently developed on the inquest, which completely exonerated all the inmates from any suspicion of complicity in the deed. There was no reasonable ground for suspecting any of them; but as the police were confronted at once with the tragedy and a strange family, they were of course compelled to closely scrutinize the character and antecedents of all those who were in the house at the time.

There were blotches of blood upon the night-gown of Frederick Nathan, and his socks were soaked in blood; but it was plain that these stains resulted from contact with the corpse after his brother had discovered it. It was equally plain that the few faint imprints of bloody feet upon the stairs, which the newspapers made vastly more numerous and conspicuous than the reality, were made by him as he ran down to the street with his brother to give the alarm. There were many little circumstances connected with both the young men and the two Kellys, which to jealous minds might be, and did become, "confirmation strong as proofs of Holy Writ," but, put into the crucible of detective experience, evaporated into utter nothingness; and before the murder was a day old all of the inmates, in the minds of those familiar with the case, were as completely cleared of all suspicion as they soon afterwards became in the public mind, after passing through a terrible ordeal of suspected guilt.

Out, therefore, into the whole wide world, the officials were forced to project the appliances of detection, with the hope of discovering the assassin. Instantly all the police force of the city was set to work watching the pawn shops and jewelry stores for the appearance of the stolen property, and searching all ship and boat yards for the identification of the "dog." This labor was also gradually extended into almost every department of mechanics, as the "dog" was in the end claimed as a tool of almost every trade. According to the confident assertions palmed upon the police, it may have been used by ship-carpenters, boat-builders, post-trimmers, ladder-makers, slaters, pump-makers, sawyers, scene-shifters in theatres, or by iron-moulders as a clamp for flasks; and lastly one person wanted all rag-pickers held for the crime because he was sure the so-called "dog" was the hook of one of that fraternity. It is plain, therefore, that an instrument that might have been used by any one of these craftsmen, must have led the detectives into an inexhaustible field for search.

That the missing property was not discovered was due solely to the prudence of the assassin. He could have offered none of the articles for sale without detection, so close was the surveillance in regard to them. A mistake was indeed made by the family in the first list furnished the police of what had been taken; but it was soon rectified and a correct statement given to the public, Jourdan saying, with rare common-sense for a policeman, that there could not be too many people looking out for these things. But although the watch has been strict and incessant up to the present writing, no trace of any of the articles has been found, and it is evident that the assassin has either thrown them away so that they shall never be found, or, if more covetous than sensible, has secreted them to await disposition when the excitement shall have died away. It seems almost morally certain, however, that they never reached the channels of habitual crime, as these were thoroughly searched for them, and moreover every known or suspected criminal in New York was required to account for himself during the night of the murder. The thieves were never so overhauled before, and never was there such a sudden and universal hegira of the professionals from the city; nor has there ever been of late years so little crime in New York as during the ten days succeeding the Twenty-third street atrocity.

The power of money was added to detective acumen as an additional means to drag the murderer from his hiding place, and the second proclamation issued by Mayor Hall offered large rewards, which were adroitly divided to make the most of every chance of finding a clue to the assassin; but although supplemented by the offer of $10,000 reward by the New York Stock Exchange, of which Mr. Nathan had been a member for thirty years, they all remained unproductive. Yet it was not for lack of knowledge of the money to be given for information, for never were rewards brought so generally to public knowledge. They were posted in huge placards all over the city, and were sent in multitudes in small hand-bills all over the country. Never was a criminal more earnestly and intelligently sought for than in this case, and never was a search more barren of results.

The pursuit certainly did not fail for lack of popular assistance, as Superintendent Jourdan was in constant receipt, for many days after the murder, of letters from all sorts of people in all kinds of places, which contained every variety of hints, theories, and supposed information. Some few of these missives were plainly dictated by an earnest and disinterested desire that the murderer should be apprehended, and a sincere purpose to aid in the efforts to that end. But of such there were very few. The perusal of these hundreds of letters would do much to convert the most skeptical to a belief in the original depravity and innate stupidity of mankind. Such eagerness to accuse personal foes of a most heinous crime, such assumptions of superior capacity, and such extreme desire to extract a little individual profit out of blood so wofully shed, I never saw before and do not desire to see again. There was indeed a satisfaction in finding that only three persons in all the nation proposed that the murderer should be hunted down by bloodhounds, and offered to furnish the animals for that purpose. It was some comfort to make the most of this comparatively encouraging fact, as I found few others even negatively good. There was one fellow, determined to do his utmost to destroy a business rival or personal foe, continually writing that a Pine street broker whom he named ought to be watched, and finally demanding his arrest and openly charging him with the murder. Another of comprehensive malice advanced his theory and vented his spleen thus:

DEAR SIR: All stock brokers are scoundrels. I have only met with one exception in all my experience. I am satisfied some miserable stock broker or operator has murdered MR. Nathan. The idea of a sneak-thief or burglar is simply absurd. Mr. Nathan may have been honest; if he was, he was surrounded on all sides with rascals, and he held some papers in his safe which some scoundrel wanted. To get at these papers he killed Mr. N. What those papers were I haven't the slightest idea. Now watch every member or any one connected directly or indirectly with the Stock Exchange.

ROBERTO.

There were scores of letters insisting upon the guilt of one of the sons or of Kelly, and indignantly demanding their arrest, and there was even an attempt to frighten Mrs. Kelly into believing that she was suspected, as she received the following note through the post-office:

They have found out that you *know more* than you tell. This makes you an accessory or party to the crime. To hide anything is criminal. Your only hope is to tell before you're arrested.

There were many clumsy and malicious attempts to aid in fastening suspicion upon the young Nathans; one of the most clumsy and despicable of which was a letter addressed to Washington Nathan and dropped in the street so that it should reach Jourdan's eyes. It reads thus:

MR. W. NATHUN. DEER SUR: In reply to your Request, all I have got to say is that if you will not do it, why, I won't of course; for I don't want to have my hand in the Bloody Work. Hoping for a reply, I remain yours,

C. BOWARD.

But the meanest of all these missives, because of its speculative purpose, read thus:

WASH: Jourdan has just received damning proofs. I am in employ. The city is not a safe place. I hope for a reward when all has blown over. In haste,

A FRIEND.

A quack doctor, holding the rules of spelling and the detectives in equal and utter contempt, sent this, with his name signed and his business card enclosed:

BOSTON, August 4, 1870.

To the Chief of Police New York.

SIR: I am of the opinion that the detectives know that Washington Nathan committed the murder upon his father and the merderer can pay twice the amount of the reward offered to screne himself. Why has the detectives not obtaned a serch warrent and serched the whole and of Washington affects in the city and out of the city. If what has been stated is true a jury would convict W— Nathan. As I look at things the detectives have done not a thing to bring the merder to punishment.

Your &Ce.

Another, sharing in the general curiosity to discover how the assassin entered the house, sent the following:

SUNDAY EVENING, July 31, 1870.

DEAR SIR: Passing the house of Mr. Nathan this afternoon, my attention was especially drawn toward the front portico over the steps. It seemed easy to my eye for a person to climb to the window of the room over the front door. There is a narrow moulding or *shelf*, may be two or three inches in width, on the front of No. 14, which ends about half the height of Mr. Nathan's portico. A person could, by using this shelf and holding to the columns of the portico, swing himself on top of the same. Once there, an entrance through the library window would seem an easy matter, especially if the window had been left unfastened. If you will have the goodness to examine the front of No. 14, you will, I think, notice a mark or marks of a boot *or scrape* on the brown-stone front of the building. I noticed such a mark this afternoon, but the officers in front of the building not allowing any one to halt, I thought I would address you a line calling your attention to this.

Yours truly,

J. B. H.

Superintendent John Jourdan.

The way by which the assassin entered the house is yet a matter of theory; but the police, for reasons that do not seem conclusive, have rejected the hypothesis presented in this letter, and the weight of opinion among them seems inclined in favor of the basement door, which is supposed to have been accidentally left unlocked.

There was another class of letters dealing in personalities, which it was evident were dictated either by an honest purpose to aid the authorities, or an intense desire to get an enemy into trouble. These were the letters from all parts of the country detailing the sudden appearance of suspicious persons in the localities of the writers. It is marvellous how many men of hang-dog faces and sneaking demeanor were to be found just after the murder. One was seen in a far-off town of Michigan, who it was subsequently found had never been in New York at all, nor done a dishonest act in his life. An old lady summering at Greenwich, Conn., wrote of the arrival at her hotel in a buggy of a man and woman who "behaved queerly." Although her honesty was apparent in every line, she had encountered nothing more serious than a taciturn gentleman and a lady in a fit of sulks. A barber in Jersey City wrote to say, that on the day Mr. Nathan was killed two suspicious-looking men came to his shop. One got shaved and had his hair cut, and the other, the hardest-looking one of the two, got his hair cut only. But this, and the fact that they said they were going to "Cincinaty," were the only suspicious circumstances mentioned. A gentleman of Princeton, N. J., wrote of a young man appearing at his door Sunday morning, who was respectably dressed, but "seemed shy, and said he was going to Philadelphia, but had no money. Some of the family remarked, 'His hands are stained,' and another said, 'With blackberries;' he then drew them down and muttered, 'Blackberries.'" This pilgrim with the stained hands was "so exceedingly reticent," and "his appearance so genteel, and his manner so false," that he must perforce be the Nathan murderer. A gentleman at Amenia, N. Y., told how he was reading the account of the murder on Saturday at the depot when a stranger asked, "What is the news from the city to-day?" to which he answered, "Nothing in particular;" but the stranger looking at him inquiringly, he said further, "There has been a shocking murder of a prominent citizen of New York." The stranger, however, manifested no surprise and asked no more questions. The reader concluded he had read the account, and proceeded to remark on the boldness and object of the crime, and mentioned the name of the murdered man, when the stranger, "without saying he was acquainted with the family, or making any other remark, said, 'Is it the old man Nathan?' and in nearly the same breath asked if there was any war news." In many ways his behavior was singular, and he departed abruptly and without apparent cause on a southern train a few minutes later. Next day he got into jail in a neighboring town as the Nathan assassin, but proved to be only a harmless lunatic.

Strangest of all the stories of suspicious appearances, was that which came officially from the detective department of the Philadelphia police, in a letter telling of "a man lurking in a thinly populated part of our city, under circumstances of a very suspicious character. He was first seen on Saturday asleep in a corner of a field, and was then lost sight of until Monday afternoon. Some two miles away from the first place mentioned, he was then seen to emerge from some bushes near the side of a road, and also close to a railroad bridge. He requested of a party passing by the loan of a newspaper. One of them had one and handed it to him, which he read, and at once proceeded to talk about the Nathan murder. While he was reading he showed signs of being greatly agitated, and in the midst of the account a train of cars appeared in sight, and without notice he jumped behind some bushes and concealed himself; after the train passed he reappeared, and when questioned about his strange conduct said that some of his friends from New York, which place he left on Friday, might be on the train, and he did not care they should see him in his sad condition." This man had stockings "with marks of blood upon them," and on his trousers were "spots, apparently blood." He also wore three studs, supposed to be diamonds, and a watch and chain, the chain partly concealed. The Philadelphia police were firmly convinced that this was the murderer, and out of these circumstances grew the report so widely published of the arrest of the assassin in that city. The story originated with two bricklayers, and they telling it to a detective, that officer rushed off and gave it to the newspapers as a first means of arresting the suspected. Naturally enough, nothing more was ever seen or heard of the man of the bushes and spots of blood.

One last case of this kind is given in the following:

READING, Aug. 3, 1870.

Dect. JORDAN, New York.

DER SIR: Last Saturday afternoon a young man arrived in this town.

He was small—a little below medium height—weight about 135 or 40 lbs—had on a gray suit with light cap. Had a large amount of money—Two large rolls of bills one of large denomination—some being 50's. His conduct appeerd strange to the writer. He evidently did not earn his money by work by the manner he exhibited and spent it treating every one—He arrived here about 4 or 5 O'clok in afternoon and left in a few hours saying he was going to Phila for a few days from there to New York stay a *month* and then to Europe—He stopped at a relatives—a german watchmaker in Penn St North side a little above 8th. the few hours he was here—he accompanny him to depot. He said he had worked nothing for five years and had just come from the *plains*, Why should he stay so short a time with his relatives here? Why such rough hands if only traveling?

There were scores of letters purporting to give information, and of these only those confined to the "dog" were found to be of value. The others either related to matters of which the authorities were more fully informed than the writers, or made distinct assertions which were subsequently, after a vast deal of labor, found to be unqualifiedly false. A single specimen of this class must suffice, and here it is:

To Superintendent J. JOURDAN.

SIR: The murderer and an accomplice of Nathan can be found in a street between Norfolk and Clinton, and between Houston and the Tenth Ward, not far from an old slaughter-house. Part of the missed articles can be found in the sub-cellar of what was once a packing-house. I would like to make the rewards, but dare not give my name for fear of revenge.

Such letters as this—of which there were several, but all the others relating to the stolen articles exclusively—added greatly to the labors of the case, as in every instance detectives were detailed to exhaust the matter; for Jourdan was determined to neglect no chance, however remote, and would not turn a deaf ear to any plausible story, however disreputable its origin. Some of these letters, however, received no other attention than a contemptuous smile, as was the case with that of the individual who, believing the sensational story of the three bloody finger-marks on the Nathan wall, told where the man with the fourth finger missing who had made those marks could be found. As there were no finger-marks whatever in the Nathan house, the joke was a failure.

Jourdan, however, had most amateur assistance in the formation of theories of the murder. It is amazing how many born detectives there are in the country unappreciated. These geniuses rushed boldly forward on this occasion to prove their value to the police service—some of them, it must be added, claiming pay for ability they rated so highly. In all these scores of theories and suggestions there was little that was original and nothing that was valuable. The most of them presumed the guilt of one of the inmates, thus naturally assuming the most obvious and least tenable theory of the case; and floundering as all did in partial knowledge of the facts, their deductions were invariably erroneous. The bulk of the letters of this class suggested that the missing property would be found in the waste-pipes of the house, but none of them were received until after Jourdan had exhausted the possibility. Some, however, were more original, as that of one citizen suggested that the "murder was committed by a man whose object was to find among the papers in the victim's pocket-book or safe the record of the combination-lock of the Broad street safe, with a view to its robbery. . . . Having been discovered by Mr. Nathan, he killed him because he was known to him." Two persons desired that the eyes of the murdered man should be examined for the image of the murderer. It is proper to say that this was not done, for the reason that Jourdan had no faith in the expedient, as it had before failed in his experience. One person in Buffalo, who was not ashamed to sign his full name, wrote thus:

I will not review anything, but simply state that by some means I am aware that the murderer is still in New York on a sick bed. He has either red or brown hair, is of middle age, stout built, and no acquaintance of Mr. Nathan. He struck so terribly only out of fright, not from hatred. His having so much money, he will not dispose of the watches. He will work hard to shift the crime upon the shoulders of another. The only available means to throw him off his guard is a sham arrest and trial of some trustworthy individual, which can easily be accomplished as there is so much money offered. This sham is to be kept from the knowledge of the public. Let the person tried be condemned and the execution be indefinitely postponed. Then hush about all and keep a wary eye everywhere.

Another, with an eye to the dramatic, had faith in the exactly opposite course, and sent the following without date or signature:

I propose; that, when the Inquest draws to a close, and there remains no evidence suficient to hold any one (although there may or may not be suspicions), That something like the following course be pursued—While an unimportant witness is on the stand, the Inquest to be adjourned, *in this way:* some one of position, as a detective, Captain of Police or other proper person, shall interupt the inquest by wispering, in an earnest and misterious way to the Coroner—The Coroner shall then adjourn the inquest. Meanwhile by the proper person and in a proper way, it must be intimated to the whole party assembled especialy to the reporters of the press, That the Detectives have *struck a trail—certain, shure, infalible!* That they can lay their hands on the criminal at a moments notice. That they ask for a little time, merly to suround the case with the proper evidence, So that when they bring their man, conviction will come with him. And meanwhile, every movement of the guilty party is being closely watched so that he canot escape. It must be broadly intimated that the *most cuning* criminal is shure *to forget something, that* something *has been discovered.* All this with startling coments will be published in the papers. The guilty party will believe himself to be watched, and if there is anything the least bit human in him, it is likely he will expose himself by some strange action.

Out of all these letters Superintendent Jourdan gleaned nothing of use but the information before referred to as to the various trades in which the "dog" may have been used. There was yet another class of letters calling upon him to invoke the supernatural to solve the mystery of the murder, and giving him the benefit of dreams. These were not numerous, but, coming as they all did from the great cities, are suggestive of the superstition yet existing in the centres of civilization. "An Interested Reader of the Particulars" announced that "a lady in Brooklyn wishes you to consult a clairvoyant with regard to the horrible Nathan murder. She has known wonderful disclosures in that way." A gentleman doing business in Broadway solemnly wrote:

On the morning of Mr. Nathan's assassination, between the hours of 2 and 4 o'clock, a "medium" of this city (a woman) had a vision of what she believes to be the whole scene. It seemed to her that there were three persons in the transaction, one an old gentleman, who was the victim, another a young man who committed the murder, and the third what she took to be a woman, whose back only appeared in view. The vision was so distinct and terrible that the medium aroused the inmates of the boarding-house by her cries, to whom after coming out of the trance she described what she seemed to have witnessed. Upon being shown, a short time after, a portrait of Mr. Nathan, she instantly recognized the face as that of the victim aforesaid. She believes that she could as quickly recognize the young man if brought into her presence, and claims that she can repeat words that passed between the assassin and Mr. Nathan immediately before and on the first assault. The parties to the murder, she declares, live in Mr. Nathan's house. She insists that the "dog" had been concealed a long time for the purpose to which it was put, and that the jewelry, etc., taken were buried on the premises, and are there to-day.

There was more to the same purport, but I pass to a dreamer who says:

I do not think it foolish to send you the dream I had the other night. I thought I was on the roof of Mr. Nathan's house, and I was attracted by a little piece of string hanging from one of the chimneys. I pulled it up and found the missing things, which consisted of a bloody shirt, in which was wrapped two watches, three studs, some money, papers and a weapon.

Another dreamer says:

NEW YORK August 1870 concerning Mr B. Natnan.
to the Sup Jordon Esq Sir
I was Dreeming 3 knights that everything that was robed of Mr Nathans safe is hiden in the yard water closeth of Mr. Nathans Primusers 23d st Bet Bricks and Seelling I hope you will Be so Kind and have it Serched in the Water closeth in yard Bet Seelling & Bricks if my dreem be found thryho & then Ill Send you another communication
yours .G. hope to see it in
Tuesdays Paper

He was as good as his word, for nothing more was heard of him. Even at a point as remote as Chicago, people were dreaming about the murder. A Dane in that city saw the servant girl of Mr. Nathan as the one who committed the murder. He also saw a clothes-brush stained with blood.

Still another class of letters were those of a taunting character from thieves who instinctively delighted in the failure of the police to trace the murderer, and who could not resist the temptation of scrawling their pleasure in anonymous notes clothed in the peculiar patois of rascality. These missives were few in number and commonplace in character, and the single specimen appended is sufficient to indicate the character of all:

HELLO, CAP. JOURDAN—How about that old Sheeny Nathan. You think you got

Wash. on that biz you and your fly cops are a set of green suckers you cant get the dead wood on nobody you think you got some one dead to rights dont you your hell you are—put Boston Jones on he knows his biz in a horn does that dog look like a cheese cutter or what—or would you sooner go a fishin plenty of caseys Say look here old fel the cove what blowd the safe got away with the ham you bet

The reader can form some idea of the amount of labor forced upon Superintendent Jourdan and Captain Kelso when told that there was no hint in all these hundreds of letters which seemed in the least degree sensible that was not acted upon until it ended in failure. As the net result of the most extraordinary search ever made for a criminal, these officials, at the time these pages are written, are precisely at the point whence they started, both as to facts and theories, except in a partial identification of the "dog." They have not gained an atom of information of any value by the labor of weeks, and their diagnosis of the case remains unchanged. They believe now, as they have from the first, that the intruder in the Nathan mansion on that terrible night was a "duffer," by which name the police mean one who, following some honest pursuit during the day, occasionally sallies forth at night to commit a house robbery. There are hundreds of these men who are entirely unknown to and unsuspected by the authorities, and are the most dangerous, because the least under surveillance, of all the criminal classes. The business of the duffer in the Nathan house was theft only, and he went there without any definite plunder in view. He was discovered while at the safe, which he would not have had the wit to open had he not found the key in the pockets of his victim, and the murder came as an inevitable event. It was consummated in a manner and with a weapon natural to a duffer, and to no one else. Nobody but a duffer would have carried the weapon from the room to drop it inside the door. The brutal coward feared that he might meet some one in the gloomy spaces of that great stairway, and when about to pass into the open streets, which were safer, he cast it from him. Nobody but an unreasoning brute, inexperienced in the detective agencies of the law, would have carried away such articles as the watches and medal, or, having done so, could have kept them concealed so long: the caution and cunning of stupidity driven to cover are unequalled. Nobody but a duffer would have gone out the front door, thus recklessly and uselessly assuming the risk of stepping from his bloody work into the clutch of a patrolman, or having done so would have neglected to close it carefully behind him, so that the next gust of wind would not thrust it ajar and give the other chance against him of hastening by hours the moment when his crime must be discovered. Nobody but a duffer in stepping from that house could have been so completely lost in the aggregate of humanity that no trace of him could be found. Rejecting, as they were compelled to do, the hypothesis that the murder was done from within the house, the officials had no choice but to seek for the murderer among either the professional or amateur criminal classes. The first they have searched thoroughly, and the second to the best of their ability. Yet among the second, according to their theory, the assassin must be found, if found at all. The truth may be far from their theory, and if time or accident ever dispels the impenetrable cloud that envelopes that terrible scene, it may be found that experience is as useless in criminal matters as it is valuable in many other affairs of life. For the present, it is sufficient to say that John Jourdan does not expect by such an event to be put on a level with the newest patrolman under his command.

With this murder and this penetrating but utterly barren pursuit before us, how shall we answer the question, "Will murder out?"

www.ingramcontent.com/pod-product-compliance
Lightning Source LLC
LaVergne TN
LVHW011229110826
845150LV00006B/1583
* 9 7 8 1 4 2 5 5 7 2 3 0 3 *